ROUTLEDGE LIBRARY EDITIONS:
THE INDUSTRIAL REVOLUTION

Volume 5

A TECHNICAL AND BUSINESS REVOLUTION

A TECHNICAL AND BUSINESS REVOLUTION

American Woolens to 1832

ELIZABETH HITZ

LONDON AND NEW YORK

First published in 1986 by Garland Publishing, Inc.

This edition first published in 2017
by Routledge
2 Park Square, Milton Park, Abingdon, Oxon OX14 4RN

and by Routledge
711 Third Avenue, New York, NY 10017

Routledge is an imprint of the Taylor & Francis Group, an informa business

British Library Cataloguing in Publication Data
A catalogue record for this book is available from the British Library

ISBN: 978-1-138-63291-2 (Set)
ISBN: 978-1-315-16309-3 (Set) (ebk)
ISBN: 978-1-138-04522-4 (Volume 5) (hbk)
ISBN: 978-1-138-04536-1 (Volume 5) (pbk)
ISBN: 978-1-315-17197-5 (Volume 5) (ebk)

Publisher's Note
The publisher has gone to great lengths to ensure the quality of this reprint but points out that some imperfections in the original copies may be apparent.

A TECHNICAL AND BUSINESS REVOLUTION ★ American Woolens to 1832

Elizabeth Hitz

Garland Publishing, Inc.
New York & London ★ 1986

Library of Congress Cataloging-in-Publication Data

Hitz, Elizabeth, 1932–
A technical and business revolution.

(American business history)
Thesis (Ph.D.)—New York University, 1978.
Bibliography: p.
1. Wool trade and industry—United States—History—19th century.
2. Wool trade and industry—Great Britain—History—19th century. 3. Woolen and worsted manufacture—United States—History—19th century.
4. Woolen and worsted manufacture—Great Britain—History—19th century. I. Title. II. Series.
HD9895.H58 1986 338.4'767731'0973 86-18325
ISBN 0-8240-8378-4

All volumes in this series are printed on acid-free, 250-year-life paper:

Printed in the United States of America

ACKNOWLEDGEMENTS

A work like this is not really possible without help and support from a whole range of individuals and institutions. First thanks must go to Dr. Brooke Hindle who started with me on this project as my advisor at New York University and then very graciously continued to oversee the research and writing when he moved to the Museum of History and Technology of the Smithsonian Institution. Professor Carl E. Prince of New York University has very helpfully acted as Dr. Hindle's surrogate in New York. He has regularly provided me with needed advice and encouragement.

The Director of the Nassau County Museums, Edward J. Smits, encouraged me from the beginning to work toward a Ph.D. and allowed me leaves of absence and short work-weeks at critical times. Nassau County provided small stipends to help pay for course work.

I was given a special opportunity by a Grant-In-Aid awarded by the Foundation Research Committee of the Eleutherian Mills Historical Library. The Director of that library, Richmond D. Williams, and the library staff including Betty-Bright Low, James White, Susan Danko, and Carol Hallman all stood by as I struggled to unravel the mysteries of the du Pont woolen operation and early nineteenth century book-keeping techniques. Dr. Eugene Ferguson, Curator of Technology at the Hagley Museum was especially helpful in providing leads for further research.

Old Sturbridge Village will always have a special place in my heart for getting me into the museum business in the first place. Frank O. Spinney, Alexander J. Wall, and Catherine Fennelly from the "old days" inspired me more than I'm sure they know. More recently, the Library and Research Departments at Sturbridge Village including Etta Falkner, Roger Parks, Ted Penn, Richard Candee, Caroline Sloat, Tina Bielenberg, and Elaine Bushnell gave me patient and helpful assistance with that library's holdings.

Mr. Robert W. Lovett and his young assistants, Susan Aborjaily and Alan Bailey helped me through the Slater Collection in Baker Library's Division of Archives and Manuscripts at Harvard. Librarians and their staffs in the Bobst Library Government Documents section (New York University), at the New-York Historical Society, the Historical Society of Pennsylvania, the New York Public Library Annex, the Rhode Island Historical Society, the Merrimack Valley Textile Museum Library, and the National Archives all showed me the way to important source materials.

Family and friends were also important; Dr. Sophie Bookhalter, Prof. Judy McGaw, and my sister Nicki Edson listened to a fair amount of moaning and groaning. Ann Cloward cheerfully put up with me and Rosebud the cat in Wilmington. Finally, my good friend Henry Harlow provided just the right atmosphere in his fine Shrewsbury house built in the 1820s and further encouraged me with his tolerant and patient presence through days of research and writing.

TABLE OF CONTENTS

LIST OF ILLUSTRATIONS

LIST OF TABLES

INTRODUCTION

The history of woolen manufacture is ancient history. While not totally undynamic in historic time, the degree of technical change in woolen manufacture hardly was profound until the eighteenth and nineteenth centuries, until that "event" loosely termed the industrial revolution.

From medieval times to the nineteenth century, woolen broadcloth manufacture was an English industry of major importance. It was highly organized, methodically regulated by the state, and a topic for parliamentary debate year after year. Because it was regulated and discussed, a great deal is known about it. Sometime during the seventeenth century its export value was superseded by worsted woolens of various types and while the woolen cloth industry continued as an important element in the English economy, it was never again to be the most important English industry.

"True" woolens continued to be of major economic significance. The North American colonies became an important market for them; so important in fact, that through 1840 the American market was the recipient of 30 to 40 percent of English production.[1]

---

[1]J. Potter, "Atlantic Economy, 1815-1860: the United States and the Industrial Revolution in Britain," in _Studies in the Industrial Revolution Presented to T. S. Ashton_, ed. L. S. Pressnell (London: Athlone, 1960), p. 267.

During the seventeenth and eighteenth centuries, American mainland colonists were dependent on English woolens. There was some folk cloth produced in colonial homes--that is, crude cloth produced by non-professionals, and by the last quarter of the eighteenth century there was developing a tradition of American "homespun" manufacture that continued through the Napoleonic Wars and after. But homespun never could displace fine English broadcloth.

Historians have always looked to England for the beginnings of industrialization. Certain important and vital seeds were there, of course, but certain other ideas--the integrated factory, mechanization as a method for saving labor and wages and increasing productivity, mechanization as a means for maintaining uniform, though not necessarily superfine, quality standards--were very early on the minds of American industrialists generally, and woolen manufacturers in particular. During the period from 1807 to 1815, an American woolen industry began; within a very short time gap American technical proficiency had surged ahead of the English.

One major difference between the English and American experiences in industrialization was the disinterest among Americans in stationary steam engines. They simply were not needed. Waterpower was cheap, plentiful, and unencumbered by problems of jurisdiction.

This reliance on waterpower made Americans seem more tradition-bound than they actually were. The woolen industry provides a particularly fine example of seeming tradition-boundness, because not only did it rely on waterpower, theoretically its manufacturing techniques were overladen with traditional methods. Yet this monograph will show that by the decade of the 1820s, American woolen manufacturing techniques became fully mechanized, and that by that point in time, those techniques were in advance of English techniques. There is even circumstantial evidence that the diffusion of this technology was not from England to America as historians have traditionally thought, but by the 1820s from America to England. This last statement cannot be proved fully without extensive exploration into English records, but there are enough fragments of evidence on this side of the Atlantic to make this a valid supposition.

American woolen manufacturers not only tried to rationalize their mechanical processes and techniques, but by the late 1820s were trying with modest success to rationalize and systematize their accounting methods, most particularly their methods for determining costs. It is nigh on impossible to determine profits without knowing costs. Yet the 1820 accounting systems used in factories were basically merchandising accounting systems. That kind of a system is fine for determining the status of individual accounts; it works fine for individual wages, for example, but it does not give its user a clue to his total costs for labor. Certain types of costs had to be separated out of manufacturing accounts--the purchase of flour to resell or to use in the boarding houses, the building of factory buildings or dwellings, for example. Other costs had to be combined in the accounting systems--labor, raw materials, building and repair, for example. By the end of the 1820 decade there is evidence that new accounting procedures were being used and developed, so that by the 1832 McLane Report, some manufacturers were able to provide a glimmer of their profitability or lack of it. The one important piece of information seldom available was the sales record. Manufacturers reported something of their costs, something of what the fabric was worth and should have sold for, but not actual sales.

There were two serious problems here--the first was the cost of wool and its fluctuation in price. Since wool was such a major ingredient of costs, a price difference of 10 percent from one year to the next could mean profit or loss to a given manufacturer. Prices of merino wool often went up or down 10 to 20 percent in a year. The other problem was the elasticity of the market for woolen cloth. Woolen cloth, broadcloth or cassimere (narrow woolen cloth) was in no way a necessity. Cheaper materials such as kersey or satinet could substitute, and as the principal use of the cloth was in men's suits and coats, new purchases could be postponed year after year.

Even though manufacturers were consistently able to lower costs, especially labor costs, their profits were dependent on the price of wool and the marketability of their cloths at high prices. It was a very fickle business subject to severe market vagaries in production costs and distribution of goods. By 1832, or roughly two decades after the start of the American industry, processes were rationalized and so were business practices. But by no means were American woolen manufacturers able to bring in steady profits. The attrition rate of woolen manufactories was very high, just how high cannot be fully known. Many went out of business in 1815, 1819, 1829, and again in 1837. Yet many factories reorganized, changed owners, incorporated, became joint stock companies, and kept going, giving employment and in many cases good livings, to operatives as well as agents. Many factories expanded seemingly in the face of annual losses. This last was possible because the economy was so completely credit based. Until situations occurred requiring banks to foreclose or call in loans, these companies could continue year after year increasing their debt and interest payments. But that is exactly what nineteenth-century panics were about--the distrust of banks by depositors and the need by banks therefore to bolster their own holdings by calling back their outstanding loans. Short term indebtedness by factories could be and was turned over and over again, but these periodic panics literally represented days of reckoning, and manufactories without substantial resources did not survive.

This monograph will develop this story of American woolen manufacture reaching far back in time to establish the very traditional nature of the fabrication of woolen cloths. Traditional techniques change slowly, and indeed woolen manufacturing technology in England did change slowly. But circumstances and conditions can change; circumstances and conditions in the United States during the Napoleonic Wars did change. Americans had more surplus capital to invest; they had abundant natural resources, especially cheap power sources; in non-slave parts of the country, literacy rates were very high; many American merchants and manufacturers sought independence from European, particularly English, goods and services. Changing times, changing technologies, social and economic change of fairly grand proportions are phenomena not only of the twentieth century; the first half of the nineteenth century in the United States saw a goodly share of such change.

Chapter I

SEVENTEENTH- AND EIGHTEENTH-CENTURY BACKGROUND

English Manufacture

From time-out-of-mind, and for century after century the great pride of England was her woolen cloth industry. English broadcloth, that prince of materials, was regulated in its length and breadth dimensions from the Middle Ages and in its weight from the time of Edward VI. Most finished broadloth (there were regional variations, but they need not be of concern here) was required to be sold in pieces of twenty-eight to thirty-three yards in length, six and one-half to seven quarters in breadth, and to weigh sixty to seventy-three pounds per piece or about nineteen ounces per square yard.[1]

The elaborate processes in the manufacture of broadcloth include sorting, scouring, picking, willowing, and carding the wool, spinning yarn, warping or measuring the yarn, sizing the yarn with glue, threading the loom with warp, weaving, fulling, scouring two or three more times, raising the nap, burling, shearing the nap, and packing the cloth in bales. There are a

---

[1]Julia de Lacy Mann, The Cloth Industry in the West of England from 1640-1880 (Oxford: Clarendon Press, 1971), pp. 313-14.

fine set of illustrations from the "Art de la Draperie" by Henry Louis Duhamel du Monceau, published in 1765 (see ill. 1-15). This level of technology had been extant in England from the sixteenth century and was to change only with the advent of the fly-shuttle.

Although John Kay patented the fly-shuttle, or spring shuttle, in 1733, it was adopted very slowly. The shuttles did not reach Yorkshire in any number until the 1760s, and it was not generally adopted there until the 1780s.[2] It was not in general use in Gloucestershire until the 1780s.[3] From this point on, technical change was relatively rapid, yet by 1820 the technical level of woolen manufacture was greater in terms of mechanized processes in the United States than it was in either of the two major woolen manufacturing centers of Great Britain--Yorkshire and the three West of England counties--Wiltshire, Somerset, and Gloucestershire.

The Lord Chancellor of England sits upon a sack of wool. Students of English history have made much of this, but there is no reason to think that the tradition predates 1500.[4] England was and is fine sheep country; it is damp

---

[2]Herbert Heaton, _The Yorkshire Woollen and Worsted Industries from Earliest Times up to the Industrial Revolution_, 2nd ed. (Oxford: Oxford University Press, 1965), p. 340.

[3]Mann, _Cloth Industry_, pp. 139-41.

[4]_The Compact Edition of the Oxford English Dictionary_, 2 vols. (Oxford: Clarendon Press, 1971), 2:2615 and 2:3816, under "Sack" and Woolsack."

SOURCE: Duhamel du Monceau's "Art de la Draperie," 1765. Courtesy of the Eleutherian Mills Historical Library.

Illus. 1. Willowing and picking washed wool.

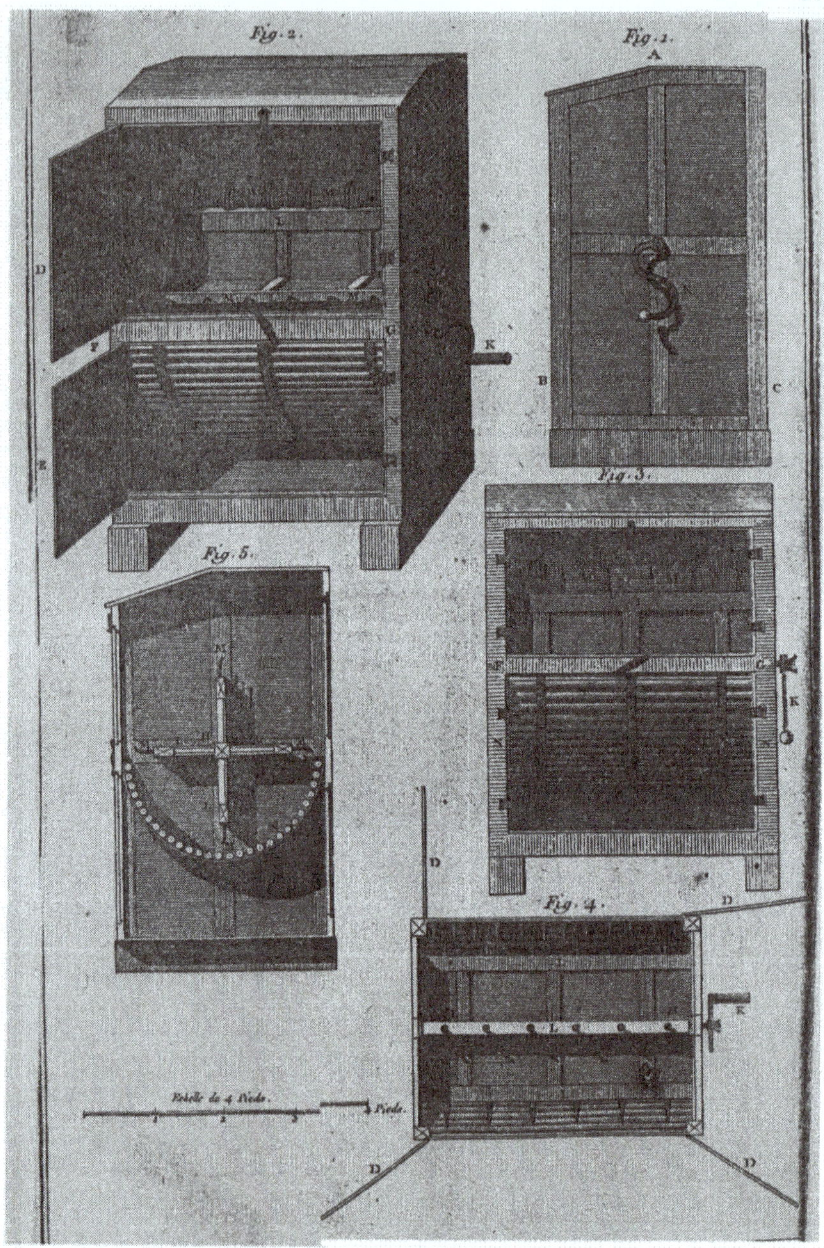

SOURCE: Duhamel du Monceau's "Art de la Draperie," 1765. Courtesy of the Eleutherian Mills Historical Library.

Illus. 2. Mechanical Picker.

SOURCE: Duhamel du Monceau's "Art de la Draperie," 1765. Courtesy of the Eleutherian Mills Historical Library.

Illus. 3. Hand Carding.

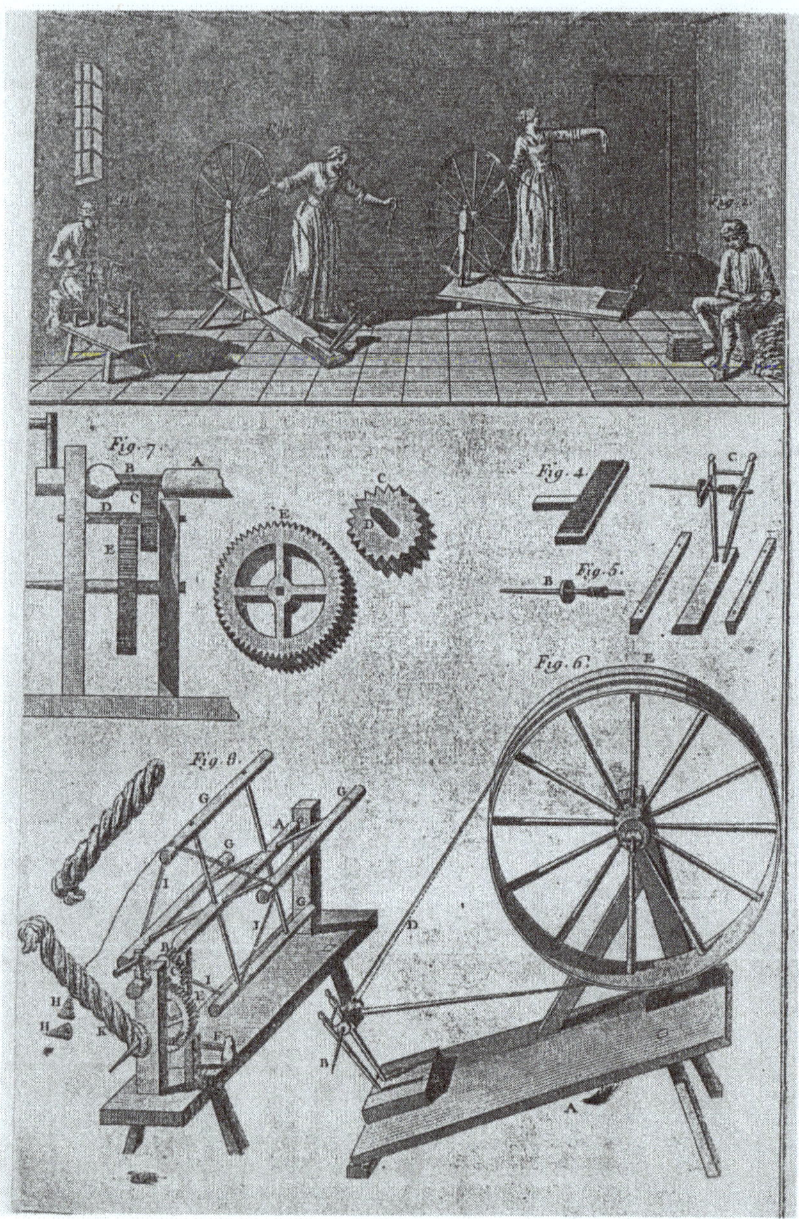

SOURCE: Duhamel du Monceau's "Art de la Draperie," 1765. Courtesy of the Eleutherian Mills Historical Library.

Illus. 4. Hand Spinning.

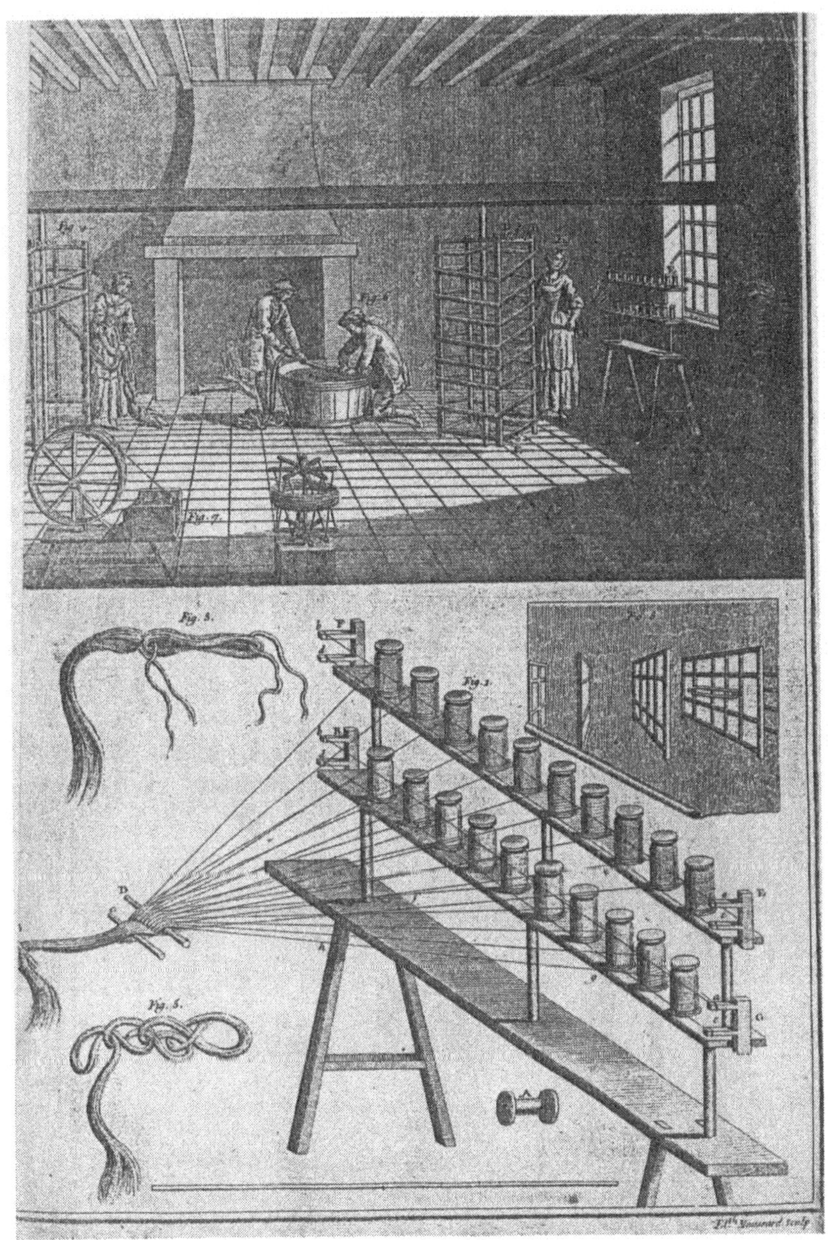

SOURCE: Duhamel du Monceau's "Art de la Draperie," 1765. Courtesy of the Eleutherian Mills Historical Library.

Illus. 5. Sizing and Warping.

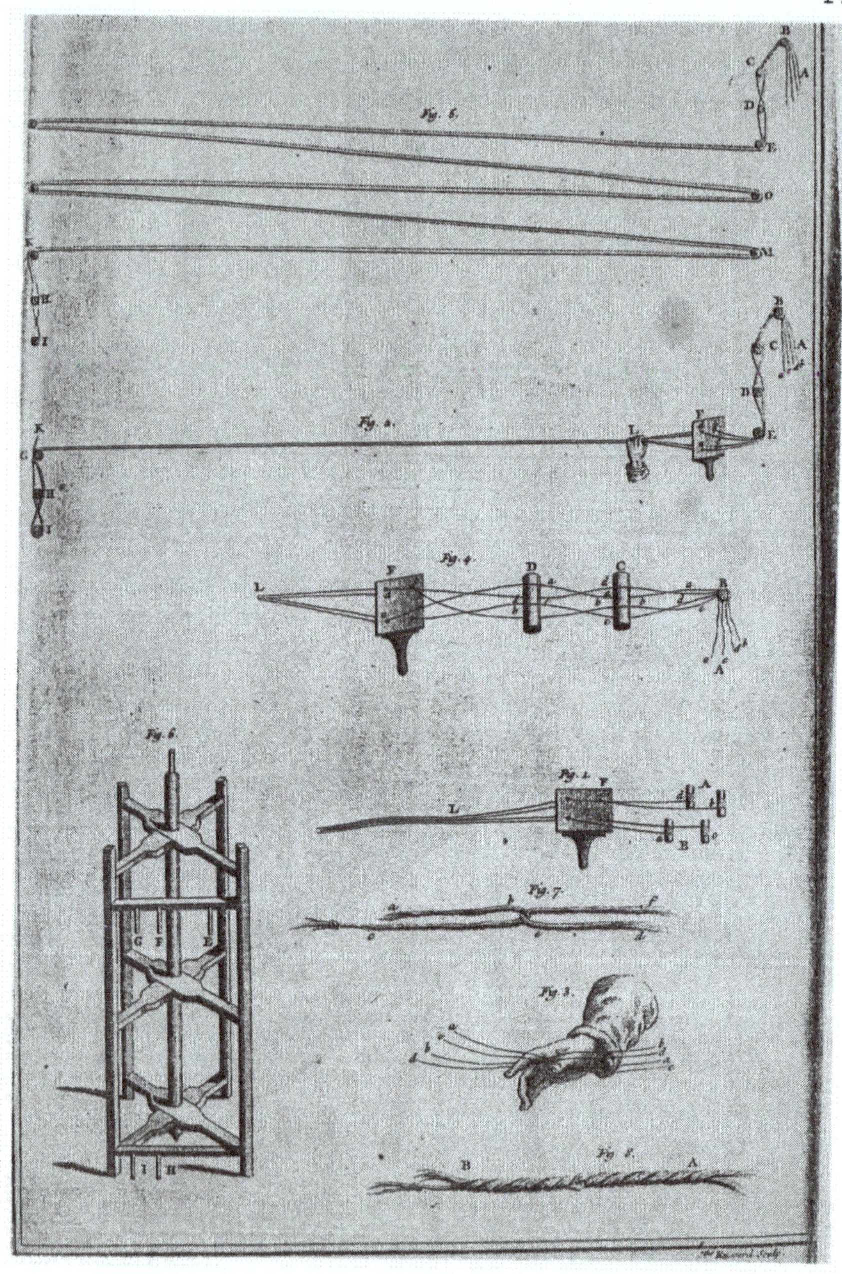

SOURCE: Duhamel du Monceau's "Art de la Draperie," 1765. Courtesy of the Eleutherian Mills Historical Library.

Illus. 6. Warping--Measuring the Warp.

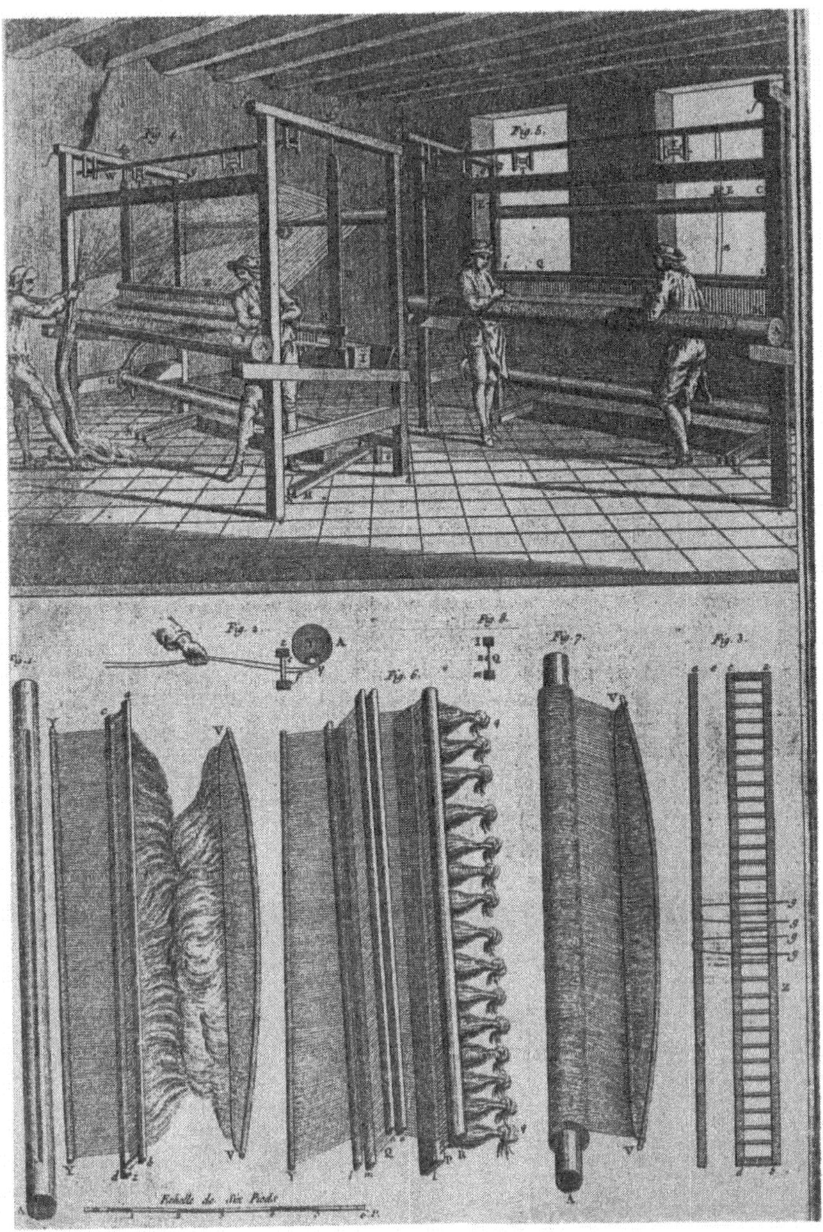

SOURCE: Duhamel du Monceau's "Art de la Draperie," 1765. Courtesy of the Eleutherian Mills Historical Library.

Illus. 7. Looming--Putting up the Loom.

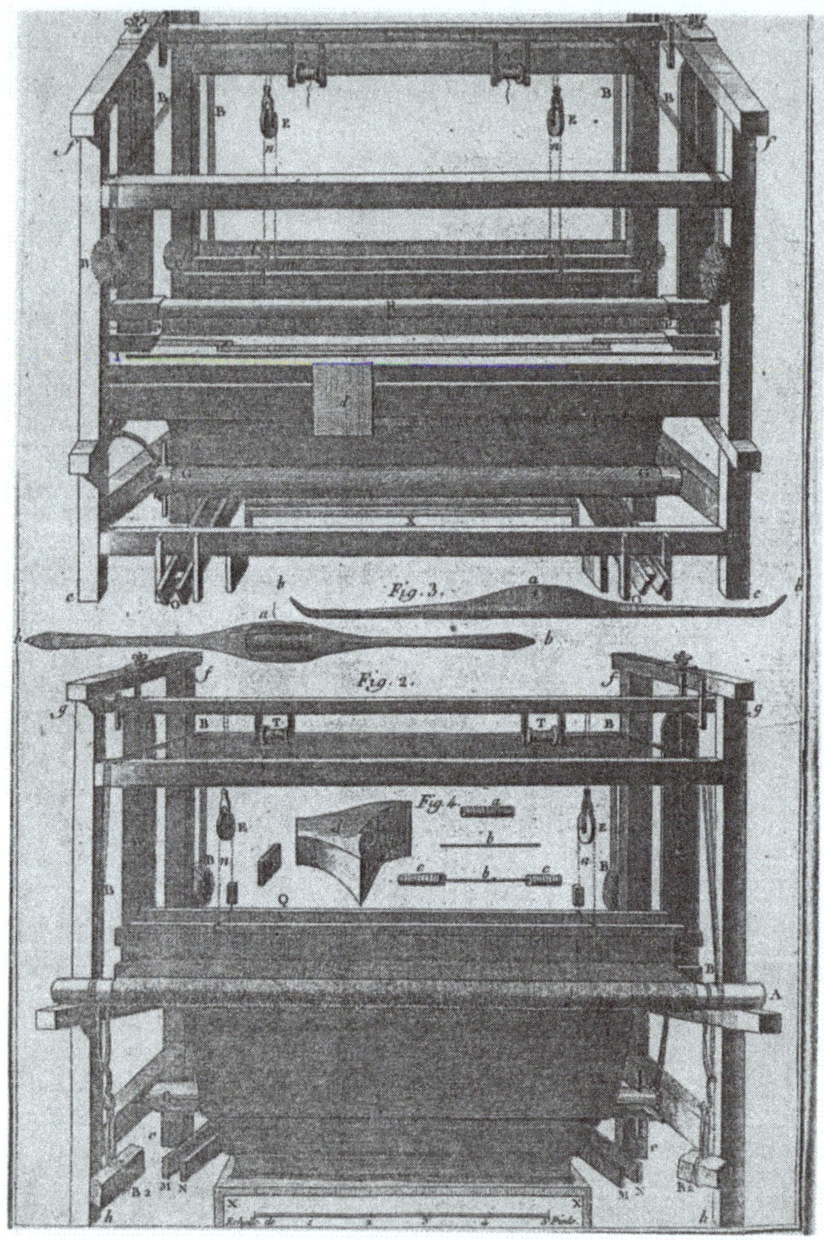

SOURCE: Duhamel du Monceau's "Art de la Draperie," 1765. Courtesy of the Eleutherian Mills Historical Library.

Illus. 8. The Broadloom.

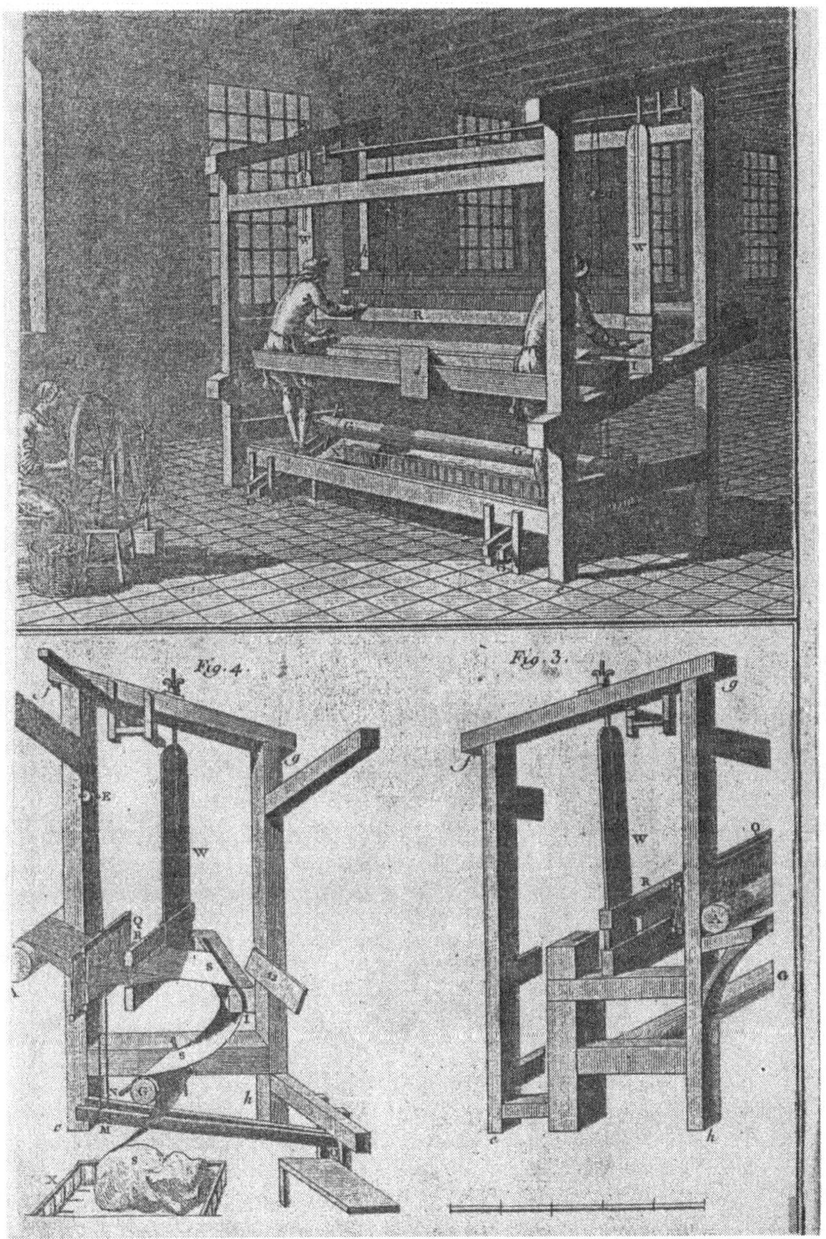

SOURCE: Duhamel du Monceau's "Art de la Draperie," 1765. Courtesy of the Eleutherian Mills Historical Library.

Illus. 9. Weaving on Broadloom.

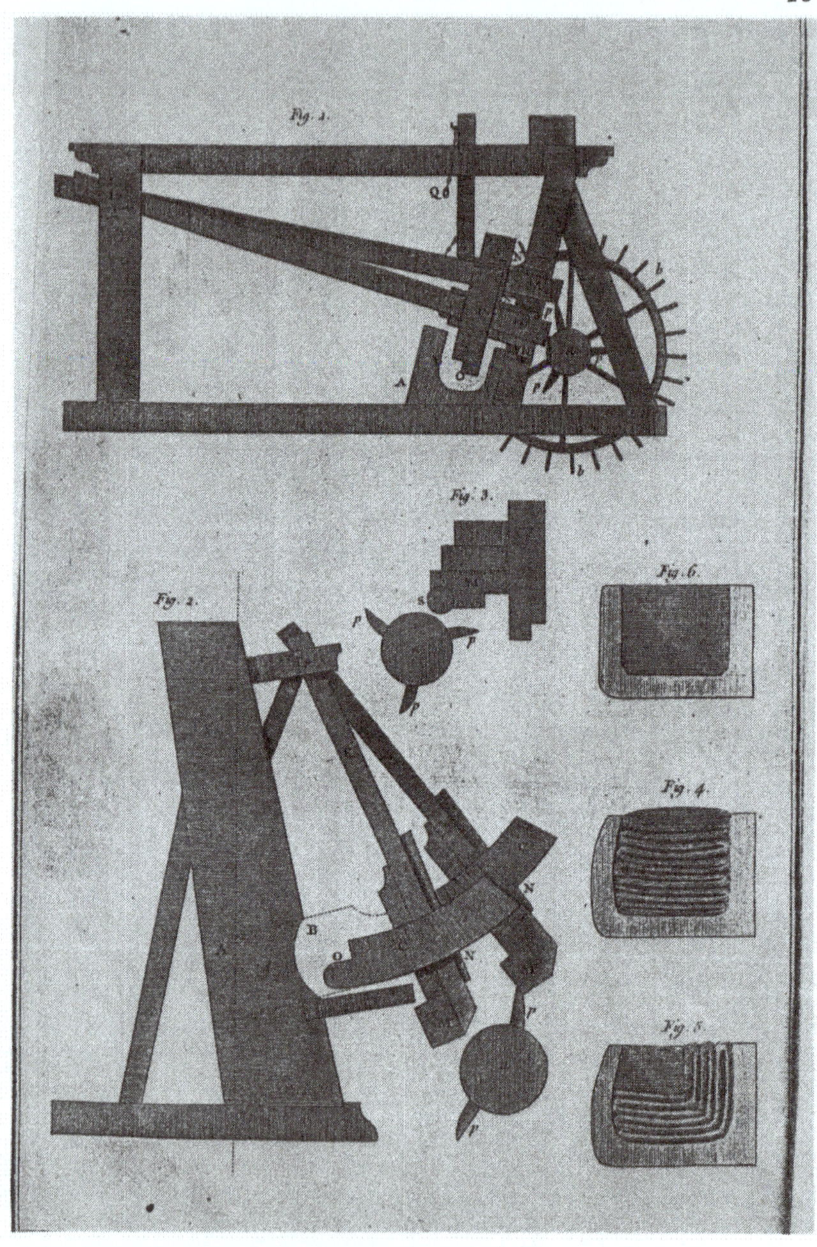

SOURCE: Duhamel du Monceau's "Art de la Draperie," 1765. Courtesy of the Eleutherian Mills Historical Library.

Illus. 10. Two Types Fulling Stocks.

SOURCE: Duhamel du Monceau's "Art de la Draperie," 1765. Courtesy of the Eleutherian Mills Historical Library.

Illus. 11. Power Train for Fulling.

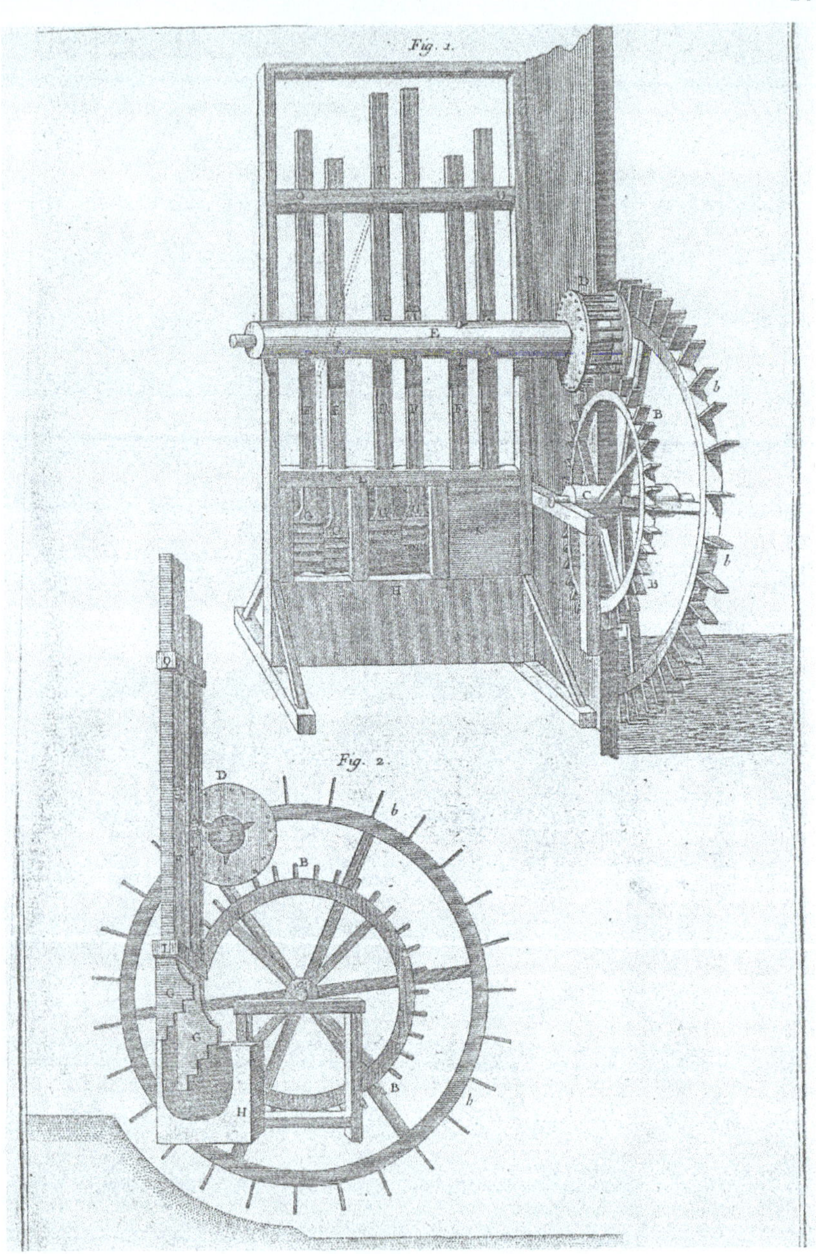

SOURCE: Duhamel du Monceau's "Art de la Draperie," 1765. Courtesy of the Eleutherian Mills Historical Library.

Illus. 12. Pounding Stocks and Gears.

SOURCE: Duhamel du Monceau's "Art de la Draperie," 1765. Courtesy of the Eleutherian Mills Historical Library.

Illus. 13. Raising the Nap with Hand Held Teasels.

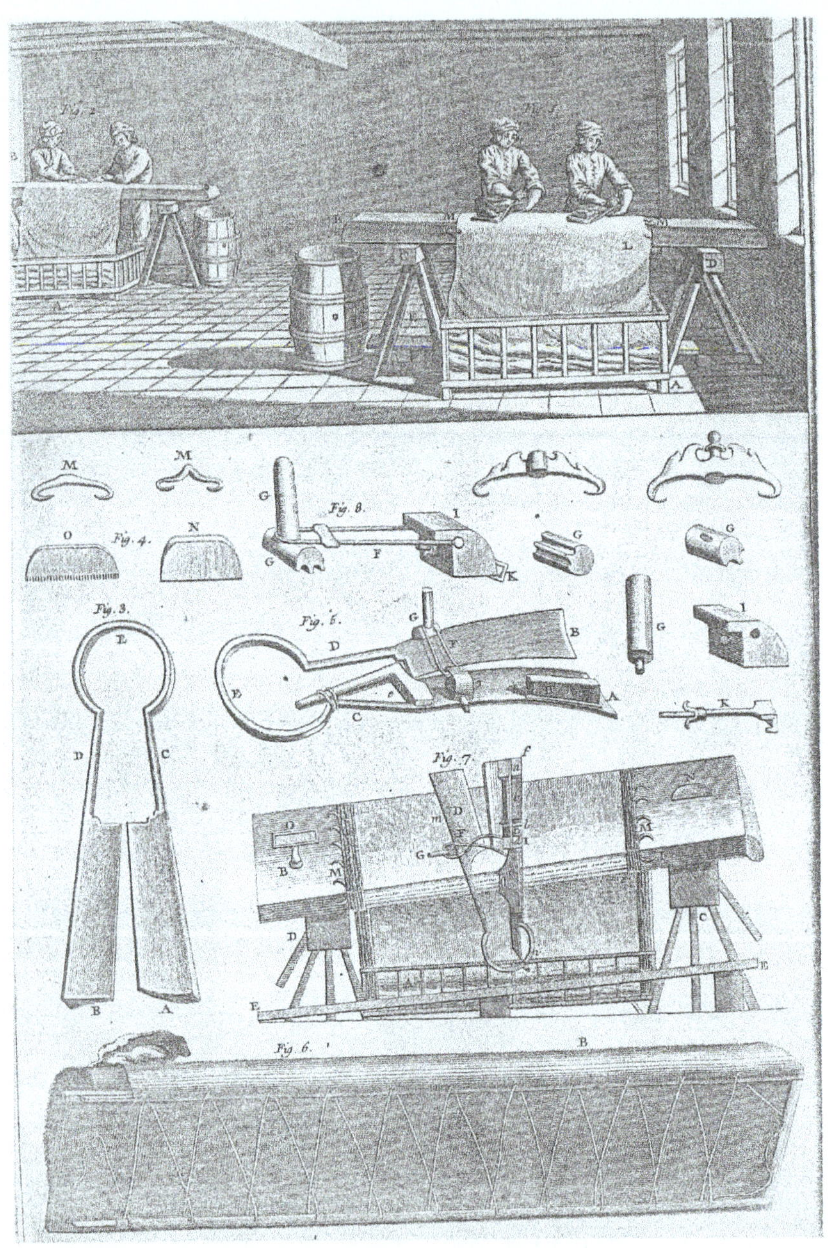

SOURCE: Duhamel du Monceau's "Art de la Draperie," 1765. Courtesy of the Eleutherian Mills Historical Library.

Illus. 14. Burling and Shearing.

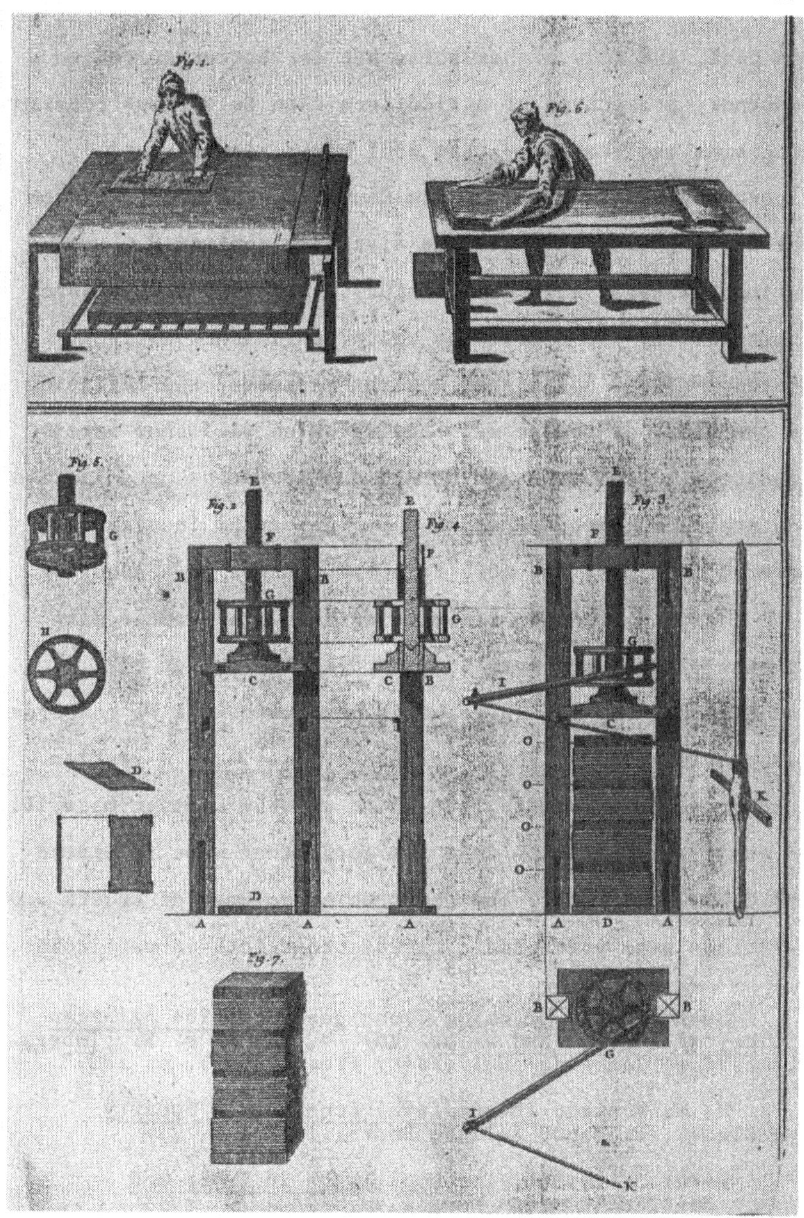

SOURCE: Duhamel du Monceau's "Art de la Draperie," 1765. Courtesy of the Eleutherian Mills Historical Library.

Illus. 15. Pressing Cloth.

and cool, and some of her soils are far better suited to a husbandry/grass type of agriculture than to various rotations of grains and grasses.[5] Raw wool was a significant export from England to the Low Countries and to Italy from the twelfth century until the sixteenth century.[6]. During the early sixteenth century, raw wool exports were superseded by the exports of white, unfinished woolen cloths.[7] These unfinished woolens represent the beginning of the story of woolen manufacture which will show how traditional processes and traditional business organization and practices were transformed by the use of inanimate powered machinery and more rational methods of accounting.

In any discussion of textiles, woolens perhaps more so than others, one must soon turn to the matter of definitions. By and large, this monograph will be concerned with woolen cloth. There may be an occasional diversion into worsteds or stuffs, but cloth was the premier material of great value; cloths were the goods that were regulated and legislated about, and about which volumes of tracts and petitions were addressed. Cloth, broadcloth in particular,

---

[5]Joan Thirsk, "Farming Techniques," in The Agrarian History of England and Wales, vol. 4, ed. H. P. R. Finberg (Cambridge: Cambridge University Press, 1967), p. 182.

[6]M. M. Postan, The Medieval Economy and Society (Middlesex, England: Pelican Books, 1972), p. 214.

[7]Peter J. Bowden, The Wool Trade in Tudor and Stuart England (London: Macmillan, 1962), p. xvii.

brought large profits both in the manufacturing and in the buying and selling. Little is marketed today, and finding surviving examples is a major accomplishment. They do exist, of course, in museums, but not in quantity, and seldom with a known provenance.[8]

The following are the main types of cloths using wool fibers:

"True" Worsteds:

1. Combed, long-stapled wools; longer and coarser than that used for woolen cloth.
2. Rock-spun with simple spindle, and after mid-sixteenth century, spun on a Saxony wheel.
3. Woven in a range of patterns including plaids.
4. Light in weight, and therefore marketable in more southern climes.
5. Not fulled; strength from long fibers.

Woolen cloth--broadcloths and kerseys:

1. Carded, short-stapled wools; used finest (thinnest) wools available.
2. Rock-spun with simple spindle, but after thirteenth or fourteenth century, spun on simple wool wheel.
3. Plain weave, though an eighteenth-century variant, cassimere, was woven in a twill pattern using three instead of two harnesses.

---

[8]Kenneth G. Ponting, The Woollen Industry of South-West England (New York: Augustus Kelley, 1971), p. 15.

4. Heavy in weight--early statutes required broadcloth to be over twenty-four ounces per square yard; very warm. Marketed in northern Europe and North America.
5. Fulled--that is, wool yarns were felted so that the weave became invisible; water resistant.
6. Finished--nap raised and sheared, brushed and pressed. Until the early 1600s, English woolen cloth was exported "white" without finishing or dyeing.

New Draperies, stuffs:

1. Mostly worsted types, but not only. Mixed with woolen yarns, and a range of other fibers including silk, linen, cotton, and other animal hairs from goats, camels, horses, etc.
2. Mostly not fulled, but there were exceptions.
3. Wide range of patterns of weave, colors, sizes, qualities, finish.[9]

---

[9]This is a compilation from various sources: Bowden, Wool Trade, pp. 41-43; Ponting, Woollen Industry, p. 27; Mann, Cloth Industry, pp. 314-15; D. C. Coleman, "An Innovation and its Diffussion: the 'New Draperies,'" Economic History Review, 2nd ser., 22 (1969):423; J. E. Pilgrim, "The Cloth Industry of East Anglia," in The Wool Textile Industry in Great Britain, ed. J. Geraint Jenkins (London: Routledge & Kegan Paul, 1972), p. 257; Melvin Kranzberg and Carroll W. Pursell, Jr., Technology in Western Civilization: The Emergence of Modern Industrial Society Earliest Times to 1900, 2 vols. (New York: Oxford University Press, 1967), 1:78.

The words for these varieties of stuffs and cloths form their own dictionary. The more common cloths known to seventeenth- and eighteenth-century Englishmen and colonials included: broadcloth, medley cloth, Spanish cloth, kerseys, dozens, penistones, friezes, and cottons.[10] For worsteds and stuffs, the names of fabrics included bays, says, serges, perpetuanas, these the most important; plus rashes, fisadoes, minikins, bambasines, grograines, buffins, russels, sagathies, mockadoes, shalloons, and tammies.[11]

All cloth making, certainly wool is no exception, has roots in folk cultures. Various types of textiles were manufactured by non-professional spinners and weavers. Most of it was very plain, roughly made, and required a minimum of skill and equipment. Most folk cloth was made for home use or for sale in the immediate neighborhood. Little or no quantitative information exists about it. Until the nineteenth century, the home manufacture of textiles of all types was more important to people in the countryside than commercial manufacture.[12] For nineteenth-century America, there are scattered data. Just at about the time home manufacture of textiles died out for good, a glimmer of its relative extent appears.

---

[10]Cottons, a coarse woolen cloth, and Spanish cloth made in England, illustrate with some clarity the complexity of the vocabulary problem.

[11]Bowden, Wool Trade, p. 41.

[12]Coleman, "Innovation and its Diffusion," p. 421.

Because of the British propensity for keeping records and writing local history, some notions of the commercial manufacture of woolen textiles can be gleaned dating from the early seventeenth century. Nothing about the English industry can be considered static. There were a variety of sheep; Joan Thirsk listed ten major breeds from sixteenth- and seventeenth-century records.[13] Raw materials changed in availability and quality; markets changed, some ceased altogether, new ones developed; technology changed; very possibly there were climatic changes; regional production shifted; personal tastes and fashions changed.

It was Adam Smith's view that by the time of Henry VIII the spinning wheel had replaced the rock and spindle thereby doubling productivity, that warping mills had become available greatly facilitating the setting up of looms, and that water powered fulling had become commonplace.[14] These machines were the bases of further mechanization.

There is probably no discernible relationship, but dramatic changes in the English woolen industry coincided in time with the early migrations to New England. From 1600 to 1640, the new draperies surged in export value to nearly that of the old cloth. From this point on worsteds

---

[13]Thirsk, "Farming Techniques," pp. 189-91.

[14]Adam Smith, The Wealth of Nations (New York: Random House, 1937), p. 246.

and stuffs became a most valuable English export.[15] This industry, unregulated or barely regulated in the case of bays, without clearly definable organization, and dispersed geographically despite East Anglian origins, probably will never be clearly understood. It should be to classical economists, a prime example of how lack of regulation and interference can stimulate the growth of an industry. But precisely because it was unregulated, not much can be known about it.[16] Suffice it to say in terms of value, that bays, says, serges, perpetuanas, and stuffs were at least as important as the export of cloths, cottons, kerseys, dozens, and penistones from 1640 on. This pattern continued until all woolen exports were surpassed by the value of cotton exports in 1803.[17]

The chaos of Stuart England was well reflected in the woolen industry. Two very crucial events almost turned the industry topsy turvy by 1650. The first, already alluded to, was the competition of the old cloth manufacture with

---

[15]Charles Wilson, England's Apprenticeship, 1603-1763 (London: Longman's Green & Co., 1965), p. 78; F. J. Fisher, "London's Export Trade in the Seventeenth Century," in The Growth of English Overseas Trade in the Seventeenth and Eighteenth Centuries, ed. W. E. Michendon (London: Methuen, 1969), pp. 66-69.

[16]Barry E. Supple, Commercial Crisis and Change in England, 1600-1641 (Cambridge: Cambridge University Press, 1959), p. 153.

[17]Elizabeth B. Schumpeter, English Overseas Trade Statistics, 1697-1808 (Oxford: Clarendon Press, 1960), pp. 34-47.

the new draperies. In East Anglia, the new types of cloth had all but displaced the old by 1650; by 1700 stuffs and serges made by Flemish and Dutch refugees and their descendents were manufactured in Devon and Dorset to the south and west. By the same time, the old woolen industry had all but disappeared in the southeast of England.[18]

The second event was provoked in some degree by the new competition, but did not result in the displacement of the old cloth industry by the new. This was the attempt to oust the old Merchant Adventurers from their monopoly of the export of undyed and unfinished woolen cloths. Alderman William Cockayne was the originator of a plan by which the white cloths would be sold to a new London group of King's Merchant Adventurers who in turn would put out the cloths to be dyed and finished in London and then exported to markets in the Baltic and Low Countries. The level of technical expertise in England in the 1610s and early '20s simply was not high enough for this project. Furthermore, it provided new opportunities for the Dutch and French to impinge on traditional English markets in the Baltic, Germany, and eastern Europe. The initial result of these experiments was that an industry that would have been in severe doldrums because of European wars, now found itself in a serious depression, made all the more serious because

---

[18]Bowden, Wool Trade, pp. 51-53.

of the competition from the new draperies.[19] In 1622 a Commission of Trade was established by Parliament who revised trading privileges so that other merchants besides the Merchant Adventurers could trade in kersies, dozens, and new draperies; now all outport merchants could handle colored cloths. The easing of trade restritions was probably helpful to the manufacturers, but by now plagues, European wars, and approaching civil war were to keep the woolen cloth industry depressed.[20]

Through the seventeenth century the woolen industry fought back to recover its position as England's premier export. In three counties: Wiltshire, Somerset, and Gloucester, British toughness and adaptability rebuilt a significant and important business in Spanish cloths or medley cloths as they were also known.[21]

As befitted an industry with a medieval heritage, fine broadcloth manufacture had been closely regulated, in part to achieve some standards for quality. There were variations within the regulations depending mostly on custom derived from geographic origins, and there was some variation over time from the 1550s to the final regulatory statute of 1624. Broadcloths were required to be twenty-six

---

[19]Supple, Commercial Crisis, pp. 135-62; C. Wilson, England's Apprenticeship, pp. 78-79.

[20]Supple, Commercial Crisis, pp. 241-42; Mann, Cloth Industry, p. 3.

[21]Mann, Cloth Industry, pp. 3-36.

to thirty-five yards long, six and a half to seven quarters in breadth (a quarter was a quarter-yard or nine inches), and to weigh from fifty-seven to eighty pounds per piece. In square yard terms this was about nineteen ounces to over twenty-five ounces per square yard; modern broadcloth weighs about 16 1/2 to 17 1/4 ounces per yard. These weights are important because the success of Spanish cloth manufacture came in great degree because of its comparative lightness and its resulting marketability in Mediterranean climates.[22]

While English data are particularly sparse for the second half of the seventeenth century, sparser even than for the first half, the state of the art of the woolen cloth industry can be summarized. The most dynamic element of the industry was certainly among the new draperies. Their principal manufacturing centers were East Anglia including Kent; in the south, Hampshire, Berkshire, and most particularly the Devon-Somerset border area; in mid-country, Worcester, Warwick, and Northampton; and in Yorkshire. By 1700 the finest old draperies--superfine cloth--were made in the West Counties and East Anglia; by 1800 Yorkshire would have a firm foothold in the competition.[23]

---

[22]Ibid.

[23]Bowden, Wool Trade, p. 49.

In the three western counties of Gloucester, Wiltshire, and Somerset, it was the changeover from undyed white cloth to Spanish cloth that saved the day after the Cockayne near-disaster. For a variety of reasons including a change in the nature of the native wool supply, changes in taste and the closing of old European markets in the north and east, this lighter cloth kept the industry afloat during the seventeenth century. The processing of Spanish cloth was much the same as for traditional broadcloth which continued as the most important West Country product. In brief, the wool was sorted, scoured, dyed and dried, carded and spun, woven into cloth on a very wide loom requiring two weavers, and finished by fulling sometimes for days, the nap raised, sheared, and the cloth finally pressed in a large screw press.[24] Kerseys from Yorkshire were made in much the same way with three major and important exceptions: the wool was much coarser; traditional broadcloth used only the finest wools. Secondly, kersey was woven on a narrow loom; usually the cloth was finished three-quarters in width. Thirdly, kerseys were fulled, but they were never finished with the same work and care that went into broadcloth.[25]

---

[24]Mann, Cloth Industry, pp. 3-37, 280-307.

[25]M. T. Wild, "The Yorkshire Wool Textile Industry," in The Wool Textile Industry in Great Britain, ed. J. Geraint Jenkins (London: Routledge & Kegan Paul, 1972), pp. 201-3.

The West Country and Yorkshire differed from each other in important ways, but for the seventeenth century this paper will concentrate on the West Country, and return at a later point to Yorkshire. In the West Country, the peak production of broadcloth had been during the reigns of Henry VII and Henry VIII.[26] The Cockayne interlude had very nearly brought the ruination of the industry although Cockayne ultimately encouraged the dyeing and finishing technologies. These technical improvements in dyeing and finishing prompted the manufacturers to concentrate on the development of fine colors and superior finishing processes. These processes, in turn, made it possible for the West Country industry to hold its own into the eighteenth century and even into the first quarter of the nineteenth.[27]

As Charles Wilson asserted, "Generally, in textiles, the finer the article, the more likely it was that the industry making it would be dominated by big capitalists capable of making the bigger outlay on finer materials, expensive dyes and tools."[28] The West counties where the finest broad and Spanish cloths were made tended to be

---

[26]Ponting, Woollen Industry of South-West England, pp. 21-29.

[27]Mann, Cloth Industry, p. viii; Wilson, England's Apprenticeship, pp. 66-78; Supple, Commercial Crisis, pp. 150-52.

[28]Wilson, England's Apprenticeship, p. 66.

dominated by clothier-fuller-capitalists. Their base of operations was the fulling mill. Clothiers bought wool and put it out to local weavers and spinsters who came to the clothier for raw materials. The clothier could become a sizeable operation with large capital invested in wool and cloth and employing as outworkers, many spinsters and weavers.

We are fortunate in having a cost analysis of the manufacturing of a piece of West Country medley cloth written by the Lord Chief Justice Sir Matthew Hale probably between 1659 and 1675. Hale came from a family of clothiers and was apparently familiar with the organization of the industry.[29]

> The ordinary process and time and charge of coarse medley cloth of our Gloucester wool at this day is:
>
> I. In every such cloth of about 32 yards long there is ninety pounds of wool which will cost at this day, at 12 d. per pound Ŀ4 10s., viz., ordinary in a grey cloth.
>
> 54 lb. of abb, 34 lb., of warp, 2 lb. of mixture

Ŀ	s.	d.
4	10	0

> II. The charge of making this cloth:

		Ŀ	s.	d.
1.	Parting and picking	0	3	0
2.	Colouring		16	0
3.	Breaking and spinning the abb, at 2 1/4d. per lb.	1	7	9*
4.	Breaking and spinning the warp, at 5d. per lb.	0	18	6*

---

[29]Mann, <u>Cloth Industry</u>, pp. 102-3, 318.

		Ł	s.	d.
5.	Cards and oil	1	0	0
6.	Weaving and spooling and warping	1	1	3
7.	Milling (fulling) and burling	0	12	0
8.	Shearing and dressing	0	18	0
9.	Drawing	0	7	6
10.	Carriage and factorage	0	7	0
	So the whole charges comes to	11	15	0

---

*The extensions for spinning are incorrect. Should be 10s. 2d. for the abb, 15s. for the warp; total should then be: Ł10 13 11 Perhaps Hale was including the breaking or carding without listing a separate price for it.

Out of which, deducting the materials of wool and cards and oil, viz., Ł5 10s., there remains entirely for the expense of work (to the) amount (of) Ł6 5s. It is true, at this day, this cloth yields not above Ł12 to be sold, which is only 5s. profit; but when trade is quicker, it may yield Ł13 or more.

III. The people that are employed in bringing about this cloth to be ready, are 14, viz., 3 weavers and spoolers, 2 breakers, 6 spinners, 1 fuller and burler, 1 shearman, 1 parter and picker; the weavers supply the office of spooler and warper.

IV. These will bring about the first cloth in about 2 months' space; but being continued in a constant tract, the cloth will be brought about in 3 weeks' time; for all the other workmen are at work and fit the cloth for the weaver in that space, that he is weaving the first cloth.

V. Consequently this one loom thus employed all the year round, allowing 2 months to the first cloth, and 3 weeks to every other, will make 14 returns the first year of cloth ready for sale, and 16 returns every year after.

> VI. Consequently that which this (loom) yields for bare wages to these 14 poor workmen for the first year is Ŀ97; and by this computation it is easy to see what every workmen can gain a week being full employed.[30]

If we can assume that the spinning and weaving was done partly, at least, by family members, then Hale's figures are not very far from Gregory King's estimate of the income of artisans. Weavers at Hale's rates would make about Ŀ17 per year. Using Hale's extensions (assuming that his wage prices for spinning are incompletely listed), the spinners would earn Ŀ37 per year for sixteen pieces. If three of the six spinners and all three weavers were members of the same family, their annual income would become Ŀ35 10s., not far at all from King's estmate of Ŀ40 for an artisan's annual income.[31]

If only two of the three weavers were part of the family, that annual income would be reduced to Ŀ11 6s. 8d; that combined with the income of three of the six spinners becomes Ŀ21 8s. This figure is very close to Julia deL. Mann's estimate that a constantly employed weaver might expect a gross return of Ŀ20 per year in the early eighteenth century.[32] The key, no doubt, was how much employment was available and how much family participation was possible.

---

[30]E. Lipson, The History of the Woollen and Worsted Industries (London: A. C. Black, 1921), pp. 256-57.

[31]C. Wilson, England's Apprenticeship, p. 239.

[32]Mann, Cloth Industry, p. 104.

The chronic problem with wage labor in seventeenth-century England was underemployment caused by the cyclical nature of the economy which in turn was dependent on the richness of the harvests and the good health of the population. Foreign conditions also played a role, often the critical role in the textile trade. During bad times, cloth manufacturing families could come very close to starvation; this became even more possible as the century went on in time, as cloth workers were recruited from cottagers who did not hold two to four acres of land for gardens and small livestock. Conditions changed in the woolen industry as in other industries, not necessarily for the better.[33]

In England in the eighteenth century, it was the northern counties that became the locus of dynamic industrial change. The major historians of that change in the woolen industry in Yorkshire--W. B. Crump, Herbert Heaton, D. T. Jenkins, and R. G. Wilson--do not suggest that Yorkshire should replace Lancashire as the leading edge of industrialization. Although the production of broadcloth more than trebled in Yorkshire in the last half of the eighteenth century,[34] the volume of production of

---

33Ibid., pp. 92, 102; L. A. Clarkson, The Pre-Industrial Economy in England (London: Batsford, 1971), p. 103.

34Derived from the figures in J. Bischoff, A Comprehensive History of the Woollen and Worsted Manufacture, 2 vols. (London: Smith, Elder, 1842; repr. London: Frank Cass, 1968), 2:app., table 4.

cotton wrought in just the last quarter of the eighteenth century was far more comprehensive and revolutionary.

One significant aspect of mechanization in Yorkshire's woolen industry was its great adaptability within the existing economic organization. Yorkshire was made up of individual families as economic units who owned a loom, or looms, and spinning wheels. These families bought the raw wool, manufactured say one piece of broadcloth per two weeks which it was able to have fulled and finished at the local mill for a fee. The cloth was then taken to be sold at one of the local cloth halls in Leeds, Wakefield, Huddersfield, or other cloth market towns.[35]

The fly-shuttle (see illus. 16) was the first important innovation to change traditional processes in the woolen industry. Invented, or rather patented, in 1733 it was greeted by hostility by English broadcloth weavers. Not until the last half of the eighteenth century did it proliferate to any degree in Yorkshire.[36] The mechanism was one that could be attached to existing looms. It not only increased productivity per loom, but allowed one weaver and a boy to weave broadcloth rather than the customary two men and a boy. In his analysis of the manufacture of the Gloucestershire medley cloth, Hale figured that two weavers

---

[35]Heaton, The Yorkshire Woollen and Worsted Industries, pp. 293-301.

[36]Ibid., pp. 340-42.

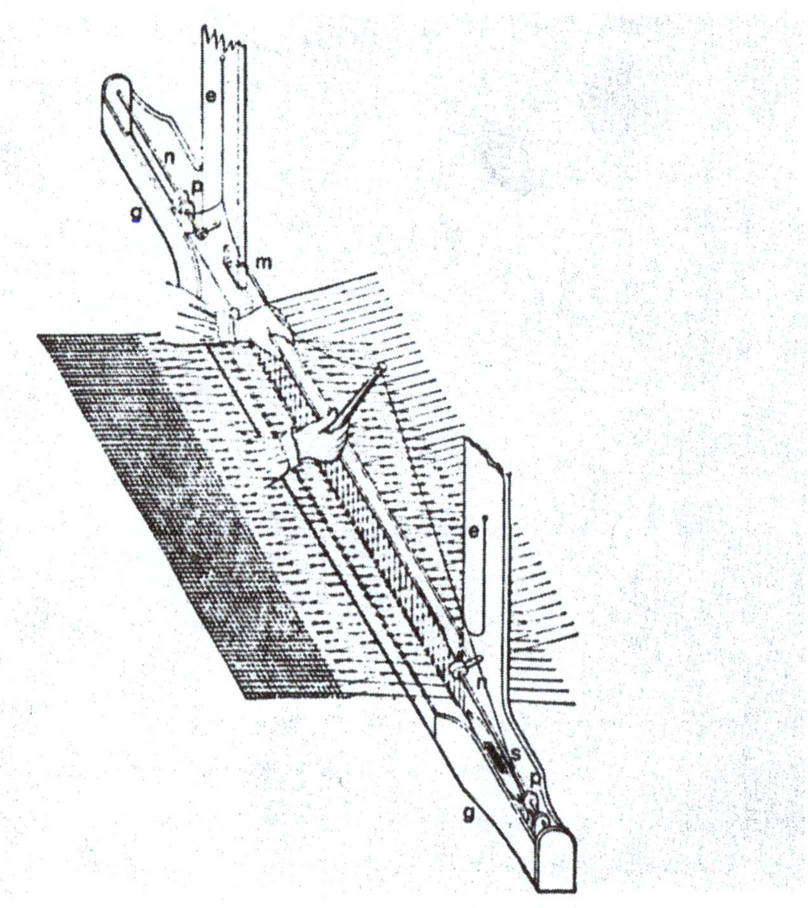

SOURCE: J. Geraint Jenkins, The Wool Textile Industry in Great Britain.

Illus. 16. Fly or Spring Shuttle.

could produce a thirty-two yard piece in three weeks or eighteen days. In the flannel, however, before fulling, this piece would have been forty-two to forty-five yards long.

The two weavers were able to produce 2 1/3 to 2 1/2 yards per day. Mann cites a weaver in 1840 who could weave, presumably on a fly-shuttle, a fifty-four yard piece of broadcloth in 150 hours. Reducing this to a twelve-hour day, this comes to 4 1/3 yards per day,[37] a figure that is very consistent with productivity figures in American woolen factories of the teens and early twenties of the nineteenth century.[38]

As weaving productivity increased so it was necessary for spinning productivity to increase. Figures for spinning seem not so clear as those for weaving. Mann calculated that one-half pound per day would be about right on the single spindled walking wheel.[39] If so, Hale's requirement of ninety pounds in three weeks would require closer to ten spinners than six.

---

[37]Mann, Cloth Industry, p. 325. Mann made an arithmetic mistake in her text by dividing the 150 hours by 54 yards; this figure gives the time required to weave one yard, about 2 3/4 hours, not 2 3/4 yards. Twelve hours divided by 2 3/4 hours equals 4.32 yards in one day. Or, the much simpler arithmetic--150 hours divided by twelve equals 12 1/2 work-days. Fifty-four yards divided by 12 1/2 work-days equals 4.32 yards per day.

[38]Infra., chap. 5.

[39]Mann, Cloth Industry, p. 322.

The most logical solution to the imbalance caused by slow spinning was a multiple spindle-head which in essence was what Hargreaves' spinning jenny was (c. 1764) (see illus. 17-19). The woolen roving was grasped by a clasp or clove which in turn was on a track of some kind. As the operator turned the engine wheel, the clove created the draft between it and the spindle. The clove was pulled away from the spindle at the same time. When the appropriate amount of twist was given to the roving, the operator stopped, wound up the spun yarns on the spindles just as he or she would have on the single spindle wool wheel. Hargreaves earliest jenny had eight spindles, and commonly the small household jennies that were used all over Yorkshire in the eighteenth century also had eight to twelve spindles.[40]

Although invented and patented earlier, the jenny did not proliferate in any of the woolen manufacturing areas until the 1780s, and its use was apparently given great impetus by the introduction of a pre-spinning machine called the billy or slubbing machine (see ill. 19). Slubbing basically drew out the carded wool giving it a very slight twist. Billies like jennies were hand powered until the teens of the nineteenth century. According to Rees, the

---

[40]Harold Catling, "The Evolution of Spinning," in Wool Textile Industry, ed. Jenkins, pp. 106-10.

SOURCE: Science Museum, London.

Illus. 17. Reconstructed Spinning Jenny.

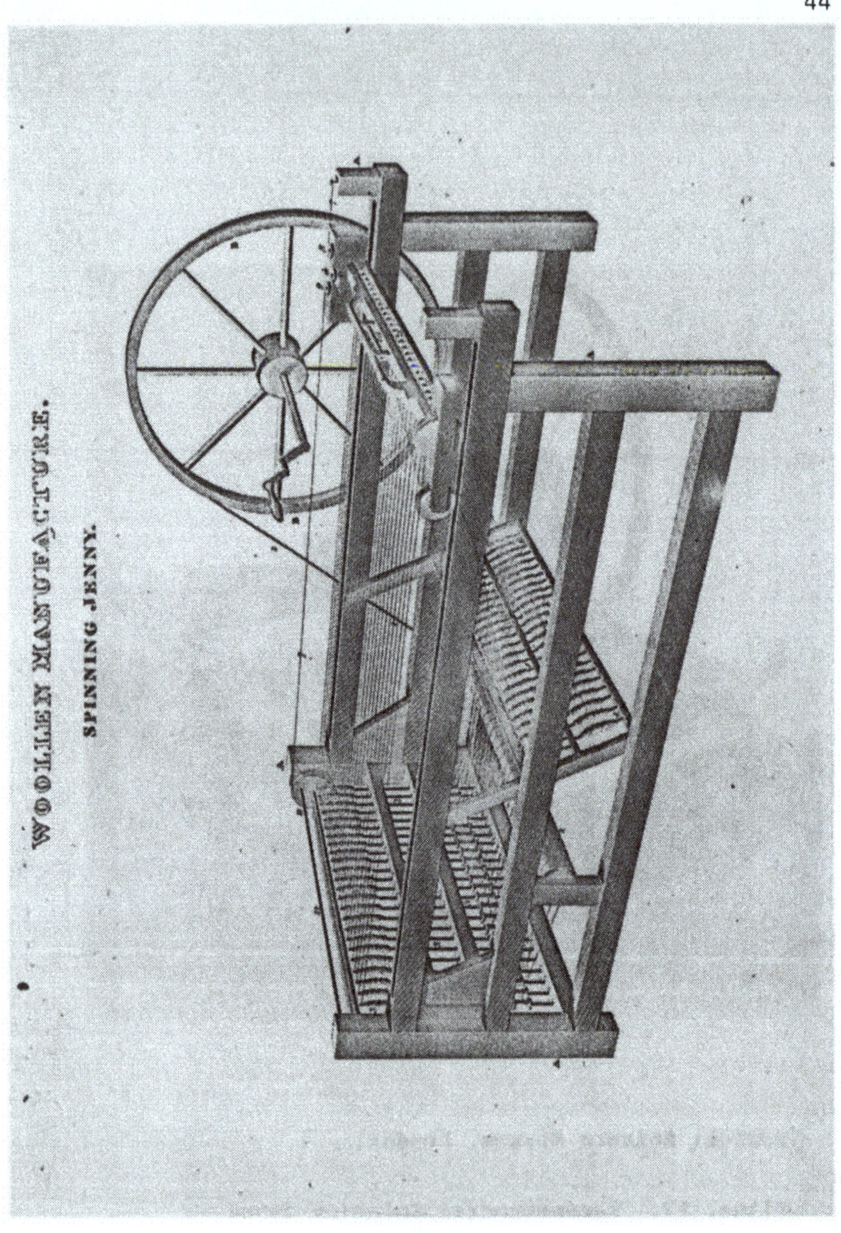

SOURCE: Rees' Cyclopaedia, 1811.

Illus. 18. Spinning Jenny.

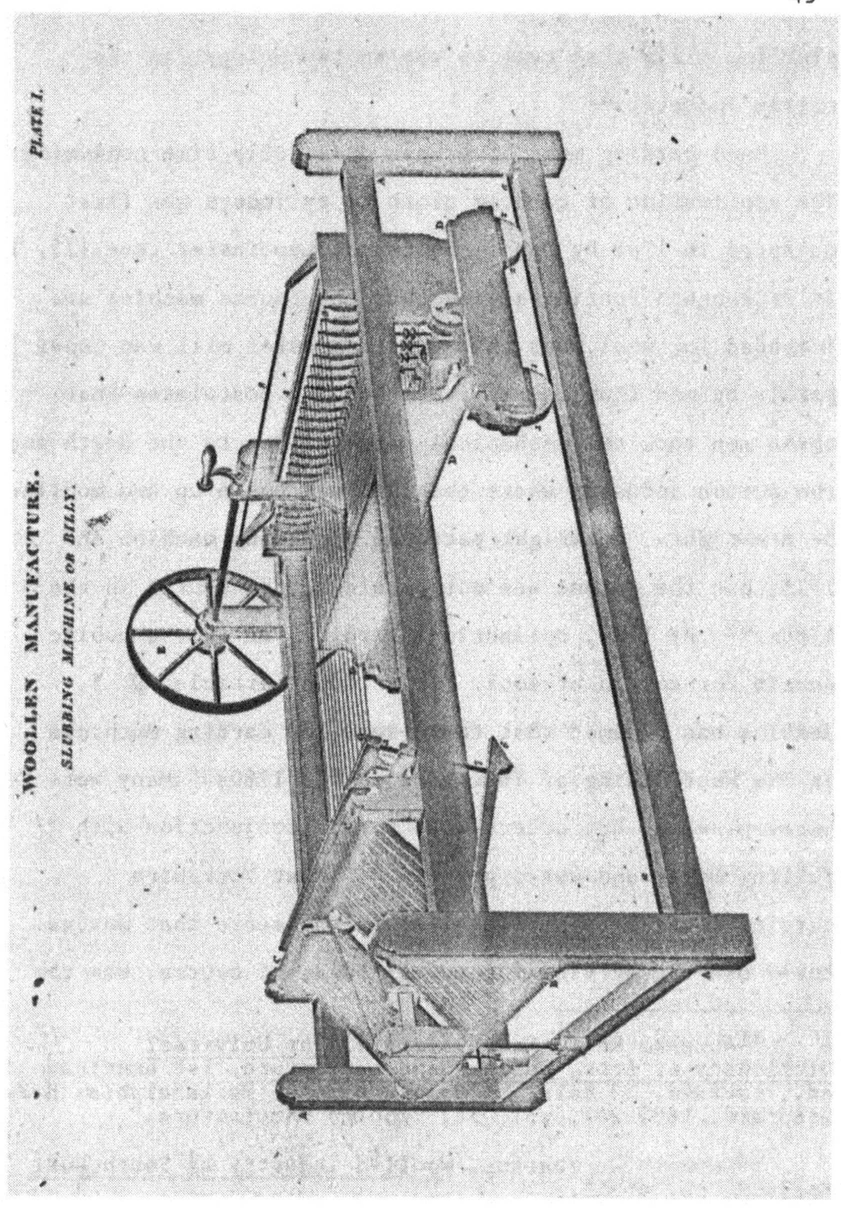

SOURCE: Rees' Cyclopaedia, 1811.

Illus. 19. Slubbing Machine or Billy.

slubbing billy also came to woolen technology via the cotton industry.[41]

Hand carding must have been dreadfully time consuming. The application of carding cloth to cylinders was first patented in 1748 by Daniel Bourne of Leominster (see ill. 20). It is Kenneth Ponting's view that the Bourne machine was intended for wool, but that the Leominster mill was owned partly by men from Lancashire. Ponting postulates that these men took the mechanical carding idea to the North and the cotton industry where the idea was taken up and modified by Arkwright. Arkwright patented a carding machine in 1775, but the patent was not upheld in the courts in the 1780s.[42] By 1785, cylindrical carding was in the public domain for cotton or wool. In a recent article, D. T. Jenkins has claimed that there were 170 carding machines in the West Riding of Yorkshire in the 1780s. Many were horse powered, but others were run in conjunction with fulling mills and water powered.[43] Most Yorkshire carding mills were public mills in the sense that anyone could use the service for a fee; this, of course, was the

---

[41]Abraham Rees, The Cyclopaedia or Universal Dictionary of Arts, Science and Literature, 1st American ed., revised, 39 vols., + 6 vol. plates (Philadelphia: S.F. Bradford, 1805-24), vol. 38, "Woollen Manufacture."

[42]Kenneth G. Ponting, Woollen Industry of South-West England, pp. 46-51.

[43]David Seward, "The Wool Textile Industry, 1750-1960," in Wool Textile Industry, ed. Jenkins, pp. 106-10.

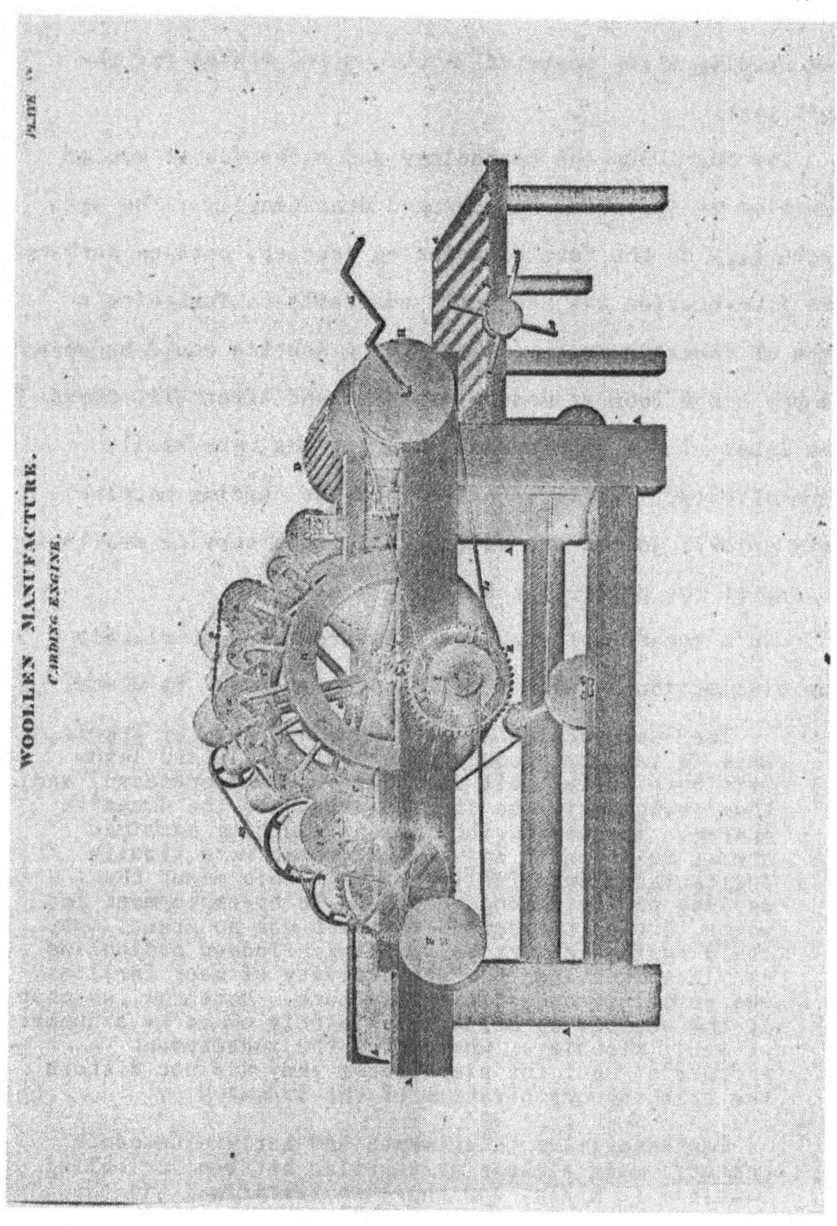

SOURCE: Rees' Cyclopaedia, 1809.

Illus. 20. Carding Engine.

way carding mills operated in the United States for the most part.

By the 1790s the technology and mechanics of woolen textiles in Yorkshire had changed dramatically. The new technology in the form of spinning jennies, carding machines, and fly-shuttles was perfectly adaptable to Yorkshire's type of domestic system. The spring shuttle could be added to any broad loom at modest expense, and after all, saved the labor of one journeyman. The jennies were small, uncomplicated, and inexpensive, and the carding machine very quickly joined the fulling mill as a service available to any of the public for a fee.

In a recent article, David Seward tried to clarify the distinction between a mill and a factory. He wrote:

> The introduction of machinery did not, by itself lead to factory production. The shuttle and jenny were both quite small and could be hand-operated, and thus could easily be incorporated into the domestic system. The new scribbling and slubbing machines needed to be power driven, but these were usually incorporated into fulling mills. This meant that carding or scribbling ceased to be by-employment for women, but as the demand for yarn was so great, they could easily convert to spinning. Indeed scribbling machines increased the productivity of many families and so helped domestic manufacture. Moreover, as most of the scribbling mills were jointly owned by a number of small clothiers, who carded the independent producers' wool for piece rates they did not disturb the existing organization of the industry.
>
> Contemporaries (eighteenth and early nineteenth century) made a clear distinction between scribbling machines in mills, and those in factories. In the former, the machine was installed by the owners to scribble wool brought in by customers; in the latter,

> the manufacturer constructed a mill with the primary intention of fulling and scribbling his own products, which was a clear break with the domestic system.[44]

Yet the famous Bean Ing of Leeds built in 1792-93 by Benjamin Gott demonstrates that even these distinctions can become blurred. As enormous as Bean Ing was--over 750 employees in 1813--Gott continued to operate as much as merchant/finisher as manufacturer, and Heaton estimated that three times more cloth was bought and finished than was actually manufactured in the factory.[45] For those who feel that industrialization depends on powered machinery (that is, inanimate power from steam which is somehow preferred over waterpower), Bean Ing did not live up to its potential for full factory status. The forty horsepower Boulton and Watt engine powered only willeys, scribbling and carding engines, fulling stocks, and some dyewood grinding rasps; that was all. Spinning, weaving, and finishing processes would wait at least until the second decade of the nineteenth century for inanimate power, and at that point the tradition-bound shearers and croppers effectively delayed their universal adoption.[46]

---

[44]Ibid.

[45]Herbert Heaton, "Benjamin Gott and the Industrial Revolution," Economic History Review, 1st ser., 3 (1931):63.

[46]Ibid., pp. 53-59; R. Offer, "The Papers of Benjamin Gott," in The Leeds Woollen Industry, 1780-1820, ed. W. B. Crump, vol. 32 (Leeds: Thoresby Society Publication, 1929; repr. New York: Johnson Reprints, 1967), pp. 178-83, 217.

By 1813 Bean Ing had burned and had been rebuilt once after a fire in 1799 and had undergone some additions. It employed 761 persons including 144 weavers, fifty-three spinners, and sixty-six bobbin winders. The mill operated three willeys, seven scribblers, and eight carders all of which required 102 workers plus two overlookers. The mill also hired four sorters, probably very well paid, and thirty-three moaters or hand pickers who had the help of five boys and another overlooker. Finishing was also accomplished by the mill itself and those processes employed eighty-one burlers, ninety-two croppers, sixteen dyers, and myriad perkers, friezers, premajers (cleaned the teasel handles used in raising the nap), scourers, sizers, and dryers. To repair and maintain machinery there was a sleymaking shop, joiners' shop, blacksmith shop with four smiths, cook, gas maker, engine man, night workers, and a watchman. There were five manufacturers who were treated in the account books as subcontractors, one wool buyer, and three salaried clerks.[47]

Bean Ing in 1815 made a profit of Ŀ5,200 on carding and scribbling for outside manufacturers; the dye house brought in Ŀ2,000 from custom work. The subcontractors paid into the firm a percentage of the value of the approximately 75,000 yards manufactured, and that totaled

---

[47]A. Yewdell, "Selections from the Mill Note-Book," in Leeds Woollen Industry, ed. W. B. Crump, pp. 306-7.

£6,500. The total profit then was £13,700, and this figure did not include profits on milling or fulling.[48]

Heaton, it will be recalled, thought the factory bought and finished three times more cloth than it produced itself.[49] Bean Ing was surely a large and lucrative business, but not strictly speaking a completely integrated factory.

Before leaving England altogether, two sources will be examined which summarize the traditional "state of the art" of wool manufacture at Trowbridge, Wiltshire in 1798 and at Bean Ing near Leeds, Yorkshire, 1811:[50]

1798. An estimate of the cost of manufacturing a superfine broadcloth from Trowbridge, Wiltshire.

	£	s.	d.
60 lb. wool @ 4s. 2d.	12	10	0
carriage @ 7d. per bag		1	9
trying @ 5d. per bag		1	3
dyeing 60 lb. @ 6d.	1	10	0
picking 59 lb. @ 1d. per lb.*		4	11*
oil, 8 lb. @ 1s. per lb. (8s. gall.)		8	0
scribbling, 59 lb. @ 2d.		9	10
carding 1 1/2d. Slubbing 1 1/2d. 59 lb. @ 3d. per lb.		14	9
cards for both per piece		1	0

48Ibid. Gott had 144 broad looms in operation. If each loom wove two yards per day for 312 days per year, this would produce 90,000 yards of cloth, less 20% for shrinkage equals 72,000 yards.

49Heaton, "Benjamin Gott and the Industrial Revolution," p. 63.

50Mann, Cloth Industry, p. 321.

	£	s.	d.
spinning warp, 440 skeins or 22 score @ 3 1/2d. per score		6	5
spinning abb, 34 lb. @ 2 1/2d. per lb.		7	1
weaving 40 yd. @ 15d. per yd.	2	10	0*
list and forrel		3	0
braying 18d. and burling 6s.		7	6
milling 3s. inspector 2d.		3	2
soap 4 lb. @ 13 1/4d. per lb.		4	5
dressing 30 yd. @ only 15d. per yd.	1	17	6
drawing 1s. carriage and postage 2s. 3d.		3	3
paper and twine			4
discount for cash on £10 @ 1d.			10
per £	22	5	0*
expenses in rent, interest, factors, charges, insurance for damages, etc. on a trade of six cloths a week			
	3	13	7 1/2
value of cloth	25	18	11 1/2
sale price of 29 1/2 yards @ 16s. 6d.	24	6	9**
loss	1	12	2 1/2

*Mistakes caught by Mann corrected by this writer.
**Mistake in extension corrected by this writer.

Benjamin Gott's Royal Prime cloth manufactured in 1811 sold for fourteen shillings per yard so presumably his costs were less than those for Wiltshire in 1798. Gott's cloth went through the following processes as listed from the "Mill Note-Book" attributed to John Dixon, Benjamin Gott's nephew:

The Processes of Manufacture[51]

(f.2) Fleece wool has to go (through) the following 29 processes before it is made into cloth ready for the Draper:--(1) The Sorting, (2) the Moating, (3) the Scouring, (4) the Dyeing, (5) The Drying, (6) Willowing & Oiling, (7) Scribbling, (8) Carding, (9) Slubbing, (10) Spinning, (11) Warping, (12) Weaving, (13) Knotting, (14) Scouring, (15) Drying 2nd, (16) Burling, (17) Milling, (18) Drying 3rd, (19) Witting & Raising, (20) Cropping, (21) Moising (Raising), (22) Drying 4th, (23) Shearing, (24) Brushing, (25) Burling, (26) Drawing, (27) Brushing, (28) Lettering & (29) Pressing.

Woolen Trade and Domestic Manufactures in the Colonies

In the seventeenth century, at least after 1630, overall economic conditions were far better in the mainland colonies of North America than in England. Land of course was the basis of economic well-being, and probably many of the professional weavers who emigrated to New England or Virginia took up land as soon as they were able. New England colonists had two sources for woolens; they made some themselves and a great deal was imported--probably all the cloth for "best clothes" for men, and for such outer garments as cloaks and coats for both men and women. The modern man's suit consisting of coat, waistcoat (or vest), and breeches can be dated from the period of Charles II, and that "best" suit with knee-length breeches plus an overcoat or cloak would have been made from woolen cloth.[52] The

[51]Crump, ed., Leeds Woollen Industry, p. 287.

[52]C. Willet and Phyllis Cunnington, Handbook of English Costume in the Seventeenth Century (Boston: Plays, Inc., 1972), p. 12.

quality of the cloth would have ranged from fine Spanish cloth to not-very-fine kersey, depending on the wealth and status of the wearer, and only would have been everyday wear for an upper class or professional person. The colonists also made and fulled their own cloth, but this was unlikely to be fine cloth.

Evidence is not abundant about any single factor relating to cloth production or cloth imports in the English colonies, but there are a few fragments that suggest a little of the relationship between the two. For one thing, there are shipping cocquets from vessels entering Boston harbor from 1645 to 1651. The following lists from the Aspinwall Notarial Records show the range of the types of imported textiles:[53]

> Woolens: cottons, Spanish cloths, Northern kerseys, frieze, Leyden duffles, broadcloth, Kentish longcloth, western kersey, penistònes, Devon dozens, plains.
>
> Worsteds and stuffs: says, chenies, shag bays, double bays, Norwich stuffs, rashes, Hampton serges, Mancheste single bays, perpetuanas, striped stuff.
>
> Linens and canvas: lockram, Kentish linen, oznabrigs, East Country linen, holland, lawns, canvas, sail cloth, Scotch cloth, slesey, Hamborough (Hamburg linen), dowlas, French linen, Guernsey linen, cambrics, ticking, Normandy canvas, Russia linen.
>
> Real cotton and mixtures: calico, taffeta, jean, fustian, dimity, vermilion, Turkey grogram.

---

[53]"Volume. . . . Containing the Aspinwall Notarial Records from 1644-1651," from Thirty-second Report of the Record Commissioners of the City of Boston (Boston: 1903), pp. 395-430.

> Ready-made clothes and miscellaneous fabric: shoes, sewing silk, boots, felt hats, stockings, belts, woolen stockings, cotton stockings, sackcloth, carpeting, ruggs (either a cloth or garment, but not small carpets), worsted stockings, vitry canvas, stuff hats, monmouth caps, upholstery, linen napkins, silk, plain gloves, blankets, coverlets spruce canvas, flannel, linen net, ribbon, lace, silk and silver buttons, waistcoats, binding.

In quantitative terms, the best course might be to examine one ship load, the Swallow which landed at Boston probably about April or May, 1650. (The latest cocquet is dated 20 March.) Twelve merchants received dry goods including woolen cloth. The number in the parentheses is the statutary requirements per piece:

30	pcs.	cottons (@12 yd. per piece)[54]
11	"	broadcloth, dressed (32)
100	"	penistones (12)
30	"	duffles (28)
320	"	goads Welch cottons (480 yd.)
2	"	frieze (12)
1 1/2	"	penistone (12)
350		goads cottons (525 yd.)
3 1/2	"	Welch cottons (12)
		Total: 4,581 yards

27	pcs.	Yorkshire kerseys
11	"	Devon
23	"	kerseys dresst (All @ 8 yd.
18	"	Devonshire per piece.)
		Total: 632 yards

50		serges
10		perpetuanas
16	pcs.	stuffs
14	"	Norwich stuff
2,000	yd.	bays
153		Norwich stuffs (All @ 8 yd.
1		double bay per piece.)
		Total: 4,760 yards

---

[54]Ibid., pp. 413-16; Supple, Commercial Crisis, p. 257.

Besides these varieties of woolens and worsteds, there were substantial quantities of canvas, Dutch, German, French, and English linens, lawns, monmouth caps, dowlas, Indian calico, worsted stockings, fustian and ruggs. All this aboard one ship; no wonder Bernard Bailyn was compelled to put this in proportion by saying that the most productive weaver in Rowley could not weave as much in the nine years between 1673-82 as one ship load into Boston.

Yet this probably is not an apt comparison.[55] No weaver in Rowley in the 1680s wove more than 100 yards in a year, probably because no one could afford to be a full-time weaver, and a man would have had to work on his own planting and harvesting or a neighbor's during those seasons. Nevertheless, Bailyn had a point: the output of the Rowley fulling mill in 1687 was only about 3,600 yards, or a good deal less than what one ship supplied in true woolen cloth in 1650.[56]

According to Arthur H. Cole, fulling mills dotted the New England countryside by 1700.[57] There were sizeable

---

[55]Bernard Bailyn, The New England Merchants in the Seventeenth Century (New York: Harper & Row, 1964), p. 74.

[56]Pearson Family Fulling Account Book, Baker Library, Harvard Business School, Boston, Massachusetts.

[57]Arthur Harrison Cole, The American Wool Manufacture, 2 vols., 2nd ed. (New York: Harper & Row, 1968), 1:10-12.

numbers of sheep raised in Rhode Island and on Long Island among English farmers. John Winthrop, Jr. started a plantation on Fisher's Island in 1643; his sons kept "several thousand" sheep there.[58] On eastern Long Island in 1675 some 1,473 sheep were reported on 271 farms, and on Romney Marsh outside of Boston thirty-one landholders were taxed for 1,544 sheep. There is some evidence that sheep like people were healthier and more prolific in the New World than in the Old.[59]

One of the first mentions of sheep in all New England is from William Bradford's "Journal," a sad little story that took place in 1642. Without recounting the gory details (Bradford spared us), one Thomas Granger, about sixteen or seventeen years of age, was executed for sodomy along with the objects of his acts--a mare, a cow, two goats, five sheep, and a turkey.[60] The loss of these livestock must have been a sizeable one for the small community.

---

[58]Richard S. Dunn, Puritans and Yankees: The Winthrop Dynasty of New England, 1630-1717 (New York: Norton, 1971), p. 259.

[59]Percy W. Bidwell and John I. Falconer, History of Agriculture in the Northern United States, 1620-1860 (New York: Peter Smith, 1941), pp. 28-29; Carl Bridenbaugh, Fat Mutton and Liberty of Conscience (New York: Atheneum, 1976), pp. 52-53.

[60]William Bradford, Of Plymouth Plantation, ed. Samuel Eliot Morison (New York: Knopf, Modern Library, 1952), pp. 320-21.

There is very little commentary related to the climatic change which émigrés from Old England to New England experienced. Coastal areas do not get the vast amounts of snow that western Massachusetts commonly endures, yet even Boston was snowier than the environs of London. The mean temperatures were colder in winter, and indeed hotter in July. There may have been somewhat less mud as for three to four months the ground would have been frozen solid and by late April, the land would have become dried out. Parts of England can be muddy all winter. There were wild animals in America, wolves in particular. From the beginning, the English colonists were forced to readjust much of their traditional agricultural behavior. Wheat was not as reliable as Indian corn; native grasses lacked the nutrition of English grass; the winters were too harsh for all but the hardiest stock who required protection in barns or sheds.

What is surprising is how quickly these colonists did adapt. Sheep presented them with difficult problems. As any student of the American West is aware, you cannot graze sheep with other livestock on the same pasture, because the sheep crop the grass so short that other animals cannot reach it. The wolf problem was solved by putting the sheep out on islands, and the problem of forage was solved by putting the sheep on necks of land that required little fencing to keep other stock out and keep the sheep in.

Most towns on Long Island, and many in New England had town flocks by the last half of the seventeenth century. During the summer the sheep were placed in the care of a shepherd who moved them from fold to fold, hopefully giving each landholder equal benefits of manure. In the spring, each farmer washed and sheared his own sheep; new lambs were earmarked and the flocks of sheep put out to common pasture until fall. Since they required some protection from the winter elements, each farmer regained his own sheep at the annual "sheep parting" in the fall when the sheep were separated according to earmark at what was by at least one description, a rather jolly October town fair.[61]

In 1642 large scale sheep farming was begun on Aquidneck Island by William Coddington. His business was such that he supplied farmers on Long Island and New Haven Colony with sheep. Bridenbaugh quoted a letter of Coddington's of 1647 to John Winthrop, Jr. arranging to sell ten queen ewes, likely twin producers, for £20 "English money." At the same time Coddington related to Winthrop that he was trading two black ewes for two Cotswold rams of Mr. Smyth of New Haven. Winthrop was starting his plantation on Fishers Island, and Coddington was taking obvious care to provide Winthrop with good stock.[62]

---

[61]Daniel M. Tredwell, Personal Reminiscences of Men and Things on Long Island (Brooklyn: Charles Andrew Ditmas, 1912), 86-92.

[62]Bridenbaugh, Fat Mutton, pp. 50-51.

Among gentlemen farmers quality was as important a consideration in the seventeenth century as it ever was; only the ordinary farmer could not afford the time or money to upgrade his flocks.

One picture shows the nature of Rhode Island sheep which coincides neatly with William Coddington's reference to Cotswolds in his letter to Winthrop. This is on the "Council Seal of Newport Rhoade Island" made in silver by Arnold Collins about 1696. It shows a long-legged, long tailed, straight-backed sheep. The fleece looks heavy and curly and therefore long.[63] Cotswold sheep were described by William Spooner of the Royal Agricultural Society in the 1850s as, "a large breed of sheep, with long and abundant fleece," prolific and hardy with superior mutton. The example pictured in Randall has a very straight back and a cropped tail.[64] Another small hint appears in the naming of the principal sheep grazing area around Boston--Romney Marsh (now Chelsea). This area was so labeled on a 1637 map. English Romney Marsh sheep are also long-wooled.[65] Of course, the existence of long-wooled sheep does not mean there were no short, fine wooled ones; yet, long-wooled sheep are seldom referred to in the American

---

[63]Bridenbaugh, Fat Mutton, p. 57 and plate 4.

[64]Henry S. Randall, Sheep Husbandry (New York: Orange Judd & Co., 1860), pp. 149-50.

[65]Bidwell and Falconer, History of Agriculture, p. 28; Thirsk, "Farming Techniques," p. 191.

colonies or the United States in the eighteenth century or the first quarter of the nineteenth.

Although the evidence is negative, it seems clear that the quality of American sheep deteriorated during the course of the eighteenth century. For one thing, there was no legal way to import sheep that could improve those that were here; England had restrictions against exports of sheep dating from Elizabethan times and these were reinstituted with other trade restrictions in 1660. In Spain, where by now the finest wool was exported as raw wool, the government long had restricted the export of sheep. Bidwell and Falconer described the common American sheep of the eighteenth century as follows,[66]

> small, long-legged, narrow in the breast and back, and also slow at arriving at maturity. They may have stood two and one-half feet high and weighed when dressed from ten to fifteen pounds per quarter, or in exceptional cases, twenty pounds. They yielded on average from two to three pounds of coarse, short-staple wool at shearing.

It seems probable that the quality of sheep reflected regional differences. These types of differences could turn around some of the negative comments by such as Peter Kalm, M'Roberts, and William Strickland. Around cities such as Boston and New York which had easy and ample access to woolen cloth imports, sheep were raised mostly for meat, and the proliferation of English hays in the latter half of the

---

[66]Bidwell and Falconer, History of Agriculture, p. 110.

eighteenth century would have been helpful in seeing the animals through the winter and fattening them for market. Their wool would have been incidental.[67] The Narragansett country of Rhode Island also was deeply involved with the livestock export market, in this case to the West Indies. Rhode Islanders marketed wool locally, but many Rhode Island sheep were shipped out live and slaughtered for meat at their destination.[68]

In both New England and New York, backcountry farms raised small flocks for sheep for their wool and for their meat, but with greater need for the wool. Around Philadelphia where woolen carpet manufacture was well-established by 1800, sheep also must have been raised for both wool and meat.[69] Yet this was not extensive; of Chester and Lancaster county farms in 1769, less than half kept sheep, averaging about seven sheep per farm. In 1782 the average was a little higher but nothing like the numbers in large English or even Rhode Island flocks.[70]

[67]Karen J. Friedmann, "Victualling Colonial Boston," Agricultural History 47 (July 1973):189-205; John T. Schlebecker, "Agricutural Markets and Marketing in the North, 1774-1777," Agricultural History 50 (January 1976): 21-36.

[68]Bridenbaugh, Fat Mutton, p. 55.

[69]Sam Bass Warner, Jr., The Private City: Philadelphia in Three Periods of Its Growth (Philadelphia: University of Pennsylvania Press, 1968), p. 69.

[70]James T. Lemon, The Best Poor Man's Country: A Geographical Study of Early Southeastern Pennsylvania (Baltimore: Johns Hopkins University Press, 1972), pp. 162, 214-15.

The immediate environs of Philadelphia still must have depended on English dry goods at least for best cloth and clothing. The early development of the Pennsylvania backcountry both as a source of marketable goods and as a market made it possible to manufacture and sell cheap Philadelphia-made cloth as well as fancy and not so fancy English cloth.

Occasionally, one encounters suggestions that Americans totally disliked lamb and mutton. The source for this is Peter Kalm who went so far as to say, ". . . Mutton was as objectionable to the Americans as pork to the Israelite."[71] He claimed that this prejudice was a greater hindrance to the development of sheep than any restrictions by the English. This is not a sound judgment. Any account of city markets in the colonial period includes something on the sale of lamb or mutton;[72] there are countless diary references to them by such as William Byrd and Washington. However, there were problems with sheep keeping besides the above mentioned wolves. Because they need grass, they are completely unsuited for forested regions where pigs, for example, thrive. For another, they lack the obvious size and hardiness of neat cattle.

---

[71]Peter Kalm, Travels in North America; the English Version of 1770, rev. and ed. Adolph E. Benson, 2 vols. (New York: Dover, 1966).

[72]Bridenbaugh, Fat Mutton, p. 102; Friedmann, "Victualling Colonial Boston," p. 191.

Probably the most significant difficulty is with preserving the meat. Mutton can be salted down, even canned in the nineteenth century, but it is not very good to eat that way. There also may be mythology associated with this presumed dislike. This myth may be rooted in the urgings during the Revolutionary War against the eating of lamb and mutton in order that the sheep could be saved for their wool production.[73] The wool, of course, was to be used to provide uniform clothing for the Continental army.

Before proceeding with eighteenth-century sources of woolen cloth, style changes in clothing that required woolen cloth should be examined. What is seen in portraits, and what has been saved from the ravages of moths and paper factories are the very best clothes that people owned. While a best suit for a man in the eighteenth century could have been made from colorful silks, satins, and elaborate embroidery, standard wear was woolen cloth. The Cunningtons said it thus:[74]

> By the end of the century woolen cloth had reached the very pinnacle; in 1795 the King himself at a Reception was wearing "a prune-coloured coat of broadcloth," and in 1797 Prime Minister Mr. Pitt "went to Court in a brown cloth dress."
>
> No doubt it was patriotic in wartime to wear English cloth instead of foreign silks.

---

[73]Schlebecker, "Agricultural Markets," p. 33.

[74]C. Willet and Phyllis Cunnington, Handbook of English Costume in the Eighteenth Century (Boston: Plays, Inc., 1972), pp. 19-20.

> But the final triumph of this material came when the arbiter of fashion George Brummel pronounced the revolutionary doctrine that henceforth a gentleman's clothes should be inconspicuous in material and exquisite only in fit; and for this he laid down the rule that the only permissible material was--cloth.

The Cunningtons also quote a receipt for a "cloth Frock suit" from 1756. The cost of the entire suit was Ŀ7.18.0; the superfine cloth, four yards, Ŀ3.12.0,[75] or 45 percent of the total.

Women did not wear as much woolen for everyday clothes as men, except lower class women in both England and the colonies who relied on kerseys or homespun. For outer wear, coats and cloaks, and riding habits, fine cloth would have been desirable although not necessarily affordable.[76]

Table 1 is designed to document the exports and per capita imports of cloth--long, short, and Spanish cloths--from England to the mainland American colonies. Some generalizations about the relationship of Britain to her mainland colonies are visible. Population was numerically small in the early days of settlement, but when it passed one million, the colonial market seems to have been discovered by English woolen merchants and manufacturers. As can be seen by table 1, the mainland American colonies and the United States were in receipt of 15 to 50 percent of the cloth exported from England in the last half of the eighteenth century. These figures correspond

---

[75]Ibid., p. 423. [76]Ibid., p. 308.

TABLE 1

PERCENT OF ENGLISH CLOTH EXPORTED TO THE MAINLAND COLONIES AND PER CAPITA IMPORTS OF WOOLEN CLOTH TO THOSE COLONIES

Year	Population of mainland colonies (000)	Yards cloth exported to mainland colonies (000)	Percent of total English manufacture exported to mainland Colonies	Per Capita imports of cloth by mainland colonies (yards)
1700	275	32	2	.113
1710	358	20	1	.059
1720	474	38	2	.08
1730	655	103	6	.157
1740	889	197	16	.221
1750	1,207	383	23	.117
1760	1,610	880	35	.547
1770	2,205	441	19	.2
1780	2,781	238	15	.086
1790	3,930	2,916	50	.742
1800	5,308	310	19	.058

SOURCE: J. Potter, "The Growth of Population in America, 1700-1860," in *Population in History: Essays in Historical Demography*, ed. D. V. Glass and D. E. C. Eversley (London: Edward Arnold, 1965), pp. 631-88; Elizabeth B. Schumpeter, *English Overseas Trade Statistics, 1697-1808* (Oxford: Clarendon Press, 1960), pp. 35-42.

nicely with the 30 to 35 percent figure that Shepherd and Walton figured so carefully for the five-year period from 1768-72.[77] During the period after the Revolution to the Napoleonic wars, the United States was taking about half of the most important and valuable of English exports. These figures will make interesting comparisons with the amounts in the 1810 national census and the New York State censuses of 1820 and 1825. A comment is in order regarding the one-half yard plus of cloth imported per capita in 1760, and the three-quarters of a yard in 1790. These cloths are 6 1/2 to 7 quarters in breadth, so each yard equalled between 1 5/8 and 1 3/4 square yards of cloth. If adult males were the major consumers of woolen cloth, and if they numbered approximately one-fourth of the population, these figures can be adjusted accordingly: 3 1/4 to 5 1/4 square yards of woolen cloth were imported per adult male. Since one man's suit required about 7 to 7 1/2 square yards, and since few men would have had more than one fine suit, it follows that cloth imports may have surpassed market needs in those years. It should be remembered that this cloth--short, long, and Spanish, can be identified and

---

[77]James F. Shepherd and Gary M. Walton, _Shipping, Maritime Trade and the Economic Development of Colonial North America_ (Cambridge: Cambridge University Press, 1972), p. 180.

measured. When the mare's nest of domestic, family-made cloth is considered, the precision of measurement cannot be nearly so neat.

Any pre-1765 analysis of American home cloth production is fraught with hazards. Trouble starts with the definition of "domestic manufacture," a term used interchangeably to mean on the one hand, home or family manufacture, and on the other, non-imported or non-foreign manufacture. Arthur Harrison Cole made a very legitimate effort at analyzing the relationship of domestic manufacture to imports, but he lacked E. B. Schumpeter's figures, as thin as they are.[78] Perhaps some sense of comfort can be achieved by taking note of certain basic aspects of life and law in eighteenth-century America and England.

English woolen manufacturers always had the ear of Parliament. The wool lobby, to use the American term, was strong and powerful from the time of Edward III through the nineteenth century.[79] What the wool lobby sought and achieved with varying results was legislation for quality control, workmanship, apprenticeships, import restrictions,

---

[78]Arthur Harrison Cole, The American Wool Manufacture 1:261, 336-49.

[79]This comment applies to manufacturers of fine woolen cloth, not necessarily to stuff and worsted manufacturers. The kersey manufacturers were on the scene later in terms of significant exports, but by the late seventeenth century, they also had their Parliamentary listeners.

and restrictions on the export of wool. Clothiers hoped to be protected from any and all competition. The Woollen Act of 1699 was primarily directed against Irish competition and prohibited the importation of Irish woolens into England. It also contained a clause directed against "Woollen Manufacture of any of the English Plantations in America." This section of the act prohibited intercolonial sale and export as well as the export of woolens out of any of the Plantations.[80]

Records showing quantities of colonial manufacturing of textiles simply do not exist. Cole felt that nearly all production was home oriented--made for families in homes and used there; but as he also knew, there were professional weavers in the towns, and he also felt that there were itinerant weavers in the countryside.[81] This notion of itinerancy is difficult to visualize, both in the colonial period and later in the early national period. The one clear reference to itinerancy is from a report by Governor Henry Moore of New York to the Board of Trade on 12 January 1767. The paragraph in full is as follows:[82]

> There is a small manufactory of linen in this city under the conduct of one Wells, and supported chiefly by the subscriptions of a set of men who call

---

[80]Merrill Jensen, English Historical Documents: American Colonial Documents to 1776, vol. 10, of English Historical Documents, ed. David C. Douglas, 12 vols. (New York: Oxford University Press, 1955), p. 414.

[81]Cole, Wool Manufacture, 1:13-17.

[82]Jensen, Colonial Documents, pp. 420-21.

> themselves the Society of Arts and Agriculture. No more than fourteen looms are employed in it, and it was established in order to give bread to several poor families which were a considerable charge to the city, and are now comfortably supported by their own daily labour, in spinning of flax. It does not appear that there is any established fabric of broadcloth here; and some poor weavers from Yorkshire who came over lately in expectation of being engaged to make broadcloths, could find no employment. But there is a general manufactory of woollen carried on here, and consists of two sorts, the first a coarse cloth entirely woollen, three fourths of a yard wide; and the other a stuff which they call linsey woolsey. The warp of this is linen, and the woof woollen; and a very small quantity of it is ever sent to market. Last year when the riots and disorders were at the height on the occasion of the Stamp Act, these manufactures were greatly boasted of, and the quantity then made greatly magnified by those who were desirous of distinguishing themselves as American patriots, and would wear nothing else. They were sometimes sold for three times their value; but the manufacturers themselves showed that they had more good sense than the persons who employed them, for they never clothed themselves with the work of their own hands but readily brought it to market, and selling it at an extravagant price there, bought English cloth for themselves and their families. The custom of making these coarse cloths in private families prevails throughout the whole province, and almost in every house a sufficient quantity is manufactured for the use of the family without the least design of sending any of it to market. This I had an opportunity of seeing during the late tour I made, and had the same accounts given me by all those persons of whom I made any inquiry, for every house swarms with children who are set to work as soon as they are able to spin and card; and as every family is furnished with a loom, the itinerant weavers who travel about the country put the finishing hand to the work.

First of all there is a normal amount of exaggerated rhetoric in the report. In no part of the country was it likely that "every family" was furnished with a loom. In the upcountry areas of New Hampshire in 1810, one out of two families had a loom, but this was the area of the country of greatest density of looms, and for reasons that will be explained below, this would have been a time of greatest home production.[83] Secondly, it is odd that Governor Moore did not know what linsey-woolsey was--or thought the Board of Trade would be unfamiliar with the term. Cole also assumed linsey-woolsey to have been an American phenomenon;[84] not so, as it was imported in the mid-seventeenth century into Boston.[85] Also the Oxford English Dictionary lists quotations using the term from Shakespeare, Celia Fiennes, Daniel Denton, Samuel Johnson, and Fielding's Tom Jones so it could not have been obscure.[86]

Most people in colonial America lived in or on the periphery of a concentrated settlement (village) within a township or parish, and in many villages a professional weaver was likely to be found. Now this man may have been highly skilled, but he may not have been able to survive with weaving as his only livelihood. He may then have been a fuller or a farmer, or he may have held down two or all three occupations. It may have been possible for a

---

[83]Tench Coxe, A Statement of the Arts and Manufactures of the United States of America, 1810 (Philadelphia: Cornman, 1814); Potter, "Population in America," pp. 664-65.

[84]Cole, Wool Manufacture, 1:29.

[85]Aspinwall Notarial Records, pp. 401, 423-24, 426.

[86]Compact O.E.D., 1:1633.

journeyman weaver to have woven in different homes, and it is also possible that the journeyman's roots never penetrated too deeply until if and when, he too became a property owner. Mobility, after all, has long been thought of as part of the American character.[87] When the factories came into existence, weavers were no more nor less mobile than other factory hands.

Fourthly, most home weaving was plain weaving; some of the home-woven wool had the capacity for being finished in the fulling mill. This would have felted the cloth and made it stronger and more weather resistant. Except for the initial turning on of the warp of a hand loom, there was nothing very difficult about the weaving operation; indeed, except that it could be frustrating, there was nothing difficult about warping and threading a loom, so there really was no need for an itinerant to "put the finishing hand to (the weaving)."[88] Also, it was perfectly possible for the weaving to have been done by women. Certainly, the eighteenth century had fewer concerns about gender roles than the nineteenth, and as women took over other types of work from men, so too they could have worked the looms. When the power looms came into the

---

87 George Wilson Pierson, "The M-Factor in American History," American Quarterly 14 (Summer 1962):275-89.

88 Edward F. Worst, Foot-Power Loom Weaving, 6th ed. (Milwaukee: Bruce Publishing Co., 1924; repr. New York: Dover, 1974), pp. 7-39.

factory, part of the purpose was to make it possible to have women tend them; no one seemed to have seen that as a startling innovation.

Finally, whatever efforts there were in this country to make really fine cloth in colonial days, those efforts could not have been undertaken by journeymen or women. So far, no records of American master weavers of superfine broadcloth have come to light. The fly or spring shuttle was not recorded in this country until after the Revolution, so whatever fine cloth there was would have had to have been narrow cloth as there is no evidence of any kind of the existence of broadlooms that would have required the labors of two men and a boy. Even the slave South would not have been hospitable to such labor intensity.

Probably most weaving was similar to that found by the Weiss's in two account books by Peter Holsart of Freehold (Monmouth County), New Jersey. The accounts are now in possession of the Rutgers University library. Holsart wove linsey-woolsey, worsted, dimity, and kersey in his 1751 accounts. In the 1769-1803 accounts, most of the textiles would seem to have been linen or cotton as the fabric was measured in ells.[89]

The English fine cloth industry in no way should have felt threatened by colonial manufacture. Americans lacked

---

[89] Harry B. Weiss and Grace M. Ziegler, The Early Woolen Industry of New Jersey (Trenton: New Jersey Agricultural Society, 1958), pp. 22-23.

the skills, raw materials, and even the interest to compete against the very fine and expensive woolens that came from the West Country and increasingly in the eighteenth century from Yorkshire. A few attempts were made to set up such cloth establishments as mentioned by Moore, but none survived as far as is known until after the Revolution. There is, however, another side to this coin. The colonies were rich in land, in livestock, in commercial profits; by 1765 the same colonials who reviled the Stamp Act were enjoying their prosperity as cooperating members of the most dynamic empire of all time, or at least since the Romans. The textile needs for over 1 1/2 million people were vast and included napkins, sacks and bags, underwear including diapers, upholstery, work clothes, bed sheets, blankets and coverlets. Certainly textile imports were large; but so was domestic manufacture. There is no way to measure the relationship.

There is no terminology to designate home textile manufacture. To describe it as a "folk industry" implies that sophisticated or urban people were never involved. They certainly were in America, especially during the bursts of home textile production that coincided with the patriotic fervor during periods of commercial boycotts and embargoes. To call it a peasant industry conveys a manorial organization that rarely existed anywhere in England or America from the early eighteenth century on. Technologically, this industry--folk textiles--was the same in America as in England and in the rest of western Europe. In the 1760s the raw wool came from one's farm or a neighbor's. As it was sheared in the spring, someone in the neighborhood with a little more expertise sorted it into three or four types; some might be for sale, especially if prices were high; some was set aside for flannel, some for cloth that would benefit by fulling. The last was washed probably with soap, and not likely with anything stronger. Then the wool was picked over by hand; the worst of the twigs and burrs were removed; the fibers were separated and disentangled. It was then carded with hand cards imported from England, and so the same on both sides of the ocean. Carding homogenized the fibers and formed them into rolls for the spinner. Spinning carded wool was done on the great or walking wheel. The wheel could have been imported but also could have been made by a proficient joiner/turner in America. Nathanial Dominy IV of East Hampton, Long Island, made at least three wool wheels in 1770, along with sixteen "Dutch" or Saxony or linen wheels. The latter cost £1, the wool "wheals" ten shillings or half as much, no doubt because they were made with less metal hardware and from a simpler design.[90] Spinning on the wool wheel was an intermittant operation, an aspect of spinning technology

[90]Charles F. Hummel, With Hammer in Hand: The Dominy Craftsmen of East Hampton, New York (Charlottesville: University of Virginia Press, 1968, publ. for the Henry Francis duPont Winthcrthur Museum), pp. 354-55.

that would continue throughout the early period of mechanization. The spinner grasped the roll as she turned the engine wheel with her other hand. As she drew out the yarn she walked alonside and away from the wheel continuing to turn the engine wheel as she walked. When she had created enough draft and corresponding twist, she gave the engine wheel another couple of turns to give a little additional twist to the yarn. She then stopped the process, and while walking toward the wheel, wound the yarn on to the very same spindle. These principles would not change with multiple head spindles--with jennies or with water-powered jacks.

The spun yarn was then ready to be woven or knitted into stockings. Woven cloth of decent quality could then be finished in the fulling mill. Fulling felted the yarns to make it possible to cut the cloth without ravels, and also to give the wearer some modest water resistance. After it was fulled, it was stretched on tenter hooks. Then a dresser of fine cloth would raise the nap of the cloth with teasels in a hand held frame, then shear that nap with giant, heavy, and unwieldy wool shears. The final process was pressing between hot iron plates in a large screw press.[91] How much of these final finishing processes were accomplished by country fullers in England or America is questionable. The cloth would hardly be worth the labor

---

[91]*Descriptions des Arts et Metiers* (1975), s.v. "Art de la *Draperie," by Henry Louis Duhamel* du Monceau. See pp. 9-23.

involved. Coloring could have been done at any one of three possible stages--in the wool, which was most common for really fine cloth, in the yarn, or in the piece. Few country dyers in England or America knew important secrets of dye recipes and mordants, and they knew even less of the precise chemistry of dyeing.

Perhaps no movement in American history was so pervasive and long-lived as that for economic independence. That in reality there can be no such thing, then or now, has never taken away its ideological and chauvinistic appeal. An independent nation required independent people, strong, hardy, individualistic and above all, self-sufficient. The personification of this ideal was ubiquitous--the Pioneer, the Frontiersman, the Mountainman, the Scout, and even more universal, the American Yeoman Farmer. No Fourth of July speech expressed it more nostalgically than Henry P. Hedges looking back at his colonial ancestors in Suffolk County, New York, in the 1880s:[92]

> From his feet to his head the farmer stood in vestment produced on his farm. The leather of his shoes came from the hides of his own cattle. The linen and woolen that he wore were products that he raised. The farmer's wife or daughter braided and sewed the straw hat on his head. His fur cap was made from the skin of a fox he shot. The feathers of wild fowl in the bed wheron he rested his weary frame at night, were the results acquired in his shooting. The pillow-cases, sheets and blankets, the

---

[92]Henry P. Hedges, Bicentennial History of Suffolk County, as quoted in Bidwell and Falconer, History of Agriculture, pp. 126-27.

> comfortables, quilts and counterpanes, the towels and table cloth, were home made. His harness and lines he cut from hides grown on his farm. Everything about his ox yoke except staple and ring he made. His whip, his ox gad, his flail, axe, hoe and fork handle were his own work. How little he bought, and how much he contrived to supply his wants by home manufacture would astonish this generation.

Homespun became the very symbol of the self-sufficient American. How much homespun was there? It should be clear from the above that there is no way to quantify it in the eighteenth century. Colonial governors' reports said there was little or none for sale; it was in their interest to say so especially during the unrest of the 1760s. Most of them said just that, Governor Bernard going so far as to say in 1768 to the Earl of Shelburne:[93]

> All the wool in the province (Massachusetts) would not make two pair of stockings a year for each person. It has always been worked up, chiefly in the families where it grows, and there used, not being fit for any market; all the advantage being its being done in the dead time of the year when there is no work to be done out of doors. There is no probability of any increase or improvement in this than what has been time out of mind.

On the other hand, newspaper reports were full during the '60s of reports of spinning bees, of record amounts spun or woven, of classes graduating from college "dressed altogether in the manufacture of this country; . . ."[94]

---

[93] Jensen, Colonial Documents, pp. 419-20.

[94] Philip Davidson, Propaganda and the American Revolution, 1763-1783 (Chapel Hill: University of North Carolina Press, 1941), p. 98; William R. Bagnall, The Textile Industries of the United States including Sketches and Notices of Cotton, Woolen, Silk and Linen Manufacture (Cambridge: Riverside Press, 1893; repr. New York: A. M. Kelley, 1971), pp. 56-59.

Rolla Tryon's data gathered in the second decade of this century indicated sizeable amounts of home spinning in the eighteenth and early nineteenth centuries, not so much home weaving; she postulated that most of the weaving was done by professionals using yarns spun in the home.[95] This coincided with the practice in England of "putting out," but it lacked the clothier/capitalist. In the American case the raw materials were owned by the consumer or commercial farmer (all farmers were commercial in that they produced for markets) although there never was much home-made cloth advertised for sale in this country. Both labor in the form of spinning or weaving and cloth were paid out as "in kind" payments to general stores and community tradesmen especially in the hinterland, but most of this was likely to be "to order" by the merchant/storekeeper or tradesman, and day books do not record resale of such cloth.

The first "real" statistics available are from the 1810 census. The 1810 figures are lacking in authority, because we do not know the marshall's instructions, nor do we have any of the original returns, although Timothy Pitkin claimed to have used them in the 1830s.[96] The

---

[95]Rolla Milton Tryon, Household Manufacture in the United States, 1640-1860: A Study in Industrial History (Chicago: University of Chicago Press, 1917), pp. 84-85.

[96]Timothy Pitkin, A Statistical View of the Commerce of the United States of America (New Haven: Durrie and Peck, 1835), p. 472.

main difficulties with them are their great discrepancies and inconsistencies; they seem to be unreliable figures. On the other hand, it is just possible that the figures reflect wide diversity in the country. Perhaps it should not be surprising if Montgomery County, New York, weavers produced 184 yards per loom while up in Washington County, they produced 357.[97]

The figures and an analysis of them make a few generalizations very plausible: there was a great deal of home cloth manufacture--apparently the marshalls were asking how much of each type of fabric was made by _families in the home_. The total averages 10 1/3 yards per person.[98]

As these figures are broken down, a few other points become clearer: in the northeastern and middle states, woolen cloth was the most valuable home manufactured textile, linen and mixed cloths were woven in greater quantity, 1 1/3 to 1 1/2 times more than wool in the cases of Maine and Vermont to four to five times more in Rhode Island and Massachusetts.[99]

If home production is considered on a per capita basis, the years around 1810 were peak years for homemade textiles

---

[97]Coxe, _Statement of the Arts and Manufacture_; Albert Gallatin, "Report on Manufactures, 1810," in _Selected Writings of Albert Gallatin_, ed. E. James Ferguson (Indianapolis: Bobbs-Merrill, 1967), pp. 240-64.

[98]Tryon, _Household Manufacture_, pp. 170-71.

[99]Ibid.; Coxe, _Statement of the Arts and Manufactures_.

(see table 2). In much of the northeast, ten or more yards per person were produced, and in New Hampshire, Rhode Island, and Connecticut over fifteen yards of textiles were produced for each person. Already, considerable quantities of cotton were woven in homes; Maine led the way in cotton weaving in the northeast, though Virginia was far ahead of Maine. It is very likely that Massachusetts, New Hampshire, and Connecticut, produced a goodly share, but the census marshalls chose to list cotton under "mixed" or "blended" fabric.[100] Most of the cotton cloth required a linen warp, as American technology concentrated on stocking yarns which lacked strength for weaving.[101]

1810 to 1814 was probably on the peak period for the home spinning and weaving of woolens on a per capita basis. More homespun was produced in later years, but population growth kept well ahead of home production. One must say "probably the peak years," because the quantifying data are not there.

New York state provided interesting data to show comparative amounts of homespun cloth. Both Rolla Tryon and Arthur H. Cole used New York state census figures to show the "age of homespun" during the decade of the twenties.

---

[100] Coxe, Statement of the Arts and Manufacturers.

[101] Caroline F. Ware, The Early New England Cotton Manufacture: A Study in Industrial Beginnings (Boston: Houghton Mifflin, 1931; repr. New York: Johnson Reprints, 1966), ch. 2.

TABLE 2

AMOUNT OF WOOLENS MANUFACTURED IN A DOMESTIC WAY IN NEW YORK STATE

	In '000's		Per Capita Yards		
Year	Fulled Cloth	Unfulled Flannel	Total Textiles	Woolen Flannel	Fulled Cloth
1810	1,802	3,252	9.2	3.4	1.9
1820	1,966	2,295	7.94*	1.0*	1.6
1825	2,918	3,468	8.95	2.15	1.8
1835	2,184	2,790	4.0	1.3	1.0
1845	1,664	2,650	2.7	1.0	.64
1855	198	380	.27	.11	.06

SOURCE: Coxe, Statement of the Arts and Manufactures, pp. xxix-xxxii; Tyron, Household Manufacture, pp. 170-71, 288-89; Cole, Wool Manufacture, 1:279; J. Potter, "Population in America," pp. 114-65.

*No doubt there was some undercounting, but it should have showed up more in 1810 than 1820.

Neither used the 1810 data to any extent, no doubt because each felt these data were incomplete and inadequate. The incompleteness and inadequacy should have shown up mostly in undercounting. Yet the 1810 statistics show higher per capita production of all types of home made cloth compared with 1820, and considerably higher per capita production of home produced woolens whether unfulled flannels or fulled cloth.

Some New York counties saw not only an increase in total home made textiles from 1810 to 1820, but some also showed a per capita increase. But these were exceptions, and even more exceptional was the county that saw a per capita increase in home production of woolens, flannels, or fulled cloth. All but a small handful saw a decline in this decade (see table 3).

As can be seen in table 2, total volume of homemade textiles greatly increased in the 1825 state census figures. Most likely the 1820 figures were undercounted, and total home production of textiles increased both in volume and on a per capita basis. Yet home production of woolens was less per capita in 1825 than it had been in 1810 in New York.

While war and boycotts including the Jeffersonian embargo of 1807 provided the most obvious incentives to family manufactures, so too did economic down turns, particularly those during periods in which the prices of raw materials like wool dropped. While there is no way it

TABLE 3

HOME TEXTILE AND WOOL PRODUCTION IN NEW YORK STATE IN PER CAPITA YARDS

County	Total Textiles 1810	Total Textiles 1820	Flannels 1810	Flannels 1820	Fulled Cloth 1810	Fulled Cloth 1820	Woolens 1810	Woolens 1820
Albany	6.7	5.0	2.5	1.3	1.7	1.1	4.2	2.4 -
Alleghany	7.9	7.0	1.6	1.9	-	1.1	1.6	3.0 +
Broom	13.1	8.2	2.8	1.5	.25	1.4	3.05	2.9 -
Cattaraugus		4.0		1.		.5		1.5
Cayuga	11.4	9.7	4.0	2.5	2.3	2.0	6.3	4.5 -
Chautaugua		6.7		1.5		1.25		2.75
Chenango	10.2	17.6	3.0	2.4	1.7	1.85	4.7	4.25-
Clinton	6.0	6.0	2.9	1.6	1.8	1.7	4.7	3.3 -
Columbia	19.0	4.6	7.9	1.7	4.4	1.9	12.3	3.6 -
Cortland	7.6	9.7	2.9	2.3	4.7	2.0	7.6	4.3 -
Delaware	10.0	7.8	3.5	2.4	3.0	1.8	6.5	4.2 -
Dutchess	7.0	6.8	2.5	2.4	-	1.8	2.5	3.2 +
Erie								
Essex	11.0	7.1	7.4	2.2	.2	2.0	7.6	4.2 -
Franklin	5.8	7.2	1.8	1.7		1.4	1.8	3.1 +
Genesee	9.6	5.2	2.3	1.3	.55	1.3	2.85	2.6 -
Green	2.8	6.2	1.1	1.4	1.9	1.4	3.0	2.8 -
Herkimer	13.5	14.0	4.3	2.2	3.5	2.0	7.8	4.2 -
Jefferson	10.6	8.4	3.4	2.3	2.6	1.7	6.0	4.0 -
King's	4.8	1.8	.5				.5	- -
Lewis	12.0	8.5	3.0	2.3	2.25	1.8	5.25	4.1 -

TABLE 3--Continued

County	Total Textiles		Flannels		Fulled Cloth		Woolens		
	1810	1820	1810	1820	1810	1820	1810	1820	
Livingston									
Madison	14.0	9.1	4.8	2.4	2.5	2.0	7.3	4.4	-
Monroe									
Montgomery	5.8	8.0	2.1	2.6	3.0	1.9	5.1	4.5	-
Niagra	16.0	1.2	4.4	.4	-	.3	4.4	.7	-
Oneida	9.9	7.8	4.7	2.1	4.0	1.7	8.7	3.8	-
Onondaga	11.8	8.0	4.1	2.0	2.7	1.8	6.8	3.8	-
Orange	9.2	9.7	2.8	.9	1.2	1.0	4.0	1.9	-
Ontario	12.5	5.4	4.7	1.6	3.0	1.3	7.7	2.9	-
Oswego									
Otsego	12.4	9.0	4.0	2.5	3.2	1.9	7.2	4.4	-
Putnam									
Queen's	9.7	4.1	2.7	1.5	1.0	.7	3.7	2.2	-
Rensselaer	10.5	7.9	4.3	1.8	2.75	1.6	7.05	3.4	-
Richmond	6.0	2.0	.4		.8		1.2	-	-
Rockland	5.7	3.0	1.0	.4	1.3	.6	2.3	1.0	-
Saratoga	11.0	8.0	5.2	2.0	2.4	1.9	7.6	3.9	-
Schenectady	.7	3.9	.25	1.2	1.0	1.0	1.25	2.2	+
Schoharie	8.8	7.0	2.8	1.8	2.1	1.7	4.9	3.5	-
Seneca	10.4	8.3	3.0	1.9	1.1	1.7	4.1	3.6	-
St. Lawrence	8.9	7.6	2.4	2.1	1.7	1.6	4.1	3.7	-
Steuben	13.0	6.9	3.6	1.8	1.0	1.4	4.6	3.2	-
Suffolk	10.1	6.4	2.4	1.0	1.3	1.3	3.7	2.3	-
Sullivan	8.2	5.7	2.2	1.3		.9	2.2	2.2	

TABLE 3--Continued

County	Total Textiles		Flannels		Fulled Cloth		Woolens	
	1810	1820	1810	1820	1810	1820	1810	1820
Tioga	12.9	8.7	3.1	1.8	2.0	1.5	5.1	3.3 -
Tompkins				2.2		2.2		4.4
Ulster	12.8	6.1	3.3	1.0	2.0	1.2	5.3	2.2 -
Warren				1.2		1.1		2.3
Washington	17.8	8.5	8.7	2.5	3.0	1.8	11.7	4.3 -
West Chester	11.1	5.5	3.7	1.0		.8	3.7	1.8 -
Averages	9.2	7.94	3.4	1.8	1.9	1.6	5.3	3.4 -

SOURCE: Coxe, Statement of the Arts and Manufacturers; Tryon, Household Manufacture, pp. 170-71, 288-89.

can be measured precisely, in good times, people tended to buy manufactured cloth, which of course was mostly imported even through the 1830s. These imports included the fine to middling woolens, worsteds, and the fine linens, fine and not-so-fine cottons, which were better than American manufacture. During bad times, people returned to their own spinning wheels and looms to produce serviceable cloth for everyday use and wear, for outdoor work, and for the myriad of other uses for textiles.

It is clearly arguable that the 1810 figures are no weaker than any of the other figures for home made cloth production. It is also clear that while total production of home textiles peaked in New York in 1825, plus or minus a few years, home production of woolens on a per capita basis peaked about 1810, plus or minus a few years. What made up the difference in woolen cloth needs were imported woolens, cloth and flannel, and some domestic manufacture, meaning in this case production from manufactories.

Arthur Cole suggested that the number of carding machines and fulling mills enumerated by the New York state censuses (see table 4) also indicated the peaking of homespun, in this case woolens, in 1825.[102] The difficulty is that the census did not trouble to differentiate between those carding machines and fulling mills in, or connected to, factories. The increase in numbers from 1810 to 1825

---

[102]Cole, Wool Manufacture, 1:185.

TABLE 4

CARDING AND FULLING IN NEW YORK, 1810-1835

	1810	1820	1825	1835
No. of carding machines	413	1,233	1,584	1,061
No. of fulling mills	427	991	1,222	965

SOURCE: Cole, Wool Manufacture, 1:185.

could, in part at least, be attributed to increase in the number of woolen factories in New York state. While McLane listed only fifty-four in 1832, Benton and Berry listed 234 woolen factories in New York in 1836.[103]

Not everyone manufactured textiles in the home. In New Hampshire there was one loom for every two families of five members; that was the most concentrated in the country. The maximum in upstate New York was 2.75 families per loom in Herkimer County, but most of the state was closer to the state average of one loom per 5.8 families. In Pennsylvania nearly every family owned a spinning wheel although only one in nine owned a loom. The vast bulk of homemade fabrics was linen, or linen mixed with cotton or wool.[104] As stated above, some cotton cloth was manufactured in homes, but it is difficult to sort out how much, because it was not counted as such. In 1814 in Rhode Island both Samuel Slater and the Hazards were putting out their own cotton yarns to be woven at home at wages ranging from 6 1/2 cents 12 1/2 cents per yard.[105]

---

[103]Louis McLane, Report to the Secretary of the Treasury, 1832: Documents Relative to the Manufactures in the United States, 22nd. Cong., 1st sess.; House Executive Document, no. 308, 2 vols. (Washington, D.C., 1833; repr. New York: A. M. Kelley, 1969), 2:89-90. Hereafter cited as McLane Report. C. Benton and S. F. Barry, comp., A Statistical View of the Number of Sheep (Cambridge, Mass.: Folsam Wells, & Thurston, 1837), pp. 118-19.

[104]Coxe, Statement of the Arts and Manufactures.

[105]Ware, New England Cotton Manufacture, ch. 3; Thomas Robinson Hazard, Facts for the Laboring Man By a Laboring Man (Newport, R.I.: James Atkinson, 1840).

Since there was so much homemade cloth (see table 5), it is important to be reminded again of the great need for textiles. The household required bedding, napkins, window and floor coverings, upholstery, pillows; the farm required a range of bags, rags, grain sacks; the individual needed stockings, underwear, diapers for part of his or her life, shirts, pants, and aprons. England and Europe could and did supply some of these needs, except during periods of economic adversity such as war or blockades. These external circumstances provided the great spur to American economic independence beginning with the boycotts during the Sugar and Stamp Act crises.

Two or three major economic events occurred in the decade of the teens which tended to cause home manufacture to decline in relative terms. In woolens, Americans gained expertise during the decade beginning in 1811 to produce by the end of the decade about three million yards of machine-made three-quarters width fine cloth. By 1817 the Boston Manufacturing Company had become a productive and financial success, providing the groundwork for the proliferation of cotton mills throughout New England and demonstrating for all to see, a model integrated factory. In the meantime the United States continued as the premier market for all English textiles. In the five-year period from 1816-20 when Great Britain dumped woolen textiles on New York and Philadelphia markets, the average annual

TABLE 5

1810: FAMILY MANUFACTURE OF NON-WOOLS AND WOOLS

State	Non-wool Textiles Per Capita in Yards	Flannels in Per Capita Yards	Fulled Woolens Per Capita Yards
Me.	8.	3.5	1.56
Mass.	8.5		1.5
N.H.	15.76	4.2	2.3
R.I.	16.	1.9	.55
Conn.	11.3	4.3	2.4
Vt.	7.	4.1	2.5
N.Y.	6.	3.4	1.9
N.J.	6.3	1.5	.8
Penna.	6.6	1.5	.8
Md. & D.C.	4.5		.1
Del.	4.1	.9	

SOURCE: Coxe, Statement of the Arts and Manufactures; Potter, "Population in America," pp. 664-65.

import of fine woolen yardage was 3.8 million yards (about one-half broad yard per person), _not_ including stuffs, blankets, satinets, carpets, kerseymeres that were also exported to the United States. In years of low import totals from 1821-30, Americans imported between 24 and 32 percent of British woolen manufacture.[106]

During the period 1811 to 1816 the groundwork was laid for American machine made woolens. There were a number of reasons that this should have occurred at this time:

1. Excess capital from foreign trade was available, particularly in New England, but also in New York state.

2. Imports were threatened, even cut off, causing prices to rise and stimulating interest in manufacturing.

3. American entrepreneurs believed that machinery would save on costs by enabling them to hire women and children for lower wages than they would have paid men. There was also an unstated sentiment that machines could become more reliable and efficient than people; machines could produce goods of more uniform quality.

4. These entrepreneurs wished to be economically independent of Great Britain.

5. The technical, mechanical, and organizational expertise was present although sometimes in the persona of recent immigrants.

---

[106]Potter, "Atlantic Economy, 1815-1860," pp. 265-69.

In the 1920s Arthur H. Cole laboriously figured the ratio of household manufactures to factory manufactures to imports of woolens to be four to three to 1 1/2 during the period of about 1828 to 1830.[107] There is no reason to dispute his figures, but it should be noted that an industry that began very slowly and from a very small base during the post-Revolutionary decades, grew so remarkably that it had achieved the position of providing one-third of American needs within a short time. The next chapter will examine these very small, and slow, beginnings that yet gave heart to such promotors of manufacturing as Alexander Hamilton and Tench Coxe.

---

[107]Cole, Wool Manufacture, 2:261.

Chapter II

THE EMBRYO CONCEIVED: AMERICAN MANUFACTURING BEGINNINGS 1787-1812

It is not possible to argue that the Revolutionary War turned the American economic world upside down. There were changes: the exodus of many Loyalists made room at the top for ambitious Patriot colonials; war inflation was inevitably followed by severe deflation; certain debts were ignored, public debt became the subject of political discussion and speculation; war profiteers made and lost fortunes. But the bases of the economy--agriculture and commerce--went on very much as before. Merchants gained in certain geographic areas, lost in others; farmers, as always, depended on weather and markets to make a living, and some were forced to reconsider planting patterns. In tobacco country, for example, soil exhaustion was commonplace in the older Chesapeake settlements, and in some wheat growing regions there were blights. For at least another twenty-five years, merchants and farmers alike would be as interested in the Livorno market as they would be in Pittsburgh. There had been considerable population and economic growth during the period from 1750 to 1775 although that growth cannot be measured on a per capita basis, because the data are not there. The data are also scanty for the period 1775 to 1800, but there was certainly some growth, particularly during the '90s, though very little evident change in basic economic functions despite war and Revolution.[1]

Until George Rogers Taylor's "great turnabout"[2] of the 1810s, American capital had gone largely into foreign trade, and American dependence on foreign trade made notions of economic self-sufficiency more immediate. Since the 1760's economic independence had been under discussion by Americans. Some of the talk, propaganda by and large, was an aspect of the various boycott schemes emanating from antipathy toward British tax legislation embodied in such as Stamp and Townshend duties. But as Samual Rezneck demonstrated some years ago, some of the discussion centered around a very critical question: whether or not it was _desirable_ to promote and develop American industry or manufacturing.[3] Now "industry" was a word like "factory" which was undergoing considerable modification in the

---

[1]Robert E. East, _Business Enterprise in the American Revolutionary Era_ (New York: Columbia University Press, 1938, repr. Gloucester, Mass.: Peter Smith, 1964), pp. 195-212; George Rogers Taylor, "American Economic Growth before 1840: An Exploratory Essay," _Journal of Economic History_ 24 (1964):427-44; Paul A. David, "The Growth of Real Product in the United States before 1840: New Evidence, Controlled Conjectures," _Journal of Economic History_ 27 (June 1967):2, 151-97.

[2]George Rogers Taylor, "American Urban Growth Preceeding the Railway Age," _Journal of Economic History_, 27 (September 1967):309-39.

[3]Samuel Rezneck, "The Rise and Early Development of Industrial Consciousness in the United States, 1760-1830," _Journal of Economic and Business History_ 4 (1932):784-811.

eighteenth and early nineteenth centuries. Neither term brought to mind belching smokestacks or mindless assembly lines. "Industry" could be combined with talent and energy to make one rich. Manufactories were enterprises in home or shop which fabricated goods. "Factory" was an old term meaning a trading station; its usage as a short form for manufactory was not general until the 1830s.[4] Grist and fulling mills, for example, were not considered manufactories, although there was some contemporary confusion and ambiguity. Mills provided services, e.g. grinding, fulling. "Domestic manufactures" was another term with ambiguous meaning in the eighteenth and early nineteenth centuries. Depending on the context, it could mean domestic rather than foreign manufactures; or it could mean home or family manufacture rather than manufacturing in a shop or manufactory.

Jeffersonians, for example, favored "domestic manufactures." What they usually meant was manufacturing in the home or home workshop that could be accomplished by their idealized version of the yeoman farmer.[5] Hamiltonians also favored "domestic manufactures"; what they usually meant was support for shop or factory production of goods in competition with foreign, particularly British,

---

[4] Compact O.E.D, 1:948.

[5] Thomas Jefferson, Notes on the State of Virginia (New York: Harper & Row, 1964), pp. 156-58.

imports. Hamiltonians and their successors not only wished to support these domestic manufactures but often to subsidize and to protect them.[6]. The whole discussion seems simple enough, but in fact was not, because farmers, after all, provided the raw materials for manufacturing--wool and cotton in particular. They, of course, favored high prices for their produce. Merchants and consumers wished domestic and imported goods at the lowest possible prices. Yet independence, particularly economic independence was an idea that required protection for industry in some form and that protection, most likely an import tax, would add to the cost. To complicate matters further what Jefferson and others had seen in England in the last part of the eighteenth and early part of the nineteenth centuries were factories full of impoverished children and adults. Some of the latter so despised machinery that they actually destroyed machines and entire factories. These conditions fueled misgivings about factories generally and provided ammunition with which to argue against protective tariffs.

While discussions of economic independence predated the Revolution, they were immediately provoked again after the war by British policies and by spokesmen for those policies, in particular, John Baker Holroyd, the Earl of Sheffield. Before the war, America had become the shipbuilder and

---

[6]Jacob E. Cooke, ed., The Reports of Alexander Hamilton (New York: Harper & Row, 1964), p. 141.

shipper of the British Atlantic empire. Sheffield hoped to see this carrying trade returned to British bottoms as well as the continued dependence of the United States on British goods. Writing in 1783, the year of the Peace of Paris, Sheffield was more than a little vindictive. A true and loyal Britisher, he wrote in the vein of an exasperated parent chastising a churlish child. The following passage is characteristic:

> By asserting their independence, the Americans have renounced the privileges, as well as the duties, of British subjects--they are become foreign states; and if in some instances, as in the loss of the carrying-trade, they feel the inconveniences of their choice, they can no longer complain; but if they are placed on the footing of the most favoured nation, they must surely applaud our liberality and friendship, without expecting that for their emolument, we should sacrifice the navigation and the naval power of Great Britain.[7]

Sheffield counseled patience to his fellow countrymen; with patience, he felt, England would regain her pre-eminence as shipper and supplier to the former colonies. His first examples were woolen goods: cheap goods such as Kendal cottons (woolens), Welch plains and flannels for slaves, fancier Yorkshire duffles and friezes for planters. These, he felt, Americans could not do without. The French were capable of offering the English some competition in qualitative terms, but prejudice and sentiment would win the day; Americans simply would prefer English goods.[8]

---

[7]Lord John B. Sheffield, Observations on the Commerce of the American States, 6th ed. (London, 1784), pp. 113-22.

[8]Ibid., p. 4.

So the English would defeat any challengers in international competition in the trading of goods to the United States. Sheffield also was convinced there was little chance of American manufacturing to offer competition,[9]

> But it will be a long time before the Americans can manufacture for themselves. Their progress will be stopped by the high price of labor, and the more pleasing and profitable employment of agriculture, while fresh lands can be got; and the degree of population (assuming disunion in the West) necessary for the manufactures cannot be expected, while a spirit of emigration, especially from New-England provinces to the interior parts of the continent, rages, full as much as it has ever done from Europe. If manufacturers should emigrate from Europe to America, at least nine-tenths of them will become farmers; for they will not work at manufactures when they can get much greater Profit by farming.

Sheffield's most immediate and persuasive American opposite was the Philadelphian Assistant to the Secretary of the Treasury, Tench Coxe. Coxe was the most vociferous and prominent early proponent of American manufacturing. His papers had long been sealed at the Historical Society of Pennsylvania, and only in 1973 did they start becoming available on microfilm. It had been known that Coxe had been an important contributor to the views of Alexander Hamilton; Jacob E. Cooke has shown in a recent article that Coxe was the _co-author_ of Hamilton's Report on Manufactures, and that together the two men had launched the Society for Establishing Useful Manufactures.[10] Coxe's piece on

---

[9]Ibid., p. 105.

[10]Jacob E. Cooke, "Tench Coxe, Alexander Hamilton, and the Encouragement of American Manufactures," _William and Mary Quarterly_, 3rd ser., 32 (July 1975):369-92.

Lord Sheffield's Observations argued that what Sheffield did not know was the "present state of our family or household manufacture." Coxe then took a series of examples from Virginia, from around Providence, and from Boston and Philadelphia. He showed that even on Virginia plantations that were supposed to be dependent on English imports, both black and white families provided many of their own textile needs. Providence, Rhode Island was a manufacturing center which produced in families in one year, 1791, over 34,000 yards of cloth. Boston produced wool cards, Philadelphia spinning wheel irons, and the entire country had a profusion of fulling mills.[11]

Coxe's reply to Sheffield relied on the same set of information that he and Hamilton used for the Report on Manufactures of the same year (1791). Hamilton, or possibly Coxe in Hamilton's name, corresponded not only with known manufacturers, but also with a network of treasury marshalls and assistants in each state. While the information returned to the treasury office hardly could be regarded as exhaustive, it contains, as edited by Arthur Harrison Cole, some of the only source material extant describing American manufacturing in the eighteenth century.[12]

---

[11]Tench Coxe, A Brief Examination of Lord Sheffield's Considerations on the Commerce of the United States, (Philadelphia, 1791), pp. 113-22.

[12]Arthur H. Cole, ed., The Industrial and Commercial Correspondence of Alexander Hamilton (Chicago: A. W. Shay Co., 1928, repr. New York: A. M. Kelley, 1968).

Among the letters returned was one from Peter Colt of Connecticut with an enclosure. This was a description of the Hartford Woolen Manufactory begun in 1788 with "the fairest prospect of succeeding." Originally capitalized at ₤1,200 (Connecticut currency, equals $4,000), this was very quickly recognized as insufficient and capitalization was increased to ₤2,800 ($9,333.33). Further description follows:

> This stock has been employed in buying wool, and working it up into worsted goods, narrow and broad coatings and cloths--after having been sorted and prepared in the manner practiced in Great Britain. This company have received some aid from government--viz. a trifling bounty the first year on spinning, then an exemption, for two years, of their workmen from a poll tax; and their work shops from all taxes for the same term of time. . . .
>
> The company at Hartford had expended so much of their small capital on buildings, implements, etc. that they found themselves under the necessity of applying to government for some aid--the Legislature being sensible of the importance of encouraging this infant establishment, granted them a lottery to raise ₤1,000 ($3,333.33),--to enable them to procure a more complete set of machinery and for extending their business. This lottery will probably net them three thousand dollars.[13]

A second letter from Elisha Colt from August 1791 graphically described the difficulties of the new factory:

> We were at that period not only totally unacquainted with the various parts of subdivisions of the labour; but equally destitute of every kind of machinery and labourers for executing such a project. But the news of this infant attempt to establish so useful a manufacture soon collected a number of workmen about us, who had been bred to different branches of the woolen and worsted business in England. These were

---

[13]Ibid., pp. 5-6.

> chiefly old soldiers who had deserted the British army, or having been taken prisoners during the late war, remained in the country. From these men we have acquired some useful knowledge tho' at a dear rate; as every one had some project to (present of) his own to propose, or improvement to make in the various implements & c. used in our business, but some of them had sufficient mechanical knowledge to give proper directions, or make themselves understood by our Mechanicks; . . . We have had to struggle with every kind of embarrassment which can attend the setting up a new business; either from the ignorance, the knavery or the fickleness of the workmen; the high price of materials; the smallness of our capital, and the prejudices of the community against home made cloths, and the interested views and jealousy of the British factors and agents in this country.[14]

At this point Elisha Colt described his company as on the brink of insolvency if it had not been for the government intervention described above.

Colt went on to list the various factory operations:

> The wool was sorted into six sorts, then passed thro' a machine called a Willow . . . afterwhich it is oiled and then Scribled by which operation it is prepared for the Spinners. This is a very labourious and expensive part of the process in making Cloths (particularly mixtures, which require to be repeated three times) and is now performed in England by machines that are worked by Water.

This quote indicates that only part of the initial carding, the scribbling, was done by machine at the factory, that the carding machines Henry Wansey saw there three years later had not yet been built or installed. The scribbled wool was put out to be hand carded and to be spun on home wheels. It was then returned to the factory to be woven on the three broad and five narrow looms. Colt claimed that

---

[14]Ibid., pp. 7-8.

the "Country Looms will not make even the narrow Cloths of sufficient width for our purpose--." The cloth then went to the fulling mill, which judging by the context of the description was a separate institution, where it was fulled and burled. The cloth again was returned to the factory and turned over to the head clothier or finisher who raised the nap, sheared the nap from the cloth, and pressed and packed it for market. The factory had the capacity for 12,000 to 20,000 pounds of wool per year which cost from 1s. 2d. to 1s. 6d. (19¢ to 25¢; this is a very low price even for country wool and indicates a slack demand.) The company made "baizes, shallons, Lastings, serge and Elastick Cloth" in the worsted category and coatings, narrow and broadcloth, and cassimeres in the true woolen category. These last ranged in price from 4s. 9d. to 13s. (79¢ to $2.166 or 3s. 7d to 9s. 7d. str.). For comparison it will be recalled that the wholesale selling price of a yard of Gloucestershire superfine broadcloth was 16s. 6d. ($3.66) in 1798.[15]

If this was not America's first woolen factory that actually fabricated wool into cloth, it was certainly the first mechanized woolen factory, as modest as that mechanization may seem. It did not do well. By 1794 the stocks of unsold cloth had become so great that the company paid a 50 percent dividend in cloth. Paying stockholders,

---

[15]Ibid., pp. 7-11.

and creditors in cloth was common practice in the early years. In 1795 Jeremiah Wadsworth, the major stockholder, bought out the company. He disposed of it in 1797.[16]

The importance of this little venture in the manufacture of woolen cloth was not lost on our early political leaders who saw in the Hartford company a significant attempt at establishing American manufacturing. Washington himself wore a suit of brown cloth from its looms to his first inauguration in New York in 1789. That suit is preserved still at the National Historical Park Museum in Morristown, New Jersey. Hamilton in the Report on Manufactures referred to this specific factory as "this precious embryo which must be cherished and brought to maturity."[17]

Much of what is known about the beginnings of mechanized American textile manufacture is from a Journal kept by a Wiltshire clothier, Henry Wansey, who visited the United States in 1794. Wansey was at least a fifth generation clothier with a thoroughly middle class background and education. In 1773 at twenty-two Wansey had finished his formal education and his apprenticeship. He was put in charge of sixteen looms and 130 employees in Salisbury, Wiltshire. His factory specialized in flannels and narrow fancy cloths. While certainly not wildly progressive in

---

[16]Bagnall, Textile Industries, pp. 100-9.

[17]Cooke, Reports of Hamilton, p. 197.

adopting new manufacturing methods, Henry Wansey was credited with introducing the jenny to Salisbury in 1791.[18]

If Wansey's trip to the United States was in any way intended as a reconnaissance for potential investment in American properties, the idea never materialized. As he said in his "Introduction,"

> The arts and improvements proceed very slow in America, from the want of that patronage so prevalent in England. The Americans being, many of them, descendants of the English, are partial to their manners and customs; yet, it must be acknowledged, that in the interior of the country, things appear, at least, half a century behind them in point of comfort.[19]

Partly Wansey was referring to his own comfort-seeking middle age and to a normal dislike for the inconveniences of travel, but also he was alluding to his American accommodations--the not so fine and sometimes very expensive meals, the mosquitos and bed bugs, the indifferent or bad bread, and so forth. But Wansey was a fair and impartial observer and most of his commentary was complimentary and positive. However, one never senses the enthusiasm of an American "convert" in the reading of Wansey; no doubt, because he never was "converted."

Wansey's description of the Hartford Woolen Manufactory is important to this story, as are his comments on textile

---

[18]David John Jeremy, ed., _Henry Wansey and His American Journal, 1794_, American Philosophical Society _Memoirs_, vol. 82 (Philadelphia: American Philosophical Society, 1970), pp. 5-6.

[19]Ibid., p. 41.

manufacture generally. Wansey was on the one hand a more specialized observer than Sheffield, and on the other hand a more disinterested commentator. Even though his own manufacturing interests could have been threatened by a thriving American woolen industry, as Wansey saw it, this was not to be in the foreseeable future. There was no vindictiveness in his commentaries. At Hartford he found a factory "much on the decay, and hardly able to maintain itself; I saw two carding engines, working by water, of a very inferior construction."[20] Later in his appendix, Wansey added,

> The carding and scribbling engines, at Hartford, were of the oldest fashion. Two large center cylinders in each, with two doffers, and only two working cylinders, of the breadth of bare sixteen inches, said to be invented by some person there. They had no spinning jennies, the yarn being all spun by hand. They were scribbling deep blue wool, of the quality of Wiltshire running fine, for making coarse broad cloth; the spinning was very bad, the wool not being half worked. I saw in the weaving shop, five looms, two on broad cloth, two on coarse cassimeres, with worsted chains, and one narrow or forest cloth. They gave the weavers nine pence per yard currency, for the cassimers, i.e. six pence three-farthings sterling (12 1/2¢); dear enough considering the largeness of the spinning. They could weave six yards of broad cloth in a day. saw there some very good well-combed worsted. They sort a fleece into seven sorts. I observed some very fine wool there, which, they told me, came from Georgia, but it was in bad condition. The concern is carried on by a company; nine thousand three hundred dollars have been lent towards the undertaking, by the state.21 None of the partners understand any thing

---

[20]Ibid., p. 68.

[21]Wansey was correct about the amount of total capital, but as far as can be learned from other sources, the State was not the lender. The State of Connecticut did authorize the lottery mentioned by Peter Colt which may have raised £900 or $3,000.

> about it, and all depends on an Englishman, who is the sorter of the wool.22

The carding machines at Hartford described by Wansey seem primitive enough, but their cost does not seem out of line. According to David Jeremy who found the bill from Zinos (Zenas) Whiting of New Haven, the two machines were installed in the spring of 1793 and cost ₤69 4s. 4d for both ($115.36 each).[23] Jeremy compared this with an improved thirty-inch carder that sold in Yorkshire at the same time for ₤26 ($115.44). While the quality of the machines may have been vastly different, one can hardly quarrel about the price difference.[24]

In New Haven Wansey was taken to the factory of McIntosh, Dickson, and Livingston. There he noted, "But what I saw of the undertaking, I am convinced, a great deal of money will be sunk to very little purpose." This was a comment Wansey was to repeat more than once. The following is the description of the New Haven mill:

---

[22] Jeremy, Wansey's American Journal, pp. 148-49.

[23] Ibid.

[24] Common-school Arithmetic (Riverhead, N.Y., 1851) cites the following currency values:

New England,	6 shillings = $1.00
New York,	8 shillings = $1.00
Penn., N. J., Del.	7 shillings/6 pence = $1.00

₤1 stirling = $4.44, fixed by Congress, 1799. At the time the pound was known to be slightly undervalued relative to the U. S. dollar; the exchange rate was raised by Congress to ₤1 = $4.80 in 1832 and $4.84 in 1840 where it remained fixed for decades.

> The building is one hundred feet long, thirty-eight feet wide, and four story high. There is not a single window placed on the north side, which is the best of all lights for a manufactory. There were two carding engines finished and at work, but both very much warped and cracked, by the heat and dryness of the rooms, as well as from being made of unseasoned wood. Two slubbing and two spinning machines of good and complete workmanship, but the cotton yarn which was then spinning, was not better than candlewick yarn. He has a wheel of thirty feet diameter, and eight feet wide, but I think they will often be in want of water to drive it; the cards were very badly made. He has erected forges there, and is making the heavy wrought and cast iron wheels, brasses, screws, spindles, etc. on the spot, at a vast expence. The coal for working and smelting is brought from Virginia. A vast number of workmen are employed in this department at very heavy expence. He has many English workmen engaged at great wages, particularly one from Sir George Young's manufactory at Ottery, in Devonshire, who engages to undertake the spinning of worsted by water; a promise I do not think he will ever perform.[25]

According to David Jeremy the company expended a capital of about $30,000 by 1795. There was no reference to it either in the 1820 Manufactures Census or in McLane, but Jeremy claimed it continued to operate until Livingston sold out in 1831.[26]

The most technically advanced factory visited by Wansey was a cotton factory in Hell Gate, York Island, New York also owned in part by David Dickson and John Robert Livingston. There he saw the "new-invented spring shuttle," which of course, was not the least bit new, but had only recently found its way to Wiltshire apparently. Also he saw a mule capable, according to Jeremy, of spinning cotton

---

[25]Jeremy, Wansey's American Journal, p. 73.

[26]Ibid.

to a yarn count of 300, a degree of fineness reached in Manchester only as recently as 1792.[27]

But even with a factory with such advanced technology, Wansey had serious misgivings, "The situation is not well chosen; they have sunk a vast deal of money in buildings and machinery unnecessarily . . . ; they are so deficient in water in summer time to keep the wheel going, that to remedy this, a thousand pounds ($2,500) is to be laid out. . . ." Wansey predicted that the English workmen would leave the moment they had saved enough to buy farms in the countryside.[28]

Wansey generally felt that manufacturing could never keep pace with the population growth in America.[29] Invariably he saw capital misused or misplaced. In citing the Society for Establishing Useful Manufactures at Patterson, New Jersey, Wansey said,

> The general error of all their large undertakings has been, their laying out their capital in large buildings and an unnecessary stock of machinery, etc. which brings a heavy mortgage on the concern, before they actually begin. They also put the whole business under the care of a chief workman (being ignorant themselves) who has no interest in an oeconomical management of the concern. The large cotton manufactory at Patterson, has almost been ruined twice by such men.

The raw materials were indifferent at best. The best wool Wansey saw came from Georgia.[31] Part of this was

---

[27]Ibid., pp. 82-83. [28]Ibid. [29]Ibid., p. 63.

[30]Ibid., p. 84. [31]Ibid., p. 100.

caused by American indifference to sheep breeding. Colonel Wadsworth told Wansey that one solution to this was in encouraging more mutton consumption.[32] The mismanagement Wansey saw was rooted partly in outright chicanery as in the case of the SUM,[33] but more commonly he saw instances of overrated abilities as in the case of McIntosh's manager a New Haven.[34]

"But with all their improvements, they must yet for a long time come to John Bull for his cloth, for at least a half century to come."[35] To hammer such a sentiment home, Wansey described the situation with Elisha Colt, the merchandiser for the Hartford Woolen Manufactory,

> He could sell them (woolen cloths) at the same price, I found, as our English goods would cost, when delivered into the stores there, but the fabric was very poor, and hard in the spinning, and very badly dressed, and therefore very inferior to, and dearer than the British loaded with all the expences of freight, insurance, merchant's profit, and seven and half per cent duty.[36]

But perhaps Wansey expressed it best when he responded to an offer by Colonel Wadsworth to settle near him in a manufactory in Hartford. A "handsome offer," Wansey said, and he felt no doubts he could "make such a scheme profitable But besides giving up family and friends,

> A concern of this kind would require thrice the exertio and fatigue, and thrice the capital; and certainly, were I resolved to leave this country (England), I would not embarrass myself with and encrease of trouble

---

[32]Ibid., p. 102. [33]Ibid., p. 127. [34]Ibid., p. 74.

[35]Ibid., p. 141. [36]Ibid., pp. 148-50.

> in another, unless my circumstances compelled it; and even in that case, there are many other concerns to be engaged in, equally profitable, without half the capital, or a quarter of the trouble and exertion.[37]

This last sentiment would be echoed repeatedly among those woolen factory owners and agents who were surveyed in 1820 and in 1832. Henry Wansey could not have been aware of it, but the one universal lament among American pioneer woolen manufacturers was that the measly profits were not worth the aggravation and hard work.

The mechanization of carding by means of carding cloth applied to cylinders and applying inanimate power in the form of water or steam to those cylinders was critical to the acceleration of textile manufacture. Carding prepared the fibers for spinning. The process had been performed using wire instead of teasels since the sixteenth century. As worked by hand, the process consists of combing the wool as with a curry comb, rolling the wool fibers, and homogenizing them randomly. Hand cards are used in pairs and each one is about four by eight inches; carding cloth is tacked to each face and handles are attached (see illus. 3). One can spin directly from hand carded rolls, but for fine woolens it was found that a preliminary mechanical spinning called slubbing was needed before the yarn could be spun on the jenny. Sir Richard Arkwright had patented cylindrical carding for use in his cotton mill in

---

[37]Ibid., pp. 102-3.

England in 1775, but after various law suits, the patent became essentially invalid, and by 1785 cylindrical carding had entered the public domain. The first wool carding engines were simple affairs with few cylinders called workers and strippers (see illus. 20). They look like fairly simple machines, but in fact are not as simple as they look. The wire staples have to be of exactly even density, and that density should vary according to the type of wool being processed. Each wire staple has a knee-bend applied which again should vary depending on the wool. The wires on the cylinders should not touch each other so that the careful engineering of the revolving axles was important, and the distance of the axles from each other should be adjustable. The staples were required to be sharp; they could become dull with the slightest abuse or overuse.

Machine cards were installed at Hartford in 1793. Wansey thought them very crude, and in fact, he saw little well-constructed carding machinery in 1794. What he did see that was well-built was for cotton. By 1810 there were some 1,600 wool carding machines counted in the census. By then there must have been a sizeable number of American carding machine builders; something is known of a few.

Some form of mechanical cylindrical carding had been sought in this country certainly before the arrival of the Scholfields in Massachusetts in 1793. Philadelphia as in many another cultural matter took the lead here, and Tench Coxe was involved as a very young man. The United Company of Philadelphia for Promoting American Manufactures was organized in 1775 to manufacture cotton yarn. It engaged one Christopher Tully to build a Hargreaves' type jenny of twenty-four spindles which apparently Tully accomplished. The Pennsylvania Assembly then authorized models of the jenny to be made available in the colony for others to copy. But the War intervened, and the United Company was dormant until reorganized as the Pennsylvania Society for the Encouragement of Arts and Domestic Manufactures with Tench Coxe as its inaugural speaker. By 1788 the Society had created a linen/cotton factory consisting of a carding machine, four jennies, and by the end of that year, twenty-six looms. The jennies in this factory were built by a local carpenter, Enoch Richardson; the carding machine by John Hauge of Alexandria, Virginia. In 1789 the Pennsylvania legislature supported the company by purchasing one hundred shares of the Society's Fund for Ł1,000 ($2,666.66 or Ł600 str.). In the spring of 1790 the factory was completely destroyed by fire presumed at the time to have been incendiary.[38]

---

[38]David J. Jeremy, "British Textile Technology Transmission to the United States: The Philadelphia Region Experience, 1770-1820," Business History Review 47 (Spring 1973):28-32, whole article, pp. 24-52.

Samuel Slater faced considerable difficulties in creating the carding capacity for his Pawtucket cotton mill. As Slater related the story to his biographer, George S. White, it was Pliny Earle of Leicester, Massachusetts who ultimately solved his problems. Earle was a member of the Society of Friends and patriarch of an important family that continued in the textile machinery business until after the Civil War. Apparently the problem that Earle solved for Slater in 1790 involved the bend of the wires and the tightness of the wire staples in their leather or canvas backing.[39] The manufacture of carding cloth was essential to both cotton and wool manufacture. Leicester became the center of such manufacture in New England. In 1832 in Leicester there were eight machine card manufacturers, six hand card manufacturers, two wire drawing factories, two machine shops, and one each shuttle factory and bobbin factory.[40]

Hand manufacture of carding cloth was described as follows: A sheet of leather eighteen to twenty inches by four was ruled by lines into cross sections as a guide. The workman used a pricker with two blades to pierce two holes at a time in the leather where the lines intercepted. The wire was bent into a staple by hand and inserted into

---

[39]George S. White, Memoir of Samuel Slater (Philadelphia, 1836; repr. New York: A. M. Kelley, 1967), pp. 96-97.

[40]McLane Report, 1:502-3.

the holes one at a time. The sheet with wire teeth was tacked on to a board for hand cards.[41]

Oliver Evans of the Brandywine River valley claimed to have invented a machine to bend and cut card wire in 1777 or 1778. He claimed that his machine which had been let out on a contract basis could make 3,000 card teeth per minute. The contracting company was said to have made one hundred and fifty pairs of hand cards per day. This company may have been Giles Richards and Company of Boston.[42]

In October 1789, George Washington paid a visit to a carding cloth manufacturer of Boston. This may also have been Giles Richards' factory:[43]

> I went to the Card Manufactory, where, I was informed, about nine hundred hands, of one kind and another, and for one purpose and another, are employed. All kinds of cards are made, and there are machines for executing every part of the work in a new and expeditious manner, especially in cutting and bending the teeth, which is done at one stroke. They have made sixty-three thousand pairs of cards in a year, and can undersell the imported cards. Many cards of this manufactory have been shipped into England.

---

[41]Charles G. Washburn, "Worcester--Manufacturing and Mechanical Industries," in History of Worcester County, Massachusetts, comp. by D. Hamilton Hurd, 2 vols. (Philadelphia: J. W. Lewis & Co., 1889), 2:1609.

[42]Greville and Dorothy Bathe, Oliver Evans: A Chronicle of Early American Engineering (Philadelphia, 1935; repr. New York: Arno Press, 1972), p. 8; J. Leander Bishop, A History of American Manufactures, 1608-1860, 3 vols. (Philadelphia: Edward Young, 1868; repr. New York: Johnson Reprints, 1967), 1:388. Bishop linked Oliver Evans, Giles Richards, and Amos Whittemore, but the linkage could not be verified.

[43]Cited in Bagnall, Textile Industries, p. 154.

A few years later Thomas Pemberton described the same factory as producing 72,000 to 84,000 pairs of cards annually and employing 1,200 women and children.[44] Tench Coxe reported that Massachusetts had exported (to southern states probably) 10,000 pairs of cotton and wool cards in 1791.[45]

Amos Whittemore of Boston and Cambridge received a patent for manufacturing sheet cards dated June 5, 1797. His was a hand powered mechanism operated by a crank and consisting of cylinders and knobs which bent and cut the wire, pricked the leather, and bent the wire staple once more.[46] Whittemore's patent was ultimately for twenty-eight years. Reuben Meriam's pictured improvements of 1831 are shown in illustration 21. In 1809 Amos' brother William reported to the Collector of Boston,

> We have made fifty-five of those patent machines, thirty-seven of which are now in use; these machines with the other apparatus necessary to carry on the business to its present extent, have cost us about forty thousand dollars. We have now employed, in the factory, upwards of forty hands; we manufacture, weekly, one hundred and eighty dozen pair of hand cards, and two hundred square feet of cards for the

---

[44] [Thomas Pemberton], "A Topographical and Historical Description of Boston in 1794," in Collections of the Massachusetts Historical Society 3 (1795):279.

[45] Tench Coxe, A Brief Examination of Lord Sheffield's Observations on the Commerce of the United States, (Philadelphia: M. Carey, 1791), p. 113.

[46] Amos Whittemore's machine for manufacturing sheet cards, patent of June 5, 1797, "Restored Patents, Specifications," 1:43-45, Record Group 241, National Archives, Washington, D.C. See Appendix B.

SOURCE: National Archives.

Illus. 21. Reuben Meriam's Improvement in the Cut, Prick and Set Machine.

> woollen and cotton factories, which, together, amount to about two thousand dollars.

Gallatin duly reported that "Whittemore's machine for making cards has completely excluded foreign importations of that article."[48] Leander Bishop claimed that the machine was introduced into England by one Mr. Dyer.[49]

This may be the first example of American technology diffusing back to England. Unfortunately, Bishop is not an impeccable source. The degree of labor-saving achieved by Whittemore's machine is impressive indeed, as is the early point in time by which he achieved it. From production of 72,000 to 84,000 hand cards per year to over 100,000 is impressive enough, but when the labor force is reduced from 1,200 hands to forty, these become extraordinary increases in productivity achieved in a relatively short period of time of perhaps twelve years. It seems entirely credible that this innovation was introduced to England from America.

Others who were manufacturing carding cloth before 1800 included Jeremiah Wilkinson, a Slater in-law of Cumberland, Rhode Island; Ebenezer Chittenden of New Haven who according to Bishop had a staple making machine in 1784, and Nathaniel

---

[47] William Whittemore to the Collector of Boston, 24 November 1809, quoted in Gallatin, "Report on Manufactures," American State Papers, Finance 2:436.

[48] Gallatin, "Report on Manufactures," American State Papers, Finance 2:428.

[49] Bishop, History of American Manufactures 1:498.

Niles of Norwich, Connecticut. Also three card manufacturers were listed in Philadelphia in 1797.[50]

Important technical achievements in the mechanization of woolen manufacture were developments in carding brought to New England by the Scholfield family from Saddleworth, Yorkshire. Both Royal C. Taft and Arthur H. Cole believed that it was not just the Scholfield accomplishment of building better, more sophisticated carding machines, but because they were a sizeable family, they managed to disseminate their technical expertise over a wide area.[51] The first shop of John and Arthur Scholfield was set up in Timothy Dexter's barn in Newburyport, Massachusetts. They next set up a water-powered factory in the next township of Byfield. The factory apparently was not successful, serving chiefly as a diversion for Boston sleighing parties who came out to watch the machinery.[52]

By 1799 the brothers left Massachusetts for New London County, Connecticut. Their first mill in Montville was very small; the Census of 1820 listed only the bare rudiments of a mill. The Census also made note that John Scholfield had been ill for the year past, and reported but 300 yards of

---

[50] Ibid., 1:388-89, 572.

[51] Royal C. Taft, Some Notes Upon the Introduction of the Woolen Manufacture into the United States (Providence: 1882), pp. 10-12; Cole, Wool Manufacture 1:92-93.

[52] Taft, Introduction of Woolen Manufacture, p. 3.

broadcloth produced in that year.[53]

Between 1801 and 1820, John Scholfield and his sons established and managed at least four factories in New London County, including the Montville factory and one in Jewett City that was sold in 1817.

The following were Scholfield Connecticut mills:

Montville Mill[54]

Established 1801 by John Scholfield, Sr.

Machinery (1820):
1 carding machine
1 billy--32 spindles
1 jenny--32 spindles
1 loom

In 1820 manufactured 300 yards broadcloth; in 1832 managed by Nathanial Scholfield, manufactured 25,000 yards satinet.

Stonington Mill[56]

Established 1806 by John Scholfield, Sr., managed by Joseph Scholfield from 1813 to 1831. It was not determined if this Joseph Scholfield was the same Joseph who "had an interest" in the Merino Woollen Manufacturing Company of Dudley, Massachusetts, or the same who was a weaver for Slater, Howard and Company of the same place in the 1820s.

Machinery (1820):
2 double carding machines
1 picker
1 billy--30 spindles
2 jennies--36 spindles, 40 spindles
3 broad)
3 narrow) looms

53Records of the 1820 Census of Manufactures: Connecticut, p. 83, Record Group 29, National Archives. Hereafter cited as 1820 Manufactures Census.

54Ibid.

55McLane Report 1:980.

561820 Manufactures Census: Conn., p. 107; Bagnall, Textile Industries, p. 424.

Waterford Mill[57]

Established 1814 by John Scholfield, Sr. Managed by Thomas Scholfield by 1820; he continued as manager until 1832.

Machinery (1820):
- 1 carding machine
- 1 billy--30 spindles
- 1 jenny--40 spindles
- 5 looms

In 1820 this mill employed one boy besides Thomas and manufactured 800 yards of three-quarter broadcloth. In 1832 it employed three men, two children, and two women and manufactured 1,200 yards flannel and 1,890 yards satinet.

Jewett City Mill[58]

Bought by John Scholfield, Jr. 1807 from John Wilson, clothier, on condition Scholfield would not carry on any custom finishing. He began with a carding mill and added machinery to it. In 1816 Scholfield mortgaged the mill to Wilson and sold it to him the next year.

Machinery (before 1817):
- 1 picker
- 1 double breaker with three feet cards
- 1 billy--40 spindles
- 3 jennies--2 40 spindle, 1 60 spindle
- 4 broad) looms
- 7 Narrow)
- 1 twisting frame--70 spindles

According to Bagnall, Wilson sold the mill to Jonathon G. W. Trumbull and John Breed of Norwich who operated the factory until 1845.

In 1820 the mill was described by the Census marshall as follows:[59]

1. - 3. 15,000 lb. wool @ $10,000
4. - 6. 20 men
10 women
5 boys

---

57 1820 Manufactures Census: Conn., p. 83; McLane Report 1:980.

58 Bagnall, Textile Industries, pp. 457-59.

59 1820 Manufactures Census: Conn., p. 101. The questionnaire used by the census marshalls asked the

7. - 8. 1 iron boiler for heating dye works
1 large blue vat
3 copper dye kettles
1 picker
4 double carding machines
1 billy
1 Brewster spinning machine, water powered--200 spindles
2 broad) looms
2 kerseymere (narrow)) looms
9 satinet hand) looms
1 napping machine (gig)
2 broad) shearing machines, Hovey's plan
4 narrow) shearing machines, Hovey's plan
1 clothiers press
1 winding machine

9. Capital invested--buildings and machinery $20,000
floating capital $10,000

---

following questions:

Account of______________in the town of_____________, county of_________________. Questions taken 1820.

RAW MATERIALS EMPLOYED	1.	The kind?
	2.	The quantity annually consumed?
	3.	The cost of annual consumption?
NUMBERS OF PERSONS EMPLOYED	4.	Men?
	5.	Women?
	6.	Boys and Girls?
MACHINERY	7.	Whole quantity and kind of machinery?
	8.	Quantity of machinery in operation?
EXPENDITURES	9.	Amount of capital invested?
	10.	Amount paid annually for wages?
	11.	Amount of contingent expenses?
PRODUCTION	12.	The nature and names of articles manufactured?
	13.	Market value of the articles which are annually manufactured?
	14.	General remarks concerning the establishment, as to its actual and past condition, the demand for, and sale of its manufacture.

10. Wages: $5,000
11. Costs: $3,000
12. Manufactured broadcloth, kerseymeres, and satinet.
13. Valued @ $25,000
14. The subscribers owners of the Griswold Manufacturing establishment purchased the property in March last and not having much knowledge of the business previous to that are unable to give any particular information respecting it.

    The property was formerly owned and the manufacturing business carried on by John Scholfield for a number of years past. He became embarrassed at the close of the late war and was finally obliged to abandon it. There has been but little done in the establishment for the last three years. The subscribers can only say that the business at present bids fair to be a living one. Woolen goods of all kinds are in good demand and of course meet with a steady sale.

While in no sense was the Schofield-Griswold-Jewett City woolen mill a very large one, in 1820, its machinery was extremely advanced. It had up-to-date dyeing equipment and the variety of looms, the Brewster spinner, the gig, and the Hovey shearing machines all were evidence of very modern practices. Unfortunately, it cannot be determined whether this machinery was installed by Scholfield or by the new owners, Trumbull and Breed.

This is perhaps a good place to suggest the possibility that Connecticut, and in particular, New London and Middlesex counties, may have been something of a technological "hearth." There were at least six, possibly eight Brewster spinners in the area in 1820; and in fact that machine probably was developed at Norwich or Jewett City. Middletown, Middlesex County, was the home of Pameacha and Sanseer, the first a fine woolen manufacturing company, the second manufacturing satinets, cottons, and ultimately machinery.[60] Jewett City in Griswold Township, New London County, not only was the site of the largest Scholfield operation (sold in 1817, see above) but also the site of two John Slater (brother of Samuel) mills, one a very large manufacturer of satinet.[61] Norwich reported the Yantic Manufacturing Company in 1832, a very large flannel factory.[62]

There are three more Scholfields to be traced; two were presumably brothers of John, Sr., the other, one of his six children. Arthur Scholfield went to Berkshire County, Massachusetts; he was involved from about 1801 to 1806 with Elkanah Watson in the latter's woolen factory, and after 1806 in his own machine shop in which he made what Arthur H. Cole maintained were carding machines of the highest possible workmanship.[63] In 1806 he advertised double carding machines for $400, or $253 without the carding cloth. But for no reason that is obvious, Arthur did not do well. Bagnall said that he bought into the Pomeroy woolen operation in Pittsfield to the amount of twenty (out of fifty) shares of stock

---

[60]1820 Manufactures Census: Conn., 215, 216; McLane Report 1:980.

[61]Bagnall, Textile Industries, pp. 595-96; McLane Report 1:980.

[62]McLane Report 1:980.

[63]Cole, Wool Manufacture 1:93.

in 1814, but lost everything by the end of the war.[64] However, Taft claimed he stayed on in Pittsfield building carding machines until his death in 1827 and in the process made Pittsfield into one of the foremost machinery centers of the time.[65] The Pomeroy manufactory was described in the 1820 Census; it was one of few factories still known to be operating in 1832.[66]

A third brother, James Scholfield spent his life in the North Andover, Massachusetts area. In 1802 he had a small forty foot by twelve one-story building with one carding machine, a jenny, and probably a billy and a loom or two. The work was done mostly by his family, including his daughter Nancy who was said to have been an accomplished weaver. In 1812, James and his brother Arthur sold their interests to Paschel and Abel Abbot for $1,900. The Abbots in turn sold out to Abraham Marland who became the organizing entrepreneur of a large flannel manufactory in Andover. The Abbots in their turn started a new satinet and flannel factory that functioned until it became insovent in 1843.[67]

In 1813 Nathanial Stevens went into the flannel business with two partners, and they hired James Scholfield

---

[64]Bagnall, Textile Industries, p. 265.

[65]Taft, Introduction of Woolen Manufacture, pp. 30-37.

[66]1820 Manufactures Census: Mass., 122, McLane Report 1:134-35.

[67]Bagnall, Textile Industries, pp. 307-8.

as their agent or plant manager. In 1815 the Stevens mill was leased to Abraham Marland and presumably Scholfield continued on as agent. In 1832, the Stevens and Marland establishments were two separate factories among five in Andover Township that were capitalized at a total of $150,000. The five factories bought nearly 250,000 pounds of wool, had a $50,000 per annum payroll, and produced 16,000 pieces of flannel (forty-six yards each) valued at $224,000.[68]

There was one more Scholfield who might have been a part of the dissemination of Scholfield technology. This was the Joseph Scholfield who was presumed to be John, Sr.'s son, and who "became interested in the Merino Woolen Factory at Dudley, Massachusetts in 1817."[69] If he did have a financial interest there, he had sold it by 1818. From 1824 to 1828, and possibly longer, one Joseph Scholfield worked for Slater, Howard and Company in Dudley as a weaver and spinner.[70]

Arthur Cole implied that there may have been a traceable network responsible for the rapid diffusion of the carding machine in the United States. For example, Moses Hale, who was Nathanial Stevens' father-in-law, set

---

[68]McLane Report 1:212-13.

[69]Taft, Introduction of Woolen Manufacture, p. 12.

[70]Daybooks 5-12, Slater, Howard & Company, Slater Collection, Baker Library, Harvard Business School, Boston, Massachusetts.

one up in East Chelmsford, Massachusetts (future Lowell) in 1800. One was established in Vernon, Connecticut, in 1802. Vernon was the home of Delano Abbot, an early manufacturer of satinet, who was possibly related to the Abbots of Andover. There were early carding machines in Poughkeepsie, New York and Worcester, Massachusetts by 1803; both towns became important wool technological centers.[71] The network is not easily traced. Nevertheless, one cannot read through Bagnall or the sources without sensing the existence of interrelationships. There seems to have been a mechanical elite made up of men who were mutually acquainted or even related. The elite was made up of partly manufacturers, but more importantly, their agents and chief mechanics. The difficulty is that the names of most of these men are not known. About all that can be done, given the state of present research, is to postulate the existence of such a network.

If American manufacturers were to have any hopes of becoming competitive in terms of quality with British fine woolen cloth, something had to be done about the raw material. Fine cloth requires fine wool, that is, wool whose fibers are very thin. Fine cloth also requires fibers that are soft and that felt well. Circa 1800, no American--farmer or cloth producer--had any illusions about the general run of American sheep. They were perfectly

---

[71] Cole, Wool Manufacture 1:90-95.

adequate for occasional Sunday mutton and for homespun cloth, but in no way able to provide the raw material for a fine cloth industry.

Early American husbandmen did not know about recessive or dominant genes. This was a serious scientific lack, but even the simplest farmer knew that good stock bred to good stock should produce good stock, and in fact, did so, more often than not. He perhaps knew even better that good stock bred to not-so-good stock stood a reasonable chance of improvement in the next generation. It was this type of thinking that induced men such as E. I. du Pont, David Humphreys, Elkanah Watson, and Robert Livingston to import European sheep. One problem these men did not recognize quickly enough was that since sheep have two quite distinct products--wool and meat--it was difficult to persuade dirt farmers to breed for one without the other. This was especially true in early nineteenth century America when the market for fine wool was minimal. There is at least one known example of an un-knowing farmer eating merino sheep. Andrew Craigie of Boston had received two ewes and a ram smuggled into the country through the good offices of one William Foster. According to the story, the Craigie family ate them; a short time later Foster ran into Craigie at an auction where merino rams were selling for $1,000 apiece.[72]

---

[72]Bishop, History of American Manufactures 2:87.

The quality of merino sheep was well-known in Europe; the English had been importing Spanish wool for more than a century. In 1765 the Elector of Saxony received a flock of two hundred merinos. The sheep had caused considerable problems in Saxony in the early years apparently because they brought a form of scab with them but by 1777, Saxony farmers were calling for more imports and some three hundred more were sent from Spain.[73]

In 1786 a small flock of merinos was sent to the French royal farm in Rambouillet, and the next year George III of England received thirty sheep. In 1801 M. Delessert, a French banker, sent four merino ram lambs to America under the sponsorship of Pierre Samuel du Pont de Nemours. The lambs were shepherded by young E. I. du Pont. Two were designated for Delessert's own farm in New York, the third for President Jefferson, and the fourth for the du Pont farm then in New Jersey. The crossing was a long and rough one so only one of the lambs survived, but that was the famous Don Pedro (see illus. 22) who sired god-knows-how-many half-blooded lambs from 1801 until his death in 1811. In 1801 Don Pedro stayed in New Jersey where he tupped nine ewes, but the next year when the du Pont family moved to Delaware, Don Pedro was sent

---

[73]Randall, _Sheep Husbandry_, p. 138; C. Benton and S. F. Berry, comp., _A Statistical View of the Number of Sheep_ (Cambridge, Mass.: Folsam, Wells, & Thurston, 1837), p. 128.

SOURCE: Courtesy of the Eleutherian Mills Historical Library.

Illus. 22. Trademark of Dupont, Bauduy and Company Showing the Ram Don Pedro.

to Delessert's farm up the Hudson. There he served a large flock until 1805 when Delessert decided to rent his farm. He sold off his flock and Don Pedro's progeny to farmers in the neighborhood. Don Pedro was bought by E. I. du Pont's agent for sixty dollars, and in July 1805 was taken down to the Brandywine. There, according to du Pont, Don Pedro served sixty to eighty du Pont and neighboring ewes per year whose lambs by 1808 du Pont was buying up as rapidly as he could.[74]

Indeed Don Pedro must have been a remarkable animal. His wooden likeness is safely ensconced in the Hagley Museum, and other likenesses abound in the various du Pont estates in Wilmington. In 1811, E. I. du Pont described him as follows:[75]

> Pedro is now ten years old; but very strong and active; he is stout, short, and woolly, and of a much better form than Merinos commonly are; and even better than that of a ram figured in a superb engraving lately received by the Agricultural Society of Philadelphia from Paris. His horns are large and spiral; his legs short, and he weighs 138 pounds; his fleece carefully washed in cold water, weighs 8 1/2 pounds, is extremely fine, the staple is 1 3/4 inches long, and lying very thick and close upon his body; it is entirely free from loose coarse hairs called jarr. Every part of his fleece, moreover, is nearly of equal fineness, even the wool of the hind legs and thighs, which is long and coarse upon many Merino sheep, is short and fine upon Pedro.

---

[74]Carroll W. Pursell, Jr., "E. I. du Pont, Don Pedro, and the Introduction of Merino Sheep into the United States, 1801: A Document," Agricultural History 33 (April 1959):86-88.

[75]Ibid.

The du Pont enthusiasm for merino sheep was rooted in three notions. For one, the du Ponts truly believed they could help their adopted country by improving the breed of American sheep. As the "merino mania" gripped the country, the business-minded du Ponts saw no reason not to make a little money. Finally, as the Embargo and Non-Intercourse legislation prevented the importation of fine woolen fabrics, the du Ponts began a sizeable factory enterprize to capitalize on that lack of fabric.[76]

Another early importer of merino sheep was David Humphreys of Connecticut. Humphreys had climbed up the career ladder during the Revolutionary War and after. A Yale graduate, he was successively an aide to General Putnam, then a private secretary to Washington himself. After the war, he became a member of the diplomatic corp first working for Jefferson in Paris, then heading his own Ministry at Lisbon. From 1797 to 1802, he was Minister to Spain, and in that capacity became involved with merino sheep.[77]

When 100 merino sheep arrived at Colonel Humphreys' Derby, Connecticut farm in the spring of 1802, he apparently had no thought of using the wool himself. He probably hoped to sell the wool and the progeny of his sheep to

---

[76]Carroll W. Pursell, Jr., "E. I. du Pont and the Merino Mania in Delaware, 1805-1815," Agricultural History 36 (April 1962):91-100.

[77]Bagnall, Textile Industries, pp. 347-48.

other gentlemen farmers like himself. In winter of 1803 Humphreys bought some land around Derby at Rimson's Falls which included two fulling mills and a clothier's shop, but it was not until the summer of 1806 that he began to equip a woolen mill.[78] By 1808 the mill had a far reaching enough reputation to gain the attention of President Jefferson. The Jefferson correspondence was through a third party, one Abraham Bishop of New Haven. Jefferson asked Bishop to secure enough of Humphreys' cloth for a suit. Bishop replied to Jefferson's request of November 13 that Colonel Humphreys would surely like to pick out the cloth for himself, that he (Humphreys) had been in Philadelphia, had only just returned, and now it would take four weeks "for finishing a piece of superior quality . . ." Jefferson replied on December 8,

> I should be glad to receive it whenever it can come, but a greater desideratum will be lost if not received in time to be made up for our New Year's Day Exhibition, when we expect every one will endeavour to be in homespun, and I should be sorry to be marked as being in default. I would sacrifice much in quality to this circumstance of time. However, I leave it to the kindness of Colonel Humphreys and yourself.

Jefferson was forthwith sent 5 1/2 yards narrow superfine cloth at $4.50 per yard.[79]

By 1808 then, Humphreys was making fine cloth. Woolen manufacture and cotton stocking manufacture were at stage

---

[78]Ibid., p. 350.

[79]Ibid., pp. 357-58. Note Jefferson's use of the word "homespun," meaning in this case domestic manufacture, not foreign.

center at Humphreysville as the manufactory was incorporated in 1810 for $500,000. Surrounding these factories were a gristmill, paper mill, and sawmill. When Timothy Dwight described the textile mill in 1811, he saw such water-powered machinery as follows:[80]

> . . . two newly invented shearing-machines; a breaker and finisher for carding sheep's wool; a machine for making ravellings; two jennies for spinning sheep's wool . . . ; a picker; two more carding machines for sheep's wool, and a billy with forty spindles, in a third building; a fulling-mill; a saw-mill, employed to cut the square timber, boards, laths, etc. for the different edifices, and to shape many of the wooden materials for the machines; two more fulling mills, on improved principles, immediately connected with the clothier's shop, and the various machinery in a cotton manufactory, a building one hundred feet long, thirty-six feet wide, and of four stories, capable of containing two thousand spindles, with all their necessary apparatus. The institution contains four broad and eight narrow looms and eighteen stocking frames.

Dwight went on to describe how boarding houses accommodated 150 persons, and gardens provided all the needed vegetables for the community. Men were paid five to twenty-five dollars per month; women worked for fifty cents to one dollar per week, and the children who served as apprentices regularly attended the common school.

Dwight did not stint in praise of his friend,

> In this manufactory, he has, I think fairly established three points of great importance. One is that these manufactures can be carried on with success; another, that the workmen can be preserved in as good health as that enjoyed by any other class of men in the country; and the third, that the deterioration of morals in

---

[80]Timothy Dwight, <u>Travels in New England and New York</u>, 4 vols. (New Haven: By the Author, 1821-22), 3:391-94.

> such institutions, which is so often complained of, is not necessary, but incidental; not inherent in the institution itself, but the fault of the proprietor.[81]

Early in 1810 Humphreys had gone to England, one has to think partly for the purpose of finding experienced workmen and of pirating them out of England. His main catch was one John Winterbotham late of Lancashire and experienced in the processes of woolen manufacture. Near Liverpool Winterbotham and three companions stole aboard the vessel *Herald* while it lay at anchor outside the surveillance of revenue officers. Later at sea the ship was searched by officers of a man-of-war, but the men escaped detection. Winterbotham's risks and skills provided him with a full partnership in the newly organized firm at Humphreysville along with Thomas Vose and David Humphreys.[82]

Humphreys was an exceedingly paternalistic operator in an age of paternalism. He was also an up-to-date technician, or at least he was interested in the most advanced machinery. David's young nephew William Humphreys invented and patented (October 4, 1811) a machine for drawing out a carded roll preparatory to spinning it.[83] This machine apparently was to take the place of the billy and was supposed to draw out rolls to any desired thickness,

---

[81]Ibid.

[82]Bagnall, *Textile Industries*, pp. 350-51.

[83]"Restored Patents, Specifications," 3:5-7, and Patent Drawing no. 1588, NA.

depending on how often the process was repeated. This may have been the so-called "Humphreysville spinner" (see ill. 23). While doing away with the need for the billy was a continuing goal among woolen manufacturers, this particular machine would not solve the basic problem of going directly from carding to spinning. Carding rolls came off the mechanical card in lengths as long as the doffing roll of the machine was wide. The Scholfield twenty-four inch carding machine, for example, produced rolls twenty-four inches long. These were pieced together by the billy or slubber tender's assistant (always a child). The billy drew out the yarn and made one continuous roving which was wound on a cop and from which the jenny spun the roving into yarn. So eliminating the billy would eliminate one nagging aspect of child labor; at the same time, the objective of going directly from carding to spinning was an objective long sought after in the early nineteenth century, ultimately achieved in 1826 by John Goulding's condenser.

Another chronicler said of Humphreys, "The machines for abridging labor lately introduced (at Humphreysville) are those of Molleneaux for shearing cloth, of Richards, for cutting dye-woods, and one for braising (raising) and finishing cloth."[84] The last two have not proven traceable, but the Molleneaux shearing machine came from

---

[84] "Humphreysville Manufacturing Company," Halcyon (Philadelphia, n.d.), as quoted in Bagnall, Textile Industries, p. 353.

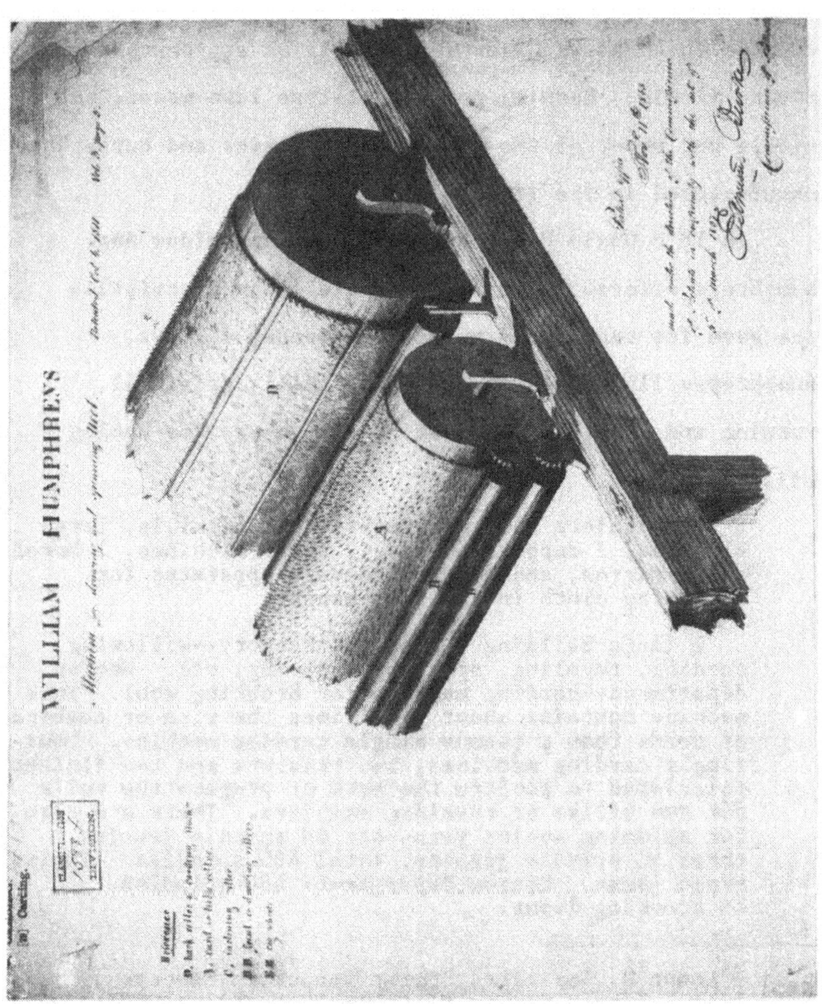

SOURCE: National Archives.

Illus. 23. William Humphreys' Machine for Drawing and Spinning Wool.

Long Island and involved one of America's most famous entrepreneurs in one of his first independent ventures: Peter Cooper. In later years, Cooper described this machine which he was licensed to sell as a precurser to a mowing machine, meaning not a reel-type lawn mower, but a sickle bar mower of the type that McCormick and Hussey had manufactured in the 1840s.[85]

In 1818 David Humphreys died, and his widow Ann Humphreys offered the mills for sale. The description she gave for the 1820 Manufactures Census follows. Humphreysville consisted of a paper mill, gristmill, turning and sawmill; the most extensive was the woolen mill:[86]

> 1 clothiers shop: 3 stocks--fulling mills, large blue vat, 2 copper kettles, 2 shear machines, 1 broad and 1 narrow, and other necessary apparatus for finishing cloth in the best manner.
>
> 1 large building called the Factory--willowing, carding, roveling, spinning, weaving, etc. Woolen department--carding machine for breaking wool. This machine contains about five times the wire or numbers of cards than a common single carding machine. Four single carding machines, two breakers and two finishers calculated to perform the work or prepare the rolls for two billys or roveling machines. There are also for spinning woolen yarn--six 60 spindle jennies, three 40 spindle jennies, total 480 spindles. Twelve broad looms. Cotton department: 480 spindles, 14 stocking looms.

---

[85]Semon H. Springer, "Peter Cooper in Hempstead, 1812-1818," Nassau County Historical Journal (Autumn 1851), pp. 9-10; Patent for Jesse Molleneaux's shearing machine, "Restored Patents, Specifications," 2:37-40, NA.

[86]1820 Manufactures Census: Conn., p. 66.

> 2 boarding houses. One to eight family dwelling house. 1 warehouse, 11 buildings in all--seven for work, 3 for dwelling.
>
> The establishment was capitalized at between $80-100,000, paid out $3,500 in wages. Manufactured cotton yarn--$2,650, woolen cloth--$150, paper--$6,076; lumber--$500. Total: $10,376. But the woolen establishment had not been in operation since the death of General Humphreys except for a little dyeing.

By 1832 the proprietor of Humphreysville, John H. DeForest, was manufacturing cottons exclusively.[87] The original factory, however, had set a pattern for textile manufacture. In the first place, Humphreysville was an integrated factory producing on the site finished woolen cloth from raw wool. The vast majority of those factories enumerated in the 1820 Manufactures Census were integrated factories manufacturing on site rather than putting out certain processes either in homes or other mills. Even those factories that continued to card yarn and full cloth for neighboring farmers manufactured cloth from scratch. This contrasts with Yorkshire's largest woolen manufactory, Bean Ing, which as late as the 1820s was purchasing three times more unfinished cloth than it was manufacturing itself.[88]

In the second place Humphreys very early established the idea of a model manufacturing town with church, school,

---

[87]McLane Report, 1:984-85.

[88]Herbert Heaton, "Benjamin Gott and the Industrial Revolution in Yorkshire," Economic History Review, 1st ser., 3 (1931):45-66.

and appropriate residence facilities for laborers. Humphreys was a well-travelled man, married to a wealthy English woman.[89] It seems very plausible that at some point he may have visited New Lanark and become familiar with the ideas of Robert Owen, before Owen came to America. A large number of his workers were orphans from the New York Almshouse.[90] Strict order was enforced at Humphreysville in part by operating the factory rather like a military school or an early form of "boys town." It is impossible to say whether conditions were harsh and severe, or whether some homeless city boys were given good food and living conditions plus steady discipline and some schooling, and thereby an opportunity for a better life. Perhaps the change from city almshouse to country manufactory was not much of a change at all. But if that is true, what kind of change did the factory represent to the farm boy or girl who came to work? It certainly must have seemed like a restricted life; yet the scanty evidence gives the impression that educational opportunities both in terms of factory skills and evening and Sunday schools may have made up for the harshness for many, especially in the early days of textile manufacture.[91]

---

[89] Ellsworth S. Grant, Yankee Dreamers and Doers (Chester, Conn.: Pequot Press, [1975]), p. 39.

[90] Bagnall, Textile Industries, pp. 356-57.

[91] Lucy Larcom, A New England Girlhood (Boston, 1889), and Harriet Robinson, Loom and Spindle, or Life Among the Early Mill Girls (Boston, 1898) cited in Robert H. Bremner, ed., Children and Youth in America: A Documentary History, 3 vols. (Cambridge, Harvard University Press, 1970), 1:601-6

In these very early years of American manufacturing, little is said about harshness, unpleasantness, disagreeableness of factory life. Modern writers seem to feel that it took these laborers one or two decades to "catch on" to how exploited and badly treated they were.[92] It seems more likely that working conditions and wages did change after the panic of 1837, the hard times following, and after the increase in immigration after 1845 that brought hundreds of unskilled men and women to the Northeast who were willing to work for very little. In these early days, the novelty of working in a factory, and particularly the novelty of shared experiences and society among the young in factories and boarding houses most surely ameliorated the harshness for many of them.

Measuring the influence of a David Humphreys is difficult indeed. Certainly his factory in Connecticut was well-known, and the man himself had a reputation for benevolence and decency. If indeed he was regarded as something of a leader, that leadership was acknowledged infrequently.

Just as the Revolutionary War had brought no startling economic or social change, neither was the two decade period after the adoption of the national Constitution a period of radical change from the past. In 1789 most

---

[92] Philip S. Foner, _The Factory Girls_ (Urbana: University of Illinois Press, 1977), pp. xiii-xxvii.

Americans lived within a few miles of the coast; so they did in 1810 although by now the country had conquered and purchased control of a vast, rich hinterland and trickles of people were responding to one of the most democratic land policies ever conceived. Foreign trade was still the major source of wealth although now China and the Far East, even Russia, became trading adversaries to Europe and the West Indies. The slave trade picked up for a while after the war but legal imports of slaves were stopped by Congress in 1808. Agriculture provided the economic base, but in New England where farming at its best was a touch and go affair, the economy was supplemented by the lumber industry, whaling, fishing, and, of course, trade and shipping. The Middle States relied on wheat and corn for home consumption and export, and the farmers with tobacco exhausted lands around Chesapeake Bay were experimenting with wheat. Further south and west a few were testing the practicality of short-stapled cotton now that a simple gin had been invented to clean it (1793). American cities were still walking cities in 1810 as well as 1790; in fact, many shopkeepers and artisans worked and lived in the same or adjacent buildings. Nevertheless, distances between cities were shortened in terms of time, and new cities along the Ohio River were booming. There were stage lines from Boston to Philadelphia, New York to Albany, and even a new canal around the falls of the Merrimack up near Chelmsford.

Philadelphia was still our greatest city, but New York which had been rebuilt completely after two bad fires during the British occupation was visibly in the process of becoming America's premier port. Baltimore was a boom town.[93]

In the 1790s it seemed that the development of American manufacturing had more of an ideological imperative than an economic one. This was perhaps particularly true in fine woolen goods which in no way could be deemed necessities for living. It was the politicians of the day--Alexander Hamilton, Tench Coxe, Mathew Carey, for example--who were urging American activity in this direction. Hamilton and Coxe were trying to prove by the example of the Society for the Establishment of Useful Manufactures, that factories were feasible and profitable. The Humphreys factory seemed guided more by ideology than economics. It was not until the last years of the Napoleonic wars, and America's participation in those wars, that economics and ideology could come together. That period was very short and presented would-be manufacturers with a perverted picture of the economic state of the world. For example, by 1814 there were serious shortages of British imports, particularly British woolen goods. By this time, British military needs for woolen cloth plus the extension of the blockade to the New England coast had effectively dried

---

[93] Ralph H. Brown, Mirror for Americans--Likeness of the Eastern Seabord, 1810 (New York: American Geographical Society, 1943), passim.

up any of the legal or illegal trade in those goods that had been going on. So prices rose accordingly. Fine merino wool was selling in Philadelphia for over three dollars per pound, and fine English cloth could bring as much as eighteen dollars per yard.[94] The many small wool factories that were established during this period ran into serious trouble as soon as the peace was signed. Most probably did not survive with their original ownership. This is a story for the next chapter. The matter for concern here are these political views that urged Americans to consider placing "the manufacturer by the side of the agriculturist."[95]

In 1791 Alexander Hamilton spent much of his writing space in the Report on Manufactures corroborating the Adam Smith view that agriculture and manufacturing could be mutually complementary. True, he was, or thought he was, foreseeing the physiocratic arguments of Jeffersonians, but it is doubtful that the prejudices against manufacturing were as rampant as Hamilton seemed to feel. Domestic manufactures, as mentioned above, had an ambivalent meaning; in certain contexts it meant manufacturing in the home, or family industry; in other contexts, it most certainly

---

[94]Arthur H. Cole, _Wholesale Commodity Prices in the United States, 1700-1861_ (Cambridge: Harvard University Press, 1938), p. 364; Bishop, _History of American Manufactures_, 2:195.

[95]Thomas Jefferson to Benjamin Austin, 9 January 1816, in Carter Goodrich, ed., _The Government and the Economy, 1783-1861_ (Indianapolis: Bobbs-Merrill, 1967), pp. 184-87.

meant domestic, not foreign manufacturing. In some cases, the meaning was never crystal clear.

Certainly some of Hamilton's arguments fell on most receptive ears. Americans were nothing if not commercially minded. There was not an American alive who did not have some notion of markets and prices. Obviously, there was no town merchant who did not. But whiskey rebels in western Pennsylvania, hemp farmers in Kentucky, and horse breeders in Rhode Island had a perfectly clear idea of the importance of markets to their own prosperity. It was no accident that Henry Clay from Kentucky became the spokesman for the "American system" that advocated improvements in transportation, in roads, turnpikes, and canals subsidized by government. The farthest backwoodsman felt his livelihood depended on getting his goods to market either to be consumed or exported further.

In Hamilton's Report on Manufactures there was a differentiation between domestic industry and home manufacture, and this differentiation depended considerably on his own notions of mechanization and labor, which, as he saw it, were inseparably related. Hamilton saw three impediments to the development of manufacturing in the United States: "scarcity of hands--dearness of labour--want of capital."[96] One solution to the first problem was

---

[96]Cooke, Reports of Hamilton, p. 192.

"the great use that can be made of women and children . . . --the vast extension given by late improvements to the employment of Machines . . . had prodigiously lessened the necessity of manual labour." As high wages were related to labor scarcity, machinery could provide enough labor savings to make up for some of labor's high price. Furthermore, Hamilton felt that perhaps higher relative (to Europe) wages had been exaggerated; he felt that the higher wage rate was "much less in regard to Artificers and manufacturers than in regard to country labourers . . . ; and the degree of disparity, which does truly exist, is diminished in proportion to the use that can be made of machinery." Finally, Hamilton felt that lower material costs, less and fewer taxes, ultimately would balance the higher transportation and labor costs faced by American manufacturers.[97]

Hamilton was fully confident that America's vast tracts of land held great potential for capital funds. But he was also aware of the difficulties in translating that potential into moving money or liquid investable capital for manufacturing. His solutions--banks and foreign capital--became the standard solutions for early nineteenth century industry,[98] but there were exceptions, and investment was seldom straight-forward. For example, some Boston merchants were heavily involved in textile manufacturing including woolen manufacture; much of their merchandizing capital was

---

[97]Ibid., pp. 144-45.

long term credit owed to English dry goods exporters and manufacturers. Some manufacturers like Samuel Slater and Victor and Charles du Pont used profits from one industry to plow back into another, but their ultimate liquid capital sources were banks or foreign creditors.[99]

Hamilton's Report was, after all, a plea for government support in the form of tariff protection, and a thoughtful, well-constructed argument against Adam Smith's free trade notions that had crossed the Atlantic in 1776. Hamilton listed sixteen industries; some like the paper industry were established and mature and already amply protected. Some, like the iron industry, needed greater tariff protection, perhaps direct government involvement in the manufacture of weaponry. Other industries required other types of support such as bounties, premiums, drawbacks, as well as tariffs on finished manufactures. On the other hand, some industries like shipbuilding and cabinet-making required only the exemption of duties on certain types ot imported woods.[100] As one might expect, the overall picture of American industry from Alexander Hamilton in 1791 was one of small scale, somewhat struggling, not greatly mechanized, industrial enterprise scattered throughout the states and territories. But the importance of the Hamilton perspective was his view of the future.

---

[99]Ibid.

[100]Cooke, Reports of Hamilton, pp. 179-201.

To be sure, he certainly never envisioned 1910 Pittsburgh or General Motors of the 1970s, but he did see clearly the potential represented by Samuel Slater, E. I. du Pont, and very likely Francis Cabot Lowell.

By 1810, twenty years later, a Jeffersonian and free-trade advocate, Albert Gallatin, Secretary of the Treasury, reported to Congress. His free-trade views were tempered; Gallatin acknowledged the need in certain instances for moderate tariffs. They were preferred certainly to prohibitory duties, and he suggested that moderate duties be established with time limits, so that given industries would not become dependent on protection. Gallatin was shoulder to shoulder with Hamilton in promoting manufactures by providing moderate subsidies including low-interest government loans, by promoting public works in the form of transportation improvements,[101] and by continued favor of the First Bank of the United States.[102]

The 1810 Manufactures Report showed considerable progress in the development of American manufactures although we will never be in a position to measure accurately the progress. Wood, and manufactures of wood "are carried to a high degree of perfection, supply the

---

[101]Albert Gallatin, "Report on Roads and Canals," in Selected Writings of Albert Gallatin, ed. E. James Ferguson (Indianapolis: Bobbs-Merrill, 1967), pp. 228-40.

[102]Gallatin, "Report on the Bank," in Writings, ed. Ferguson, pp. 264-74.

whole demand of the United States." "Tanneries are established in every part of the United States." "Soap and tallow candles yield a profit, it is said, of fifteen per centum on the capital employed." "The number (of hats) made in the State of Massachusetts is estimated, by the hat company of Boston, at four times the number required for the consumption of the State. . . ." "Although it is not practicable to make a correct statement of the value of all the iron and manufactures of iron, annually made in the United States, it is believed to be from twelve to fifteen millions of dollars."[103] These quotations indicate clearly that American industry already was broadly based and playing a significant economic role.

America's early nineteenth-century economy was, of course, agriculturally and commercially based, but it was clear to both Hamilton and Gallatin that that base could and must expand into manufacturing. The twentieth-century problem in understanding this commitment to manufacturing is mostly related to its very small scale. Even though few can truly conceive of the huge sizes of capital, of plant space, of numbers of employees or stockholders required by modern industry, few now can imagine the _smallness_ of factories, of their capitalization, their few employees, and the limited partnerships of the early nineteenth

---

[103]Gallatin, "Report on Manufactures," in _Writings_, ed. Ferguson, 240-64.

century. Within five years of the 1810 Report, the Boston Manufacturing Company revolutionized American industry by creating an integrated plant, with an initial $100,000 in capital (1811) and twelve partners (1815).[104] This was the small start that very quickly would become a very large industry, that by 1837 had the productive capacity of 300 million yards of cotton cloth.[105] If this beginning was ever so small in cotton, in woolen manufacturing, it was even smaller, and for various reasons would not grow into anything like the cotton giant.

Hamilton reported that the woolen manufactory in Hartford had "reached a considerable degree of perfection" in the manufacture of broadcloths and cassimeres. But he knew that the industry needed encouragement and especially needed to improve its raw material supply. To do that he recommended premiums on the finest domestic supply of wool, and bounties for increased foreign supply of fine wool. The country's climate insured that woolen cloth would always be necessary; but some kind of encouragement was needed "to

---

[104]Robert V. Spalding, "The Boston Mercantile Community and the Promotion of the Textile Industry in New England, 1813-1860" (Ph.D. dissertation, Yale University, 1963), pp. 17-19.

[105]Robert Brooke Zevin, "The Growth of Cotton Textile Production after 1815," in The Reinterpretation of American Economic History, ed. Robert W. Fogel and Stanley L. Engerman (New York: Harper & Row, 1971), p. 124, whole article, pp. 122-47.

[106]Cooke, "Reports of Hamilton," pp. 193, 196.

cherish and bring to maturity this precious embryo."[107]

In 1810 Gallatin reported eighty-seven cotton mills, sixty-two of which were in operation. These mills had the potential to employ 500 men, 3,500 women and children. They consumed 3.6 million pounds of cotton and produced 2.8 million pounds of yarn.[108]

The Gallatin Report claimed that almost all woolens were spun and woven in private families although Gallatin did know of fourteen mills around Philadelphia and Baltimore which produced on the average 10,000 yards of serviceable to fine cloth ranging in price from one dollar to ten dollars per yard. According to Gallatin,

> All these cloths, as well as those manufactured in private families, are generally superior in quality, though somewhat inferior in appearance, to imported cloths of the same price. The principal obstacle to the extension of the manufacture is the want of wool, which is still deficient, both in quality and quantity. But these defects are daily and rapidly lessened by the introduction of sheep of the merino and other superior breeds; by the great demand for the article; and by the attention now every where paid by farmers to the increase and improvement of flocks.

The Embargo of 1807 and the Non-Intercourse act of 1809 presumably stopped the importation of woolen cloth to the United States from England. The merino sheep "mania" peaked in 1809-10. Neither one nor both together provided

---

[107]Ibid., pp. 197-98.

[108]Gallatin, "Report on Manufactures," in Writings, ed. Ferguson, pp. 246-48.

[109]Ibid., pp. 248-49.

the necessary stimulus for American mechanized manufacturing. They did stimulate, however, domestic industry; in this case meaning manufacture in the home by families of woolens, woolen-cotton, woolen-linen mixtures, and other linen and/or cotton homespuns. Alexander Hamilton did not mention machine carding in 1791. In 1810 Gallatin claimed that water-powered carding machines were everywhere in the eastern and middle states, and that jennies, spinning machines, and flying shuttles had been introduced in many places. Gallatin said about household manufactures,[110]

> The information received from every state, and from more than sixty places, concurs in establishing the fact of extraordinary increase, during the last two years, and in rendering it probable that about two-thirds of the clothing including hosiery, and of the house and table linen, worn and used by the inhabitants of the United States, who do not reside in cities, is the product of family manufactures.

What seemed to have happened in the period just before 1810 was that the capacity to card wool by machinery proliferated. The Scholfields might take some credit, but so too might many others--men like Amos Whittemore and Pliny Earle. No doubt there were a dozen or so technicians in the eastern states who were capable of building carding machines. This capacity plus the merino "craze," and the high price of wool induced many farmers to invest more in their sheep herds.

---

[110]Gallatin, "Report on Manufactures," in _Writings_, ed. Ferguson, pp. 249-50; Coxe's _Statement on the Arts and Manufactures_ reported 1,630 carding machines in the nation in 1810.

It was never true that <u>every</u> family manufactured its own cloth at home in America. The 1810 Census enumerated looms, although it neglected to describe the type of loom it was counting. By taking the total population by state and by dividing by five members, an approximate figure of the number of families in a given area can be reached. Using those numbers, and the 1810 Census, it was found that only in New Hampshire was the ratio of looms to families one to two. The national average was one loom for every five families, and the range was one for every twelve in Maryland, to the one for two in New Hampshire. The ratio was highest in the middle states; that is, there were less looms per family. In the South and in New England looms numbered one in three or four families. Most home weaving was linen or linen mixtures.[111]

In 1810 more than 6.6 million pounds of domestic wool was carded in the states from Massachusetts to Maryland, and this was probably over 95 percent of the national total. In the same year 5.5 million yards of wool were fulled in those states, averaging on a per capita basis 1.4 yards per person. High per capita woolen cloth production existed in New Hampshire, Vermont, Connecticut, and New York; the range was 1.9 to 2.5 yards per person. There was much less per capita wool production in New Jersey and

---

[111]Coxe, <u>Statement of the Arts and Manufactures</u>, passim; Pitkin, <u>Statistical View of Commerce</u>, pp. 472-73; Potter, "Growth of Population," pp. 664-65.

Pennsylvania. It should be noted, however, that there was much more production of textiles other than woolens such as mixed and blended fibers of cotton and linen. Some, no doubt, were mixed with woolen yarns.[112]

The period of lowest imports from Great Britain was not during the legal boycotts and embargos. The bottom of that cycle came during the years 1813 and 1814 during the War of 1812. In 1814 British imports were less than 10 percent of what they had been from 1805 to 1807.[113]

At one time it was conventional wisdom to assume that war provided an economy with important stimuli that served to increase production and productivity. Certain industries can benefit from intensive research and development efforts during war time that can spin off into very profitable techniques during peace time. In the case of the American woolen industry, the War of 1812 had a stimulating effect, partly from the increase in demand from the military and its need for uniform cloth, partly from the shortages caused by the lack of British imports of woolen cloth. The requirements of war made the woolen cloth market behave very elastically, and the great increase in prices caused manufacturers to look for improved raw materials, to

---

[112]Coxe, <u>Statement of the Arts and Manufactures</u>, passim; Potter, "Growth of Population," pp. 664-65.

[113]Emory R. Johnson, <u>History of the Domestic and Foreign Commerce of the United States</u>, 2 vols. (Washington, D. C.: Carnegie Institution, 1915), I:20.

increase investment in research and development of machinery, and to look for durable but cheap products that could be manufactured with the goods and tools at hand. The rise in prices caught the attention of farmers who now raised more sheep and made greater efforts to improve the quality of the wool they raised. In Philadelphia, full-blood merino wool averaged $3.31 per pound during the last half of 1814. Fine broadcloth sold for eighteen dollars per yard in Philadelphia at the same time.[114] American clothiers who had invested in carding machines now further expanded into spinning machinery, wide and narrow looms with fly shuttles, and finishing machines such as gigs and mechanical shearers. For many, this was a small investment, but others like the du Ponts saw opportunities for the longer range. During this period the du Pont investment in woolen manufacture was over $50,000. Even though much of this capital went for the purchase of raw wool, it probably represented the largest capitalization for any woolen company until the 1820s.[115]

Tench Coxe seemed to have caught the spirit of the times when he wrote a piece called "Supplementary Observations" to add to A Statement on the Arts and Manufacture of

---

[114]Cole, Wholesale Commodity Prices, p. 364; Bishop, History of American Manufactures, 2:195.

[115]Ledger 54, Charles I. du Pont & Company, Accession 500, Eleutherian Mills Historical Library, Greenville, Delaware.

the United States for the Year 1810. The "Observations" were written in 1813 or 1814, and were particularly apt and prescient on the subject of wool:[116]

> The manufacture, which is next in rapid improvement and extent, to cotton is that of wool. It is very considerably aided by the new carding and spinning machinery, by the introduction of the Barbary, Merino and long woolled sheep, by improvements in the breeding and tending of the general flocks of the country, by the superior care of the growing of the fleece, by the increase of the value of the carcase of mutton, by the sorting of wool, by improvements in the stocking and cloth looms, by the acquisition of the fly shuttle and of machinery to dress and finish cloths, by increased skill in the workmen, and by improvements in the arts and business of fulling and dying, to acquire which great exertion and expense are applied.

Coxe went on to discuss the desirability to increase the wool supply and quality, and mentioned the prevailing stylish colors for cloth--drabs, bottle greens, grave mixtures, maroons, and browns.[117]

Coxe recognized that "nice skill in using fulling machinery is of the greatest importance to the success of the woollen branch. The skill is wanting in many places." As a man of his time, Coxe also felt wool provided a universal substance for all phases of well-being and comfort:

> There is no other good and safe material for carpets; no other capable material for common hats and winter stockings. . . . No material, for cloths, for

---

[116]Coxe, Statement of the Arts and Manufactures, p. xxix.

[117]Ibid.

furniture and for apparel, is so safe as wool in respect to fire. No abundant one for these purposes is capable of so economical and elegant colorings and dyes. . . .

---

118 Ibid., pp. xxx-xxxi.

Chapter III

AN OVERVIEW OF AMERCIAN WOOLEN MANUFACTURE, 1813-32

During the brief twenty-year period following the American involvement in the Napoleonic wars, Americans created an industry in the mechanized factory production of woolen goods. It is, no doubt, too extreme to describe this creation as revolutionary. Yet considering the kind of change involved in such a tradition-bound industry and considering the short length of time needed to institute the change, it may not be too far amiss to think of the mechanization in woolens as something of a major skirmish in the overall concept of industrial revolution. In 1860 woolen goods production ranked eighth in terms of the value added in production of American manufactures.[1] While it cannot be argued that woolen cloth was the leading American manufacture, it obviously was an important one.

Although it cannot be proven, the likelihood is that the great majority of the woolen factories represented in the returns from the 1820 Manufactures Census were founded in the years 1813 to 1815. Most of the earlier mills can be identified, and while there were probably more than the

---

[1]Peter Temin, "Manufacturing," in American Economic Growth: An Economist's History of the United States ed. Lance Davis, et al. (New York: Harper & Row, 1972), p. 433.

fourteen enumerated by Gallatin in 1810, there surely were less than fifty and probably not many more than thirty.[2] The industry was stimulated primarily by the shortages of woolen goods and their consequent high prices during the brief period of the War of 1812. Army needs played a small part for a few companies. After the peace in 1815 the market for fine woolens was deluged by British imports, and those manufactories which survived with their original ownership made large cutbacks in production. Many did not survive and factories were leased, sold, reorganized, and in extreme cases abandoned.

Many of the early factories placed major responsibilities on English immigrants with presumed advanced skills in the manufacture of broadcloth, cassimere, kersey and satinet. The immigrants came mostly from Yorkshire and the West of England, plus a few from Lancashire. Many seem to have had more than a trace of wanderlust in their character. William Partridge, for example, came from Gloucestershire and from 1810 to 1816 worked at Middletown, Connecticut, for Du Pont, Bauduy and Company in Delaware, and the Providence Woolen Manufacturing Company in Rhode Island. At some point after the War, he returned to England, and by 1822 was back in New York importing dye stuffs and writing _A Practical Treatise on Dying of Woollen, Cotton, and Skein_

[2]Cole, _Wool Manufacture_, 1:232.

[3]William Partridge, _A Practical Treatis on Dying of Woollen, Cotton, and Skein Silk with the Manufacture of_

Silk.[3] Partridge would seem to have been an honest man; others if they were not outright dishonest were certainly shady characters. Jemmy Anderton left his wife and children in Leicester, Massachusetts for one Fanny Wilby; William H. Clifford was a bigamist.[4] These men did not help a fledgling industry to fly on its own. Perhaps one problem was simply too rapid growth.

One neglected source that indicated considerable change in the woolen industry is the 1820 Census of Manufactures. Available from it are individual manuscript returns on microfilm. The census procedures are unknown, but the questionnaire was used as the return, so at least the questions are known (see chap. 2, fn. 59).

Knowing the questions does not solve the problem of meanings. Starting with basics, what were manufactories? Carding and fulling mills clearly were not factories if all they did was card wool and full cloth for country farmers; but they were mechanized, and so some census takers included them. On the other hand, tanneries produced a saleable product from raw materials that were purchased; but they

---

Broadcloth and Cassimere Including the Most Improved Methods in the West of England (New York: H. Walker and Co. for the Author, 1823; repr. Edington, Wiltshire: Pasold Research Fund Ltd., 1973), pp. ix, 10.

[4]Thomas W. Leavitt, ed., The Hollingworth Letters: Technical Change in the Textile Industry, 1826-1837 (Cambridge, Mass.: Society for the History of Technology and the Massachusetts Institute of Technology Press, 1969), pp. 48, 92; John Beverly Riggs, A Guide To the Manuscripts In the Eleutherian Mills Historical Library (Greenville, Del.: Eleutherian Mills Historical Library, 1970), pp. 75, 275.

were not mechanized. Most but not all census takers included them. When did a workshop become a factory? A question worth pondering as many a census taker may have pondered, but one that cannot be answered comprehensively. For the purposes of this monograph, this definition will be used: a woolen factory had the capacity to both spin and weave at the factory. Carding and fulling establishments provided a service; they carded wool into rolls for which they charged five to eight cents a pound, and/or they fulled and finished cloth at from fourteen to twenty-five cents per yard. Clothiers or finishers usually dyed wool and/or cloth. Dyers were sometimes, but not always, clothiers.[5] Factories did not necessarily have the capacity to full and finish cloth, in which case they will be categorized as flannel manufactories. Satinets used cotton warps but were fulled and finished. Factories making satinets exclusively will not be considered woolen factories, but factories making satinet along with broadcloth and cassimere will be included here. The satinet yardage will be counted as three-quarter width cloth with half the square yardage of broadcloth of equal length. Unfortunately, this will make satinet equal to cassimere in the overall figures. Cassimere is a much finer cloth than satinet;

[5]Seward, "The Wool Textile Industry," p. 43.

cassimere could be considered a narrow three-quarter width broadcloth.

The clearest differentiating aspect of a factory as opposed to a mill is that the factory bought raw wool. Some proprietors bought wool and manufactured cloth while also continuing to offer carding and fulling services. In some instances these establishments provided the most comfortable and secure livelihoods for their proprietors, because they could count on the service business. National averages for carding mills in 1810 was 4,160 pounds of wool carded per mill; for fulling mills, the average was 3,580 yards. At the lowest prices, this meant $208 for carding, $501 for fulling, $709 altogether. If operated year-round, a clothier could have hired one man at say $250, one boy for half that, or $375 per year for wages and $334 for the proprietor.[6]

The New-York Historical Society owns a "carding book" from what must be an upstate New York mill. (The shilling equivalents are in New York money.) In 1827 the mill carded 3,334 pounds of wool for £61 2s. 9d. ($152.84) and dressed 233 pieces of cloth, dyed old garments and stockings for £109 5s. 1d. ($273.13) for a total of $425.97. The mill operated from June 4 to December 10, charged four to five pence for carding, ten pence for

---

[6]Coxe, Statement of the Arts and Manufacturers, passim.

dyeing, one and six to two shillings per yard for dressing, and one shilling per pound for dyeing yarn. The range of dye colors from this country mill included drab, black, sand on brown, dark bright red, claret, snuff, dark wine, olive green, green, blue, cinnamon brown, smoke, dark claret, light claret, and sea green. It worked mostly in quantities from four to eight yards. As it was apparently a partnership, the income would have had to be divided in two, but $213 is not bad for a year's by-employment.[7]

In the returns from the 1820 Census of Manufactures enough special pleading for the tariff went on in the commentary sections to lead one to think that this was at least part of the purpose behind the census. Just precisely how this bias affected the data is fairly clear when it is realized how seldom any agent or proprietor admitted to a profit. However, it should be noted that 1820 was a down year in the business cycle. In 1819 a serious monetary panic had occurred, and that could have accounted for some of the dissatisfaction. Also, wool manufacturers had had a very difficult time competing with imports since 1815. Better times returned in the 1820s, but one finds almost as much pro-tariff bias, and moaning about lack of profits, in the 1832 McLane Report.

---

[7]Isaac Young and Solomon Fancher, Factory Day Book A, 1827, New York Historical Society Manuscript Collection, New York, New York.

Even such a word as "profit" could be ambiguous in the eighteenth and early nineteenth centuries. One aspect of this ambiguity revolved around the notion of interest. Money or capital always had a potential to earn at the legal interest rate which varied slightly from state to state. In most of New England it was 6 percent; in New York it was 7 percent in the 1820s. While this did not always mean an individual lender received 6 or 7 percent interest, as demand for money fluctuated then as now, in terms of figuring profits, the legal interest rate was _presumed_ to be the base earning power of money. The question for "profit" was whether or not to include interest rates in one's profit estimations. If capital was borrowed, interest became a significant cost; also if capital was tied up and frozen--_not_ earning interest, interest became a "loss" or a part of costs or expenses. In practical terms, a given agent might be bemoaning his poor 2 percent when what he was really bemoaning was his 8 percent profit, because he assumed the 6 percent to be "given." There were other difficulties surrounding the meaning of profit, but this example will suffice as a warning.

The six New England states and the five middle states which comprise the area under discussion had in 1810 1,600 carding machines and 1,542 fulling mills. Both figures represented more than 90 percent of the national total of such mills. In 1820, these eleven states boasted approximately 250 woolen factories. The total capital employed was 2.8 millions of dollars, making the average capitalization of each woolen factory something over $11,000 per factory. This capital consisted of land, water rights, buildings, and machinery--fixed capital. There were some problems of meanings and definitions here: capital could also include stock--raw materials as well as finished goods--in theory, liquid capital, but not necessarily in practice. Total employment in these factories numbered 3,755 people; about half were men, 30 percent were children (again, a definition problem--children seemed to have meant mostly boys under sixteen, girls under fourteen) and the rest, 20 percent were women. These averaged 15.1 persons employed per factory: 7.8 men, 4.7 children, and 2.6 women.[8]

The qualifying factors for these woolen manufactories were the capacity to spin and weave and the purchase of wool. There were a few factories that manufactured only satinet or only flannel; some of those tended to be more profitable than broadcloth/cassimere factories. Many of the latter continued to do "country work" for local farmers; that is, carding and/or fulling wool and cloth as a service.

It is not possible to tabulate the data from the 1820 Census or from McLane any more than the marshalls were able

[8]Coxe, Statement of the Arts and Manufactures, passim; 1820 Manufactures Census, passim.

to do themselves. In a limited way change and comparisons can be indicated on a state by state basis by using both 1820 and 1832 information, plus testimony from the hearings in Congress in 1828. Too often the comparisons become like those between apples and pears, and then become incomprehensible. Satinet factories, flannel manufactories, broadcloth and cassimere producers were different in machinery and labor needs. Carding and fulling mills which added jennies and looms were in yet another category.

The following is a summary of the data from the 1820 Manufactures' Census:[9]

Maine: Manuscripts for five factories were found for Maine. The average capital reported was $7,600, and each factory employed on the average three or four men, one woman, and two or three children.

Vermont: Eighteen factories reported an average capital of just over $6,000 and thirteen employees broken down to seven men, two women, and four children.

New Hampshire: Manuscripts for six factories in 1820 still exist. Their average capital was $6,600 and they employed eleven people each. In northern New England in 1820, two satinet factories reported very large profits.

Massachusetts: In 1820 in Massachusetts already nearly $400,000 had been invested in the woolen industry--in thirty-four factories with an average capitalization of

---

[9] 1820 Manufactures Census, passim.

over $11,000. Four were satinet factories and three of those had water powered satinet looms for a total of twenty-two power looms; there was one flannel factory. Each factory employed on the average ten men, four women, and four children.

Rhode Island: Out of eleven woolen factories in Rhode Island in 1820, six were satinet factories. The average capitalization of nine of the eleven was $9,100. There was an average of sixteen employees in each, or seven men, three women, and six children.

Connecticut: Capitalization in Connecticut was larger than in Massachusetts for woolen manufacture in 1820, a total of $619,600 in forty-three factories, or an average of $14,400. Fourteen people were employed on the average--six men, three women, and four or five children. Already in 1820 there were six factories in Connecticut making satinet exclusively, and two of those factories had water powered looms.

New York: New York was the state with the greatest amount invested in woolens in 1820--$741,500 in fifty-five factories, averaging $13,500. Fifteen hands was the normal complement in a New York factory with eight or nine men, two women, and six children. One factory listed thirteen power looms, probably for satinet.

New Jersey: Only fourteen factories were accounted for in New Jersey. Twelve thousand dollars was the average invested, and each factory employed ten or eleven hands.

Pennsylvania: Sixteen hands were the average in forty factories--eight men, two women, and six children. The average capital was just over $11,000.

Maryland, District of Columbia, and Delaware: In the two small southernmost states of this survey plus the District, there were twenty-three woolen factories with a total capital of $238,000, or $10,300 each. Twenty-one people on the average manned the factories with ten men, three women, and eight children.

Between 1813 and 1832 New England and New York became the centers of American wool manufacturing. There were differences between the two areas; New York, for example, was not nearly as agriculturally desolate as New England, but both areas had considerable advantages for manufacturing. The following is a summary of geographic considerations that gave New England and New York such advantages. It is adapted from a recent work by Robert G. Leblanc:[10]

1. Waterpower was widely available in New England and New York. There seldom were conflicts over riparian rights as land claims and riparian claims were not overladen with multiple ownerships and jurisdictions. Demand for the power was not so great that down stream dam builders were in constant conflict with those taking power from upstream locations.

---

[10] Robert G. Leblanc, Location of Manufacturing in the Nineteenth Century (Hanover, New Hampshire: Geography Publications at Dartmouth, 1969), passim.

2. New England and New York had surplus capital derived from foreign and domestic trade. Even men in rural areas were learning the advantages of such institutions as banks and insurance companies, and New York and New England legislatures, albeit not particularly consistently, favored corporate organizations and limited liabilities. Manufacturing itself provided capital that was plowed back into expansion and new machinery.

3. In competition with agriculture, almost any other means of making a living would soon prove superior. There were exceptions--sheep raising in Berkshire County, Massachusetts and Dutchess, Columbia and Oneida counties in New York for example, but compared to the rest of the country, New England's fertility was wretched. New York was not as rocky as New England and soils were not quite so thin, but New York felt agricultural competition from the Old Northwest very early in the nineteenth century.

4. Within New England, roads were no better than the rest of the country, but distances were short, and many towns had access to the Atlantic Ocean. By 1815 the canal period had begun, expanding access to the country's interior. New York's early commitment to the Erie Canal (completed 1825) assured that state of leadership in the transport of goods.

5. New England and New York had ready access to raw materials via inexpensive water routes. Sheep were raised

right there, and cotton was easily shipped from the South. The mobility of the raw material may have had something to do with the fact that woolen factories were dispersed much more widely than cotton textile manufactories.

6. There was no shortage of entrepreneurship or technical expertise although some of it had to be imported. Whether because of slavery, or other reasons, New England and the Middle States attracted greater immigration, and textile technicians were among those immigrants even when their emigration from Britain was illegal. Technology was stolen, borrowed, and copied fairly easily; much of it was not very complicated, and there was little real protection by patent laws. Some undoubtedly tried to keep industrial secrets, but this would have been futile in the face of the mobility of American labor.

New York was home to a considerable woolen industry. There agricultural fertility was not so extremely bad, and sheep were very important commercially in such counties as Columbia and Dutchess up the Hudson River. In 1820 a number of small factories that continued to offer carding and fulling services were located in New York. For example, William and James P. Brown of Newburgh (Orange County) reported that they leased a factory for $600 per year. As rent normally was 6 percent of capital, this probably meant an original capital investment of about $10,000. The Browns invested another $1,000 of their own money. In 1820 they manufactured 1,000 pounds of wool into cassimere worth one dollar per yard. For the country trade they finished 3,000 yards of cloth for which they might have charged twenty cents per yard, and they dyed 3,000 pounds of cotton yarn for forty-two cents per pound. They listed their total costs including raw materials and wages as $2,100 while they claimed the value of their work and manufacture to be $2,860.[11]

In 1820 Connecticut was ahead of Massachusetts not only in numbers of woolen factories but also in the mechanization of those factories. Connecticut was the location for more Brewster spinners and more satinet power looms than any other part of the country in 1820.[12] By 1832 Massachusetts had surged ahead of both New York and Connecticut both in numbers of factories and the degree of mechanization. Philadelphia too has been cited as a woolen center in the early nineteenth century, but her manufacture of woolens was almost entirely carpeting and some flannels. Western Pennsylvania counted numbers of very small combination carding/fulling and manufacturing mills in the 1832 McLane Report.

---

[11] 1820 Manufactures Census: New York, p. 1441. This assumes contingency expenses included wool and wages.

[12] 1820 Manufactures Census: Connecticut and passim.

Capitalization/the Physical Plant and Machinery

On December 19, 1822, Zachariah Allen of Providence, Rhode Island, recorded in his "Diary,"

> My machinery at the mill is now all arranged in readiness for operation with the drums and belts attached to turn. I have now only to wait for spinners to commence. The carder and roper is ready with his three boys to commence tomorrow and shall get well underweigh by Christmas . . .

Work on Allen's factory had begun back in February of 1822. At that time Allen had itemized his initial capital expenses as follows:

Feb. 22, 1822

Land, privilege, and trenches for 16 foot fall		$ 5,000
A stone building for the factory, cellar or basement complete	Say	4,000
Dye house and blacksmith shop		1,200
3 dwellings, about $660 each	Say	2,000
Levelling off ground, covering trench and raceway next to the mill and sundry jobs of finishing off, not less than say		800
		$ 8,000
Cost of necessary buildings and levelling ground &c. Allow for unexpected expenses and short estimates		1,000
Real estate for factory		$14,000
Woollen machinery, fulling stocks, dye vats, and kettles &c--say,		7,000
Allowing capital in trade probably		20,000
		$41,000

---

[13]Zachariah Allen, "Diary," Zachariah Allen Papers, Rhode Island Historical Society, Providence, Rhode Island.

Carpentry work in factory	$ 634.86
Each dwelling house @ $224.73	674.19
Picking house	62.87
Blacksmith shop	16.57
Dam &c.	243.70
	$1,632.19

In October, 1822 Allen recorded a short trip to Worcester, Oxford, Dudley, and Southbridge to view different woolen mills. On that trip he ordered his dye vats and kettles, and contracted with a Southbridge man to build his fulling stocks. By the first of November the first shaft had been set and turned by the water wheel, and the dye house was nearly completed. His shearing machines had been delivered from White and Boyden of Worcester, and he was expecting delivery of his carding machines by the following week.

By mid-December Allen recorded his first moments of anxiety--

> Dull foggy day. I have not yet commenced spinning-- I have felt rather dull respecting the undertaking of making woolen goods. The expenses I have been at are very heavy and the prospect of reimbursement uncertain. I hope for the best, and must prepare for the worst.[14]

A few days later workmen had finished installing his machinery and power train. The factory was ready. By Christmas eve, Allen succumbed to a little nostalgia,

> The church bell is now ringing a merry peal. To me it is rather melancholy - as it recalls days long since past, when I hailed the return of Christmas as one of the happiest days of my life. How cheaply was my

---

[14]Ibid.

> happiness procured by the little presents I received. Now anxious thoughts and deep enlaid schemes of future aggrandizement engross my mind. . . . The carding and roping machinery has been in operation nearly a week and I shall probably begin to spin tomorrow.

The fixed capital of Allen's mill--$21,000--was, of course, somewhat higher than the average investment of 1820. The factory building in stone might be considered extravagant except for the frequency of fires. The $7,000 for machinery is more than would be expected since Allen was weaving with only five spring shuttle broad looms and two or four water powered satinet looms.[16]

From the end of 1822 through 1824, Edward Howard bought about $2,800 worth of machinery to start the Slater, Howard & Company woolen factory.[17] What was not included were dye vats, wool press, and power train equipment, easily adding another one to $2,000 to the Slater, Howard & Company purchases. The $7,000 of Allen is very high by those standards; it is not clear just why Allen posted such a large amount for machinery. Machinery usually, although not always, increased in price through the period of the '20s, primarily because it was built more solidly as machinery manufacturers became more confident of the workability of their equipment.

It is possible to project a model for a woolen factory

---

[15]Ibid. [16]Ibid.

[17]Infra.

with the minimum available machinery capable of performing all of the processes required in the manufacture of fine broadcloth in the early 1820s. This model is not unlike many enumerated in the 1820 Manufactures Census except that often those factories omitted one element or another, possibly because they did not have it, but more likely because the reporting agent neglected to note it down. Many factories had a mechanical picker; one cost about fifty dollars and was not much different from the one pictured in Duhamel du Monceau except it may have been larger and water-powered. Some companies put out wool picking into local homes well into the twenties. Three carding machines or one set should have cost about $1,000 new. Billies were $2 per spindle, jennies $1 so that one forty-spindle billy and two sixty-spindle jennies should cost $200. Every town had a carpenter or joiner who made looms; narrow ones cost $15, broad looms, $20, both with spring shuttles. A complete fulling mill with dye vats as well as two types of fulling stocks could cost as much as $700 to $1,000. The dye vats could be costly as some clothiers felt it necessary to dye certain colors in copper vats. Finally, the finishing machinery--gig, one each broad and narrow shearing machines, and the screw press with iron plates might cost $350. All this adds up to $2,500 for machinery and ten spring shuttled broad looms and with a theoretical capacity of 1,000 to

1,300 woven broad yards per month or about 800 to 1,000 broad yards finished.

One had to house this machinery in some type of building. Allen's cost of $4,000 was not outrageous for a stone or brick building, but a wooden clad building could have been built for half. Because it needed to be purchased in pieces, the power train cost is difficult to estimate. Gears including crown wheels, shafts, and boxes (bearings) were bought and sold by the pound as they were iron castings. In 1827 Slater, Howard and Company spent $454.68 for cast iron in various forms, $16.25 for forging and turning thirteen bearings and $27.06 for drilling and turning gudgeons. It seems probable that a decent power train could be installed for about $500, but this would not have included the work for the millrace for say another $100.

A bare minimum mechanized woolen factory could have been built in the early 1820s for between $5000 and $6000. But there were other variables in the total cost that are more difficult to price. Land and water rights was one set of prices that depended on the area itself. Small dwelling houses for hands could be built for $250, but boarding houses for single people cost more, and certainly a mill village required a tavern for transient salesmen and mechanics. Most mills had at least a blacksmith shop for repair work, but some had elaborate machine shops in which to build machinery. Mills owned farms and farm land which were usually leased and provided truck for villagers and grass and hay for animals. So two elements tended to change the cost of the factory: one was simply the size of the works and multiples of the basic machines necessary. The other also related to size was the amount of land, number of dwellings and type for hands, and the need for machinery repair or machinery building.

Sometime in 1825 an unknown watercolorist chanced by Joel Cranston's woolen mill in Stow, Massachusetts Middlesex County (see illus. 24). This was the Rock Bottom Woolen Factory described by Cranston in 1820 for the census takers as follows:

1 - 3	8,000 lb. wool and 5,000 lb. cotton consumed at a cost of $6,350.	
4 - 6	13 men) 7 women) employed. 4 children)	
7 - 8	For wool:	2 broad looms 2 narrow looms 2 carding machines 3 jennies 1 billy 2 fulling mills 3 shears
	For cotton:	5 carding machines 20 spinning frames 1 mule and drawing frames, &c. &c.
9	Capital Invested: $23,000	
10	Wages: $4,000	
11	Costs: $200	
12	Manufactured broadcloth, cassimere, satinets, kerseys, &c.	
13	Market value: $12,700	
14	Comment: In good demand.[18]	

[18]1820 Manufactures Census: Massachusetts, p. 32.

SOURCE: Photo Collection, Old Sturbridge Village.

Illus. 24. "A SE View of Rock Bottom Woollen Factory and Village in 1825 Owned By Messrs. Cranston & Hale, Situated in Stow, County of Middlesex, Massachusetts."

There are other pictures of mills from the first quarter of the nineteenth century, but few of woolen mills, and this was the only picture found in which people are shown actually at work.[19] The factory building is in the center, a three-story clapboarded building complete with cupola and bell. It is not clear how the water power reached the factory; probably through a channel in the basement area. There are a large number of pieces of cloth on the two ramps leading to the first floor. These cloths, like the one carried in the wheelbarrow, are wet and have just been scoured. These cloths are returning to the factory to be burled--to have the knots, double yarns, and other imperfections corrected; that cloth then will be dried and then fulled. After fulling, the cloth will be dried on the tenters; the long cloth carried by the three men is being taken to the tenters to be dried. The wet cloth also could be waiting to have its nap raised and sheared. This was done after fulling and tentering. Then the cloth was scoured once again.

The factory building housed carding machinery, billies and jennies for spinning, shearing machines, and benches for burling. The small building held fulling stocks, and in the case of Rock Bottom, may have housed the dye vats

---

[19]Photo Collection, Old Sturbridge Village, Sturbridge, Massachusetts. The watercolor is owned by Howard Folsom Gleason.

and other accoutrement for that process. The weaving most likely was conducted in the low one and one-half story building seen to the right of the factory.

In 1832 the Stow Woollen Manfacturing Company reported $20,000 in real estate and building capital and $15,000 in machinery. With twenty men, two children, and twenty-nine women, the factory produced 30,000 yards of six-quarter cloth. Wages and raw materials cost Stow about $53,000 in that year.[20]

As the water color's title so clearly states, Rock Bottom was a village as well as a factory. In view is a sawmill and residences, at least one of which on the far right was very likely a tavern. What are not in view, or what are not identifiable, are a store, church, or schoolhouse, but most mill villages were not built far from town centers. Sometimes proprietors provided something for a church or school--land for example, but just as often the town itself furnished these institutions. Samuel H. Babcock, for example, did not wish to donate land for a Methodist church. In Merino Village of Dudley, Massachusetts Babcock did build a store, dwellings and boarding houses, but for profit, not amenities for hands.[21]

---

[20]McLane Report, 1:356-57.

[21]Samuel H. Babcock to Major John Brown, 28 July 1828, Box 21, Dudley Woollen Manufacturing Company, Old Sturbridge Village Research Library, Sturbridge, Massachusetts.

Housing was built to attract labor, especially skilled labor. In the early days housing was cheap and probably comfortable, and although there must have been some crowding, the crowding may not have been worse than for any large family trying to make do with small quarters. Boarding may not have been ideal, but many boarded, both men and women. Boarding kept a limit on spending as charges were simply taken out of one's credit from wages, as were rents and charges for commodities at the company store. Profits went to the boardinghouse keeper who in turn paid rent to the company, or profits went directly to the company itself.[22] One could work, live in the boardinghouse, have an occasional, or more often, glass of gin or rum, buy an occasional luxury--a new hat, a little ribbon, a Sunday ride in the company chaise, and still come out ahead. The community at large gained as the mill village required carpenters and masons for building, blacksmiths for metal work, farmers to run company farms, and providers of lumber, firewood, belt leather, foodstuffs, and hay for the company horses and cows or those owned by agents or operatives. The town gained canal diggers and rock blowers, and a whole galaxy of arts and skills besides the geniuses who were the technicians, machinists, and artisans who would build the very guts of the factories.

---

[22]Ledgers 55 and 56, Dudley Woollen Mfg. Co., Papers, OSV.

Physically, then, the mill village for a woolen manufactory contained circa 1820 to 1830, a factory building or two, of wood, stone, or brick, and comprising three to six stories, a fulling mill and/or dye house, a dry house, a blacksmith shop, store, tavern, boarding-houses and dwellings. The factory buildings were immediately accessible to a stream for water power. Nearby or in the village proper were a church and school. A progressive mill in terms of technology in 1820 would have housed the following machinery: picking machine, a set of carding machines (three--scribbler, breaker, and carder), billy or slubber, two jennies or a Brewster spinner, looms, fulling stocks, gig, one broad and one narrow shearing machine, screw press, and dye vats.

Wages and Hands

The difference between wool and cotton factories and between large and small woolen factories (the largest of which by 1825 was as large as the cotton operation at Waltham, Massachusetts had been in 1817) were matters of scale. In employment, woolens required more skill and more strength (hence more men) than cotton. Most woolen agents looked for family labor, supplemented with a few young single men and women. There were a few jobs for children in all woolen mills. By 1832, most factories showed a preference for women and girls over boys, because their wages would be less, but also because women were presumed to be more tractable and to have a greater capacity for routine and humdrum work. Also factory proprietors were more subject to criticism for hiring boys to work cheaply than they were for hiring girls. The sexist attitudes of the day preferred to see young boys in school.[23] The great demand for young girls as spinners and weavers did not develop in woolens until after the 1830s. Young women did tend power looms, and power looms were used regularly in woolen mills after the mid-1820s, but not nearly on the magnitude that they were in cotton mills.

Among the larger New England factory complexes were two Wolcott factories in Southbridge, Massachusetts and nearby Woodstock, Connecticut. Perez B. Wolcott was agent for the factories in 1820; James Wolcott, Jr. took over later in the 1820s. In 1820 the two companies employed forty-seven men, three women, and ten children; the average daily wage paid to each of the sixty people was seventy cents. As can be seen in table 6 the composition of the labor force was altered considerably from 1820 to 1827, and again from 1827 to 1832.[24]

Wages were determined for the most part by the supply and demand of a particular skill. Certain jobs in the woolen factory--sorter, for example--required a great deal

---

[23] McLane Report, 1:583, 611.

[24] 1820 Manufactures Census: Massachusetts, p. 63; Connecticut, p. 163.

TABLE 6

COMPOSITION OF WORK FORCE AND WAGES, HAMILTON MANUFACTURING COMPANY

	Men	Aver. Wage	Women	Aver. Wage	Children	Aver. Wage	Total Employees	Daily Payroll	Aver. Wage	Annual Wages 311 days
1820	47		3		10		60		$.70	$13,000.00
1827	71	$ .75	38	$.40	12	$.25	121	$71.45	.59	22,221.00
1832	36	1.00	60	.37 1/2	8	.25	104	60.50	.58	18,816.00

SOURCE: 1820 Manufactures Census: Massachusetts, p. 63; Connecticut, p. 163.

U.S. Congress, House, Committee on Manufactures, Minutes of Evidence on Woollens, 20th Cong., 1st sess., 1828, pp. 114-116. Hereafter cited as U. S. Congress, Evidence on Woollens, 1828.

McLane Report, 1:536.

of experience; other jobs--scourer is another example--an unpleasant job requiring no great skill which was apt to be paid in the middle range. Weaving usually went for a going rate in the community, but those rates depended on the quality of the cloth being manufactured. Because wages were viewed as part of the whole market system, there tended to be similarities in pay rates from factory to factory. There was some collusion on the part of owners to keep certain wages down. Slater, Howard and Company and the Dudley Woollen Manufacturing Company apparently agreed to reduce cassimere weaving rates from eight cents per yard to seven in March, 1827.[25]

Yet woolen manufacturers would seem to have approached the matter of factory operations and wage scales from entirely different vantage points. Possibly this was a factor of collective inexperience, but that is difficult to substantiate. Certainly part of the problem must have derived from traditional ways of payment. Spinners and weavers were paid by the piece; spinners by the run (length related to fineness) or by the pound, weavers by the yard. Payments to those engaged in preparation of the wool were paid by the day or month as were those involved in the finishing processes. In practice it actually did not matter if you were paid by the month or by the day; months

[25]Slater, Howard & Company to Dudley Woollen Manufacturing Company, 16 March 1827, Box 23, Dudley Woollen Mfg. Co., OSV.

were figured as twenty-six days--if a worker was absent, he was docked a day's pay. Women were paid by the week as were children, unless they were apprentices and were paid by the year. Sorting was a highly skilled job and at two cents per pound, very well paid as 100 pounds in a day was not out of the question. Picking was a very tedious job, paid three cents per pound, but few could pick more than 100 pounds per week (see payrolls in Appendix A).

In August 1823 Zachariah Allen's recorded his payroll in his "Diary," as follows:[26]

		Daily Wage
Dye House Carding Room	John Payton, overseer, sorter, and bookkeeper, tends the shop (9s. 6d./day)	$ 1.58
	Darius Sherman & Duncan Forbes @ 7s./day to scour and dye wool	2.33
	William Arnold carder & roper @ 6s.6d./day	1.08
	David Carpenter to tend cards @ $7 & board/month .	.54
	Richard Allen board & $30/year	.30
	Eliza Payton board & $30/year.	.25
	Jarvis Smith warp spinner (10s./day)	1.66
	Friend Dudley filling spinner (8s./day)	1.33
Weaving Room	Stephen Luther Moses Arnold Stephen Cooke Benjamin Forrestall Jarvis Payton Thomas Guinea They average 27 yards/day (@ 25¢)	6.75
		$14.74 (wrong, should be 15.82)

26Z. Allen, "Diary," Allen Papers, RIHS.

Room	Item	Cost	
Fulling and Knapping Room	Luther Lyon, satinet spinner @ $10/month and board . . .	.72	
	Peter Buckley @ 7s.8d./day .	1.28	
	Edward Briggs @ 5s.6d./day .	.96	
Finishing Room	3 women Burling and Picking @ 15s./week	1.26	(1.25)
	1 weaving satinet with power looms @ 2 1/2¢ per yard is per day averaging 29 yards	.72	
	Chester Mann tends three shears	1.50	
	James Payton boy, picking over wool	.30	
	24 persons total employed at daily expense of	$21.48	(22.55)
	3 persons average on wool put out to families to pick @3¢ per pound on 40 pounds	1.20	
		$22.68	(23.75)
	Deduct for cost of 18 yard satinet for labor carding, roping, spinning @ 6¢	1.08	
	Weaving 18 yd. @ 4¢, dressing and finishing @ 5¢	1.62	
		$ 2.70	
	(Total daily labour costs) . . .	$19.98	($21.05)

The six weavers averaged twenty-seven yards per day. As this would be reduced by finishing to 21.6 yards (less 20 percent), the labor cost per broad yard came to just less than $1, 97.5 cents figuring $21.05 per day.

Colonel James Shepherd of Northampton, Hampshire County, Massachusetts, was an acknowledged leading and respected woolen manufacturer. Aaron Tufts, in testimony before the Congressional Committee on Manufactures, said that he believed that Colonel Shepherd's woolen factory was "the oldest one of any extent" in Massachusetts.[27] From 1809 to 1831 Shepherd was the active superintendent of the Northampton Woolen Manufacturing Company. During that period the company was reorganized at least four times. Joseph Lyman, McLane's marshall in Hampshire County said of it in his 1832 report, "The business might be considered calamitous, but for the number of people to whom it has given employment and livlihood."[28] When Shepherd himself gave testimony in 1828, in theory, he was one of the men who could view the industry with something like long-term perspective. Yet in that hearing, Shepherd testified that, "On the 1st January, 1827, on bringing up our account, we found that we had sustained great losses."[29] In the context of the testimony, this statement implied that the company had not "brought up their accounts" with any regularity or frequency in the past and suggests that the bookkeeping in Shepherd's company was, at best, a very casual affair. But Shepherd was not a casual business man. If anything, Shepherd's way of analyzing wage costs was more sophisticated than Zachariah Allen's, but neither one of them had advanced very far from the costing techniques of Justice Hale in the seventeenth century. There simply had not been developed any cost accounting systems applicable

---

[27]U. S. Congress, Evidence on Woollens, 1828, p. 97.

[28]McLane Report, 1:310-11.

[29]U. S. Congress, Evidence on Woollens, 1828, pp. 88-90.

to manufacturing. These men did the best they could within existing systems based on estate systems, mercantile systems, and those systems developed by manufacturers who put out work.[30] The following is Shepherd's payroll in 1826:[31]

<u>Assorting</u> -- 1 1/2¢lb., but since the chief assorter is a superintendent, the costs are really 2¢/lb.

<u>Roving</u> -- (oiling, carding, and roping) @ 6¢/lb. for fine, 5¢ for middling. (They don't manufacture coarse.)

<u>Spinning</u> -- 1st quality - 14¢/lb. for warp; 7¢ for filling
2nd quality - 12¢/lb. for warp; 6¢ for filling
3rd quality - 10¢/lb. for warp; 5¢ for filling
4th quality - 8¢/lb. for warp; 4¢ for filling
(Two-thirds of Shepherd's spinning was spun on jennies; one-third, the lower qualities, on a Brewster spinner.)

<u>Warping and dressing</u> -- 1 1/2¢/lb. for 12 quarter broadcloth

<u>Weaving</u> -- 18-28¢/yard before power looms
10¢/yard for broadcloth on power looms
5¢/yard for cassimere on power looms

<u>Scouring</u> -- 1 scourer @ $21/month including board

<u>Fulling</u> -- I man @ $32/month; a boy @ $16/month including board

<u>Raising or knapping</u>, "commonly called gigging" -- 1 man @ $26/month + $6 for board plus 9 young men @ average $14/month board included

---

[30] Sidney Pollard, <u>The Genesis of Modern Management: A Study of the Industrial Revolution in Great Britain (Cambridge: Harvard University Press, 1965)</u>, p. 209.

[31] U. S. Congress, <u>Evidence on Woollens</u>, 1828, pp. 88-90.

<u>Teasel setter</u> -- @$10/month + $6 for board

<u>Shearing</u> -- superintendent @ $32/month including board; 20 pairs shears operated by 7 girls @ $8/month including board

<u>Burling, linting, and marking</u> -- 7 girls @ $8/month including board
Carding superintendent -- @$39/month including board
2 loom superintendents -- @$24/month including board
Clerk @ $500 per annum, boards self
Myself and brother receive 2 1/2% of gross sales; from Jan. 1, 1826 to Dec. 31, this amounted to about $1,600. (It is unclear from the context if this was the total for two, or for each brother. For their sakes, one hopes it was the second, in which case gross sales would have been about $128,000.)

Summary of wages:

32 men @ $21/month (81¢/day) . . .	$ 8,064.
16 men, 13-20 years old @ $14/month (54¢/day)	2,688.
16 boys, 8-12 years old @ $6/month (23¢/day)	1,152.
54 girls and women @ $13/month (50¢/day)	8,425.
Carding superintendent @ $39/month	468.
2 loom superintendents @ $24/month each	576.
Clerk (no board)	500.
Myself and brother, 2 1/2% gross sales each	3,200.
	$25,072.

(Of this total, $7,618 was board.)

41% men over 13
13% boys under 13
46% girls, women

In 1826 Shepherd produced 37,616 yards of broadcloth, 4,168 yards of cassimere, or a total of 39,600 broad yards. In 1826 Shepherd with power looms employed sixty-four men and boys plus fifty-four girls and women. His cost per yard was 63¢ even including the $7,618 board bill. Compared to

Allen's operation of three years earlier, Shepherd produced about four times more cloth with about four times more manpower, but Shepherd's labor costs were 21 percent less than Allen's (80¢ versus 63¢) because 59 percent of his labor were women and young boys and girls. In Allen's case in 1823, 26 percent of his labor force were women and young boys and girls.

Both of these establishments made prize winning cloth.[32] Neither one could be classified as efficient in terms of labor. Shepherd should not have been paying so much board; if those costs had not existed in 1826, Shepherd's per yard labor would have been 44¢ per yard. Allen should have had more machinery and hired less men.

The new management of the Northampton company reported in 1832 higher average wages to men and women, no board, and for 120 hands payment of $18,485. Production in 1832 for Northampton was 43,800 yards broadcloth, 37,650 yards satinet, or 62,625 broad yards.[33] The cost per yard was only 30¢; 57.5 percent of his hands were women and boys. Allen by 1832 was producing about 32,000 broad yards with sixty-seven hands. He had reduced his costs to 48¢ per yard, and by then 60 percent of his labor force were women and boys.[34]

---

[32] Manufacturers' and Farmers' Journal: Providence and Pawtucket Advertiser, 9 November 1820, 21 October, 1822, 25 November 1824, 20 October 1823, 11 October 1824.

[33] McLane Report, 1:308-9. [34] Ibid., 1:951, 975.

Wool manufacturers succeeded in trimming wage costs during the decade of the twenties. As they mechanized, they hired proportionally more women to tend the machines, and of course, paid the women less. Men's wages on the average actually went up during the period, but this statement does not take into account the almost universal elimination of board payments. Wage costs per yard declined, and while wages were certainly an important cost item in the manufacture of woolen cloth, it was not the only item, and it probably was not the most significant. It was, however, the one item over which manufacturers had the most control.

Skilled men did not fare badly working in the woolen factories. This was especially true when the men came from the same families and could share living quarters. One fine example of family labor in woolen textiles has become available through the recently published Hollingworth letters.[35]

In 1820 James Anderton was the agent for a woolen mill located in South Leicester, Massachusetts (Worcester County). He had leased the mill from Ashael Washburn and described his operation to the census marshall as follows:[36]

---

[35]Leavitt, ed., Hollingworth Letters.

[36]Rev. A. H. Coolidge, "Leicester," in History of Worcester County, Massachusetts, comp. by H. Hamilton Hurd, 2 vols. (Philadelphia: J. W. Lewis & Co., 1869), 1:718.

1 - 3	3,000 lb. merino wool @ $2,250
	8 men)
	1 woman) employed.
	4 children)
7 - 8	1 picker
	2 carding machines
	1 billy)
	2 jennies) 110 spindles. Only half operating.
	3 broad looms
	4 narrow looms
	1 broad shearing machine, 2 narrow
9	Machinery cost $6,000, now (worth) no more than $3,000.
10	Wages: $2,500
11	Costs: $ 600
12	Manufactured broadcloth, satinet, and cassimere.
13	Market value: $5,500.
14	Comments: At this establishment great quantity of custom work (is) done for their neighbors--dressing of cloth and carding of wool.[37]

This was the company that George, John, and Jabez Hollingworth and other members of their family came to work for in the winter or early spring of 1826. The mill complex as described in 1828 showed considerable growth from the above 1820 description and now contained three major buildings. The main factory building was 100 feet long by 40 feet wide and four stories high and the company also owned a dye house, store, and eleven dwellings for employees.[38] The Hollingworth family had emigrated to America with the intention of removing to a farm in upper New York state. The deal that they thought they had made fell through, and six male Hollingworths worked in the southern Worcester

---

[37]1820 Manufactures Census: Massachusetts, p, 58.

[38]Jerimiah Spofford, A Gazeteer of Massachusetts (1828), cited by Leavitt, ed., Hollingworth Letters, p. xxiv.

County area until 1833. In June, 1828, the father, George Hollingworth who was probably a weaver, described their situation to his brother-in-law, William Rawcliff, of the Hollingworth's native Huddersfield,

> We all live together in a double house. We have plenty of room. The House contains 8 Rooms besides a Cellar under the whole. We pay 60 Dollars a year Rent. George Mellor James Hollingworth and J. Kenyon boards with us. Son James is a Filling Spiner viz. a bobing Spiner and can earn 8 or 9 dollars per week. Son John has been a little time a Condensed Spiner. This is a new miserable business for making money. He is now a Slubber which is a fare better Job. He will make better than a dollar a day. Son Joseph has been a Gigger every since he came at only 15 1/2 dollers per Month. As the Job was a new one to him and I wished him to learn I was not particular about wages at first, but now has he got an expert hand I am thinking of asking for more wages not less than 20 dollers per month. Edwin is a Warp Winder or Spooler winder for the Warping machine at 1 1/2 dollers per Week. I am intending to have his wages advanced also. There is not much in America I dislike (exep)ting the too general conduct of Emigrants, and the Factory Sistem I hate with a perfect hatered as being only calculated to create bad feeling bad principles and bad practices; . . . I forgot to mention son Jabez. He is working in the machine Shop at 25 dollors per month.39

As a gigger, Joseph Hollingworth would have been tending a gig mill to raise the nap on cloth. As a weaver, George Hollingworth would have made about twenty dollars per month.

---

[39]Leavitt, ed., Hollingworth Letters, 26-28. The description of John's work sounds like the factory was trying a new condenser on one of their carding machines to form consecutive rolls of wool that could be spun on jennies directly. Perhaps, the innovation failed and John Hollingworth was able to return to his old job as a slubber, one of the highest paid jobs in any wool factory. Because it was so highly paid, slubbing was a job factory agents were eager to get rid of.

		per year
James "$8 or $9/week" ($8.50 x 52)	spinner	$442
John "better than $1/day" x 311	slubber	311
Joseph "$15 1/2/month" x 12	gigger	186
Edwin "$1 1/2/week" x 52	winder and spooler	78
Jabez "$25/month" x 12	machinist	300
George (father) $20/month x 12	weaver	240

The annual wages for the Hollingworths amounted to $1,557, not accounting for absences.

By 1830, Jemmy Anderton, native of Lancashire, had skipped town leaving wife and debts, bound for "somewhere between Albany and Buffaloe" with one Fanny Wilby.[40] The factory was purchased by Joshua Clapp, but in the meantime, in looking for other employment the Hollingworths were faced with that universal tendency of American textile mills--the replacement of men by machines and women at half wages, or less. As Jabez Hollingworth wrote to William Rawcliff in March 1830:[41]

> Now you see the Fruits of Large Factorys. Here we are supplanted by Females that is expected to perform the same quantity of work for one half the wages the quality being out of the Question.

They were able to find jobs, however, in what had become one of the largest woolen factories in the country--the Hamilton Manufacturing Company, whose prior agent had been James Wolcott, Jr.

At Hamilton, George, the father, was warping on a machine, as was Joseph. James was spinning at a jack

[40] Ibid., p. 92.   [41] Ibid., p. 66.

(possibly Wolcott's old Brewster), and Edwin was still spooling.[42] If the three adult men averaged one dollar per day as reported in McLane and Edwin received 25¢, their gross would have been $1,007.50. At those pay rates it is not difficult to see how such a newly arrived family group might be able to seriously contemplate running their own factory, as indeed the Hollingworths were.

On July 1, 1830, John, Jabez, and James Hollingworth began paying rent to Sayles and Hitchcock for the other Wolcott factory in Woodstock, Connecticut.[43] The Boston merchants were trying to sell the property for $6,000, a considerable depreciation from its 1820 value of $20,000.[44] The lease was for three years at $500 per year. There was a degree of haggling between Sayles and Hitchcock and the Hollingworths about machinery, who would furnish what, for example. One comment about the gig mill by Sayles and Hitchcock corroborates that that machine was not particularly a significant item,

> As respects a napper if we correctly understand you, it is merely a cylinder clothed with cards, same as the clothing of the carding machines, & so if you can find enough of these about the factory at Southbridge & a plenty of the second hand clothing which you will have for the same.[45]

---

[42]Ibid., pp. 76, 88.

[43]Ibid., p. 80.

[44]1820 Manufactures Census: Connecticut, p. 163.

[45]Ibid., p. 70.

Joseph Hollingworth commented on the wire gigs, "We do not use any teazels, but do all our Napping with Cards, though I am perswaided some teazels would be better."[46]

In another letter to William Rawcliff who had followed his in-laws to America and was soon to be working for Wadsworth's in Poughkeepsie, New York, John Hollingworth described the newly leased Muddy-brook-pond Factory,[47]

> The factory consists of 2 Buildings connected together 3 storys each. They are about 18 feet wide and 36 or 40 feet long. We have 3 Double Carding Machines and 1 Billy 1 Jenny (a) Picker and Fulling Stock 2 Shearing Frames 1 Press and 1 Dye Kettle. We are to have 6 power Looms which is to be ready By 10 inst. There is about 2 Acres of Land a Pond of about 100 or 150 Acres which we can draw down 10 feet. . . . I forgot to say that there is 15 hand Looms at the place which we can use if we want. There is a Barn and other outbuildings.

Some more detail and some additions were described in a letter three months later from Joseph Hollingworth to Rawcliff:

> There were 2 billys, 4 Jennys, 13 broad hand looms, 4 new satinet power looms, 1 fulling stock called a poacher, 1 picker, 2 broad shears, 1 press, 1 dye kettle, 1 satinet Napper and 2 shears which we have had to buy, and several other things. There is a most exelent watter weel, an over shot weel the best I ever saw.48

Without the company records, we know little more than that the Hollingworths did not buy the factory although John Hollingworth, a farmer in Woodstock as of 1835, was involved in the bankruptcy of the Muddy Brook Manufacturing Company

---

[46]Ibid., p. 100. [47]Ibid., p. 80.

[48]Ibid., p. 89.

in 1837 so he must have retained some investment in the company.[49] But young Joseph, a sometime family renegade, and certainly the most outspoken member of his family can be quoted in revealing ways in various letters to Rawcliff written in 1830 and 1831:

> But dont you think farming the best, and surest way of getting a living? Manufacturing is a very unsteady business, sometimes up, and sometimes down, some few gets Rich, and thousands are ruined by it. Roques, Rascals, Knaves and vagabonds are connected with it.[50]

Or here is another letter:

> For my own part I have no doubt, but that farming might do well, if well managed. I think it is the surest (if not the easiest) way of getting a livelihood. I think a small farme, with a mill on it, for doing custom work such as Carding and Cloth-dressing; (or a saw mill and Grist mill) would do very well for such folks as you and I.[51]

The Hollingworths did very well monetarily, and they do not seem to be an exceptional case. All three factories studied in depth had some employed families who did well financially. The common threads among them were the number of men in the family and their skills. But even families with greater proportion of women and less skills could make money. The Hollingworth dream of escaping the factory for a farm must have been a commonplace one. Generally, one senses that no one in the early nineteenth century thought working in a factory ideal, although for some it must have meant positive change.

---

[49]Ibid., pp. xxv, 109. [50]Ibid., p. 93.

[51]Ibid., p. 104.

Thomas R. Hazard described operatives in his Peace Dale factory as follows in the 1820s:[52]

	Per annum
Father @ $14/month & board	$168
Adult son @ $17/month & board	204
Daughter @ $2/week & board	104
Daughter 15 @ $2.50/week, boards at home .	130
Son 13 @ $1/week & board	52
	$658

mother and youngest daughter (age 11) keep house	
Board for father and son @ $1.75	$182
Board for daughter @ $1.50	78
Board for son @ $1	52
	$312

Hazard, of course, represents the proprietor's view and says nothing of the physical conditions of work. Just how bad physical working conditions were is a very difficult estimation. Hands worked long hours, and during the winter the dim candle light and wood-stove heat combined with ammonia smells and a damp air filled with woolen fibers must have created a nasty environment. It must not have been very safe. With candlelight and wood stoves, anxiety about fire must have been constant, and unguarded drive shafts and belts increased the chances for accidents. For example, Mary Kenyon, a Hollingworth cousin, lost her right forefinger in a power loom at Southbridge.[53] Yet

---

[52][Thomas Robinson Hazard], Facts for the Laboring Man By a Laboring Man (Newport, Rhode Island: James Atkinson, 1840).

[53]Leavitt, ed., Hollingworth Letters, p. 88.

unpleasantness is relative. Very few people worked the full 311 day year. (The two or three holidays included the Fourth of July, Thanksgiving, and Fast Day for some factories.) Many employees were absent at least one day per month out of the twenty-six, and some hands took one or two weeks vacation during the summer. Farming, on the other hand, is a seven-day week although most farmers did only necessary milking and mucking on Sundays. The work on a farm is dawn to dusk at least half the year. For one-fourth of the year in some parts of the Northeast traveling was difficult because of snow or mud. The factory village at least provided some society. The Hollingworths claimed they did not like factory life. Yet when they did earn a small stake, they did not become farmers but factory proprietors, so it seems quite possible that what they did not like was the restrictiveness of factory life rather than its unpleasant and unsafe working conditions.

Raw Material Costs, Production and Profits (or Losses)

Turning to the raw materials for woolen manufacture, one of the best lists is from the Northampton Woolen Manufacturing Company's figures to the McLane Report in 1832:[54]

---

[54]McLane Report, 1:308-9.

127,000 lb. wool, 3/4 foreign, 1/4 from the vicinity (@65¢)	$ 82,550
5,000 lb. woad	400
3,200 lb. glue	448
1,000,000 teasels	1,000
100 bbl. soft soap	300
900 bbl. sig	450
600 cds. wood	1,050
240 bus. lime	144
Alum, vitriol, copperas	300
Transportation	1,500
Wrapping paper, tapes, twine, sewing silk, wickyarn, tallow, nails, tow cloth, stationery, brooms, & brushes	600
Iron, steel, screws, wire, tacks, nails, lumber, casks, reeds, shuttles, leather, &c. materials used in repairs	900
Leather	300
1,000 bu. charcoal	50
37,560 yds. cotton warp	2,065
500 gls. lamp oil for mill	450
Total domestic	$92,507
2,845 lb. indigo	$ 4,552
2,500 lb. madder	625
62,800 lb. logwood & fustic	1,403
3,120 gal. olive oil	3,130
6,280 lb. castile soap	753
Total foreign	$ 10,463
Total raw materials	$102,970

The key expense item, of course, was wool itself. A variation in price of just 10¢ could mean over $12,000 in costs for a company of the size of Northampton. Not much, if anything, was done by manufacturers about raw material costs. Perhaps nothing could be done, but one might have expected greater efforts at encouraging better and cheaper wools and cheaper dye stuffs. There was agitation for protective tariffs on woolen goods that in some views was too successful since there were blatant and outrageous violations of the laws after 1828.[55] To some extent those tariffs were counter balanced by duties on raw imported wool.[56]

On August 11, 1823, the Manufacturer's and Farmer's Journal quoted a small piece from the Salem Register complaining that it was the "high price of labour" that prevented American manufacturers from making a "decent cloth" for less than four dollars per yard. In England, the article claimed, fine cloth could be manufactured for three dollars per yard.[57] Cost accounting was in its barest infancy in the early twenties in the United States. In 1823 Zachariah Allen made a couple of estimates of the cost of manufacturing a yard of cloth based on the very same system that had been used in Gloucestershire in 1798 and similar to that used by Justice Hale in the seventeenth century. In his "Diary" Allen calculated the cost of labor for one yard of second quality broadcloth:[58]

---

[55] Herbert Heaton, Yorkshire Cloth Traders in the United States, 1770-1840 (Leeds; Thoresby Society Publication 37, 1941).

[56] F. W. Taussig, The Tariff History of the United States, 8th ed. (New York: Capricorn Press, 1964), pp. 68-108.

[57] Manufacturers' and Farmers' Journal, 11 August 1823.

[58] Z. Allen, "Diary," Allen Papers, RIHS.

Picking and sorting, 2 pounds @ 5¢	$ .10
Scouring and dyeing	1.08
Roping and carding @ 7¢	.14
Spinning	.17
Weaving 1 1/2 yards to make 1 yard	.37 1/2
Fulling, napping, shearing, tentering, &c.	.20
Overseers wages (@$1.40 for 20 yards) . . .	.07
Cartage and other expenses	.06
Labour	$1.24

In this example, Allen was using the traditional methods of cost accounting. There are differences between this analysis of his labor costs and Allen's actual payroll as listed above (pp. 186-87). In the payroll, John Payton was listed as overseer, sorter, bookkeeper, and the man who "tends the shop." If he was paid $1.58 per day, and production was twenty yards per day as shown here (close to the 21.7 yards from p. 187), his cost would have been just short of 8 cents per yard rather than the 17 cents shown here, combining picking and sorting and overseers wages. In the payroll, cartage and "other expenses" were not listed. If shrinkage was closer to 20 percent that was estimated above rather than the 33 1/3 percent estimated in this example by Zachariah Allen, this would reduce labor costs another 5 cents. With these small items excluded, Allen's estimates in the traditional manner are very close to his payroll figures: $1.04.

Allen made two or three estimates of his cost of stock or raw materials per yard. The following is one such estimate:[59]

---

[59]Ibid.

Cost of stock:

2 pounds wool for yard cloth @ 85¢		$1.70
2 lb. indigo	.55	
Soap and potash	.08	
Madder and woad	.05	
Sig	.02	.70
Oil (olive)	.02	
Soap, scouring &c.	.03	
Glue for sizing	.02	
Fire wood	.03	.10
		$2.50

The major variable in Allen's stock estimates was again the cost of wool. The 85¢ posted above would seem very high, but probably represents cleaned and picked wool; manufacturers often added as much as 20 to 25 percent to the value of the wool if it was clean.

Allen's next diary entry was to recapitulate these costs in the following manner:[60]

Labor cost 1 yard	$1.00
Interest on capital, 6 months	.15
Interest on buildings (includes wear and tear on machinery)	.25
Stock, dyeing 1 yard	.70
Oil, glue, firewood, soap	.10
2 lb. wool	1.70
	$3.90

In this example, Allen clearly is trying to come to grips with some of his other expenses that neither his payroll could cover adequately nor his traditional cost analysis. However, what is not clear is whether the two listed interest items were actual costs (interest from borrowed money) or a rough estimate of frozen assets that were not interest bearing, and hence "losses." But Allen's real innovation here is his effort to break down costs into

---

[60]Ibid.

labor, raw materials, factory expenses (firewood), and even wear and tear on machinery. It perhaps could have been more refined, and it is impossible to know how he reached his particular figures, but it does show how one man tried to pull together a somewhat more realistic cost analysis.

Allen corresponded with Frederick Wolcott of Litchfield County, Connecticut. Wolcott sent Allen a more precise cost analysis than Allen himself had done, but while he did not include interest, depreciation, commissions, he did include some of the clerical and managerial expenses. This set of figures was made up in 1823:[61]

2 1/2 pounds in fleece, shrinks 28%, will make a yard and costs 65¢ OR	$1.46
1 pound, 10 ounces clean wool @ 90¢ (= 1.625 lb.)	
Assorting @ 2 1/2¢	.05
Dyeing and scouring @ 28¢, shop and repairs 2¢	.49
Carding and slubbing @ 8¢, oil 4¢ = 12¢	.20
Spinning @ 3 1/2 plus use Brewster's machine @ 1 1/2¢	.08
Listing and heading 4¢/yard, glue 1 1/4¢, say all	.09
Weaving and bobbin winding, 26¢, shrinkage 6¢	.32
Soap and other materials for milling and scouring	.04
Labour in fulling mill 7¢, use machinery &c.	.09
Warping 2¢/yard, and harness & shuttles 1¢	.03
Burling & picking 4¢, teasels and canvass for leaders (1¢)	.05
Twine & tape, wrapping paper & fire wood	.03
Labour in finishing room	.10
Clerk hire say $340/year, other incidental expenses	.08
Salary of superintendent $1,000/year	.09
	$3.20

[61]Ibid.

Both Allen and Wolcott took considerable care in the analysis of their costs, and although Allen's was rougher and cruder, he included items Wolcott did not. Within the year, Allen had cut back his work force by half. From May to October he calculated he had manufactured 2,487 broad yards of broadcloth and cassimere, that it had cost $3.33 per yard, and that that represented 20¢ more than the selling price of the cloth. For another year the situation did not improve. Allen's "Diary" entry for 25 November 1824 was as follows:

> My business does not improve cloths being quite as low as ever, and as unprofitable. I feel utterly depress(ed) and discouraged an unfortunate result of an undertaking, to which I have devoted my whole time and care for nearly three years. If it should not improve in the spring I am determined to make no more broadcloth, but confine my attention to the manufacture of satinets, which pay a tolerable profit at present, or if I have an opportunity, to sell my mill at once.[62]

The following spring found Allen in Europe inspecting textile mills in England and France with Abraham Schenck of New York. There are no day by day accounts, but his business must have improved. As reported to McLane in 1832, Allen's capital investment had more than doubled to $94,000. His work force in 1832 consisted of sixty-seven people of which twenty-seven were men, thirty were women, and ten were children. He claimed his wage costs were $13,000, so that if his production was about 32,000 broad yards ($80,000

---

[62]Ibid.

worth at \$2.50/yard), his wages per yard were closer to 40¢ rather than the dollar or more figured in the early twenties.[63]

The period from 1809 to 1820 saw the woolen industry break with certain traditions. Technology represented the most obvious break with English manufacturing processes. This was not a case of one national group, say the Americans, taking one road, another national group, the English, another road. It was more a matter of the degree of mechanization. Yorkshire woolen mills were mechanizing their processes in the early nineteenth century. They were borrowing processes from the neighboring cotton mills in Lancashire, and they were concentrating on the adoption of steam power to the manufacture of woolen cloths.[64] Manufacturers in Yorkshire applied steam to the obvious carding and fulling processes, but lagged seriously behind the United States in applying inanimate power to spinning, weaving, or any of the finishing processes besides fulling.[65] This aspect of industrialization should have given the Americans some advantages: since waterpower was so abundant and inexpensive, capital was freed to be

---

[63] McLane Report, 1:951, 975.

[64] D. T. Jenkins, The West Riding Wool Textile Industry, 1770-1835: A Study of Fixed Capital Formation (Edington, Wiltshire: Pasold Research Fund, 1975), pp. 93-94.

[65] Ibid., pp. 120-31.

available for mechanizing these other processes. Furthermore, because American mills did not require fuel for power, comparable mills in America should have had need for proportionally less working capital.

A small factory could be built and equipped for less than $10,000 in the United States in 1820. A typical working force for the small factory could be employed at between $2,000 and $3,000 per year, depending on how much board for the hands the employer was willing to pay. Wool was the expensive item. For 3,000 broad yards of superfine cloth, wool would have cost from between $3,300 and $5,000.[66] None of these moneys were required in cash; these factories normally did not need a cash flow of any magnitude, but they did need credit. Since the tendency for manufacturing was to be undercapitalized in the first place, one or two bad years were apt to stop the credit flow, and that tended to be fatal. By and large, the credit for wool came directly from the factory's commercial dealers. If those dealers could not sell the factory's cloth, or were forced to underprice it, they were unlikely under those circumstances to continue to supply credit for wool.[67] At four

---

[66]1820 Manufactures Census: passim.

[67]Glenn Porter and Harold C. Livesay, Merchants and Maufacturers: Studies in the Changing Structure of Nineteenth-Century Marketing (Baltimore: Johns Hopkins University Pess, 1970), pp. 1-36.

dollars per yard, this model might have made a profit; at three dollars, profits were much more difficult. As American markets became inundated with British woolens from 1815 until the tariff of 1824, prices for American woolen cloth could not and did not hold.

Americans accused the English of "dumping," that is, exporting and jobbing goods at prices less than actual manufacturing costs.[68] Wool manufacturing costs were not much different in Great Britain from the United States. Common wool averaged 33¢ per pound in New York from 1816 to 1837;[69] in Great Britain, the average price of common wool was 31¢ from 1805 to 1834.[70] In 1825, Zachariah Allen reported that imported Saxony and Spanish wool was priced in England at two shillings to two and nine pence or 49¢ to 67¢, about the same as American full-blood wool.[71]

As for wages, mule spinners in woolen factories in both Yorkshire and Gloucestershire made on the average twenty-five to twenty-six shillings per week in the 1820s. This was equivalent to $1.00 to 1.04 per day in the United

---

[68]Robert G. Albion, *The Rise of New York Port, 1815-1860* (New York: Scribners's, 1939; repr. 1970), pp. 12-13, 60-62, 276-80.

[69]Cole, *Wholesale Commodity Prices*, p. 364.

[70]Phyllis Deane and W. A. Cole, *British Economic Growth, 1688-1959*, 2nd ed. (Cambridge: Cambridge University press, 1969), p. 196.

[71]Z. Allen, "Travel Journal," pp. 6, 61, Allen Papers, RIHS.

States based on the pound equal to \$4.80; according to Zachariah Allen, wages for mule spinning in the United States were \$1.08 to \$1.40 in 1825.[72] Actually, Slater and Howard of Dudley paid an average of \$1.13 to three jenny spinners in 1824;[73] Victor and Charles du Pont of the Brandywine paid \$1.04 in 1822.[74] In 1825 one spinner, probably on the jenny, was paid what amounted to \$1.30 per day by the Dudley Woollen Manufacturing Company,[75] but in 1826, two spinners in the same company were paid only 96¢ per day on the average.[76]

---

[72]J. Bischoff, A Comprehensive History of the Woollen and Worsted Manufacture, 2 vols. (London: Smith, Elder, 1842; repr. London: Frank Cass, 1968), 1:416; Zachariah Allen, "Upon the Relative Advantages Possessed by England, France, and the United States of America as Manufacturing Nations," in White, Memoirs of Slater, pp. 339-44; Z. Allen, "Travel Journal," pp. 113, 152-54; Nathan Rosenberg, "Anglo-American Wage Differences in the 1820s," in Rosenberg, Perspectives in Technology (New York: Cambridge University Press, 1976), pp. 50-58.

Wages in the West of England may have been considerably lower. The figures used here are from Bischoff, and Allen's "Travel Journal." Elsewhere in the "Travel Journal," Allen had excerpted a London newspaper article of July 1825, indicating that mule spinners in the West were paid \$1.44 to \$1.92 per week plus board. Assuming board at twenty-five cents per day, per diem work rates would have been only forty-nine to fifty-seven cents.

[73]Daybooks 5-7, Slater, Howard and Company, Slater Coll., BL.

[74]Petit lodger 63, Papers of Charles I. du Pont and Company, Acc. 500, EMHL.

[75]Time book 74, Ledger 55, Dudley Woollen Mfg. Co., OSV.

[76]Ledger 55, Dudley Woollen Mfg. Co., OSV.

There were variables other than supply and demand in the labor picture, especially for a specialist such as a spinner. These included the quality of the wool, the condition of the machinery, the experience of the workman, what he was spinning--the fineness of the final yarn, whether it was to be used as warp or fill. These variables accounted for the discrepancies in wages as much certainly as the supply of skilled labor. All in all, the Americans were paid slightly more; labor costs in American mills were perhaps 10 percent greater than in Yorkshire mills, or English woolen mills generally in the 1820s. However, this amount easily would have been consumed by the cost of coal in England. Using Zachariah Allen's figures of 1825, a small ten horsepower steam engine would require 4 1/2 tons of coal per week. At eight shillings per ton, the cost for coal and repairs on the engine would be about $450 per year, easily making up for the wage differences in a small factory.[77]

The question this poses is whether the American woolen manufacturers in the 1820s had it within their power to overcome English competition. The manufacturers did not think so, and were virtually unanimous in their support for the tariff on woolen goods. It is impossible to tell how many woolen factories failed between 1815 and 1832; there is no way to determine how many factories extant in 1820

---

[77]Z. Allen, "Travel Journal," p. 149, Allen Papers, RIHS.

still existed in 1832 under the same management. Most likely, less than one-third. Many new factories were started in the 1820s although most were probably on the physical sites of older factories or mills. Woolens must have seemed like a logical investment. Americans needed woolen cloth. Most was imported which added shipping costs to the selling price. Surely, Americans could manufacture such a product more cheaply than importing it. Yet it is not clear that they could. The evidence seems to show that costs were not that different. Americans made rapid advances in mechanizing the entire woolen manufacturing process during the 1820s. Mechanization did increase American productivity as will be seen in coming chapters. Perhaps the tariffs of 1824 and 1828 helped some. For a short five-year period, English exports of woolen cloth to the United States did decline, but by the 1830s, export volume from Great Britain to the United States was even greater than earlier.[78]

Cassimere and broadcloth cannot be considered necessities. Demand for them was very elastic. When their price reached less than three dollars per broad yard, they sold well, but often the market price was actually below manufacturing costs. What was learned eventually on both sides of the Atlantic was that you did not have to make such a long-lasting, beautiful and fine product to sell.

---

[78]J. Potter, "Atlantic Economy, 1815-1860," pp. 264-267.

Satinet was a product that was developed after the American War for Independence. By 1832 nearly all the woolen factories in Connecticut and New Jersey manufactured satinet, and many in Massachusetts had added satinet to their lines of woolens. The British caught on to this in the early '30s, and from then through the 1850s exploited a larger and larger share of this market.[79]

In 1832 the published McLane Report revealed the following information on a state by state basis:

Maine: There were six factories using wool as a primary raw material in Maine in 1832. Four manufactured satinet, and their average capitalization was $6,125. Their average number of employees was four men, four women, and one child, and each factory produced 16,000 yards of satinet. One small cassimere factory produced 8,400 yards of the narrow cloth, and was capitalized at $4,400. This factory also carded wool and fulled cloth in its locality for $996. One factory made 1,500 yards of broadcloth, 3,000 yards of satinet, and 400 yards of flannel. It employed ten men, four boys, and two women, and claimed a fixed capital of $5,600.[80]

Vermont: There were eight factories in Windsor county manufacturing 41,000 yards of broadcloth, 36,000 yards of cassimere, and 70,000 yards of satinet. The average numbers of employees were thirteen men, and sixteen women

[79]Ibid.

[80]McLane Report, 1:1-65, 4, 22, 56.

and girls, and the average capitalization of each factory was $12,000. In the rest of Vermont there were nine small factories manufacturing satinet and narrow cloth. Three factories were making broadcloth, one reporting 32,000 yards of blue broadcloth per year. Average capitalization in these factories was $11,000. One Caledonia county factory produced 150,000 yards of flannel.[81]

New Hampshire: Somersworth (Stafford County) was home for two enormous factories, one a combination woolen and cotton mill, the other manufacturing broadcloths exclusively. The two combined, manufactured 170,000 yards of broadcloth. The Great Falls Company defies analysis because the cotton and wool statistics were unseparated. Salmon Falls was capitalized at $225,000, employed seventy-one men, 138 women, twelve children, and produced 52,600 yards of broadcloth. Great Falls manufactured broadcloth valued at $320,000 by its agent; this should have been about 117,400 broad yards. There were two small satinet factories, and two flannel factories in the rest of New Hampshire.[82]

Massachusetts: Massachusetts was the center of the woolen industry in 1832 with forty-six factories producing over a million broad yards of kersey, cassimere, and

---

[81]Ibid., 1:877-926, 884-86, 890-94, 918-24.

[82]Ibid., 1:579-875, 636-41, 648-49; Victor S. Clark History of Manufactures in the United States, 3 vols. (Washington, D. C.: Carnegie Institution, 1929; repr. New York: Peter Smith, 1969), 1:566.

broadcloths. The factories were much larger than they had been in 1820. Then the average capitalization was just over $11,000; in 1832 it was nearly $37,000. In 1820, thirty-seven factories employed an average of ten men, four women, and four children; in 1832, forty-six factories employed an average of twenty-one men, twenty women, and five children. There were also fifty-five satinet factories in Massachusetts producing 2.8 million yards, and ten flannel factories producing over 3 million yards. The Middlesex Woollen Company of Lowell claimed to produce 135,000 yards of cassimere in 1832; reduced by dividing by two this would have come to 67,500 broad yards.[83]

Rhode Island: Sixteen woolen and satinet factories were reported from Rhode Island. Most were small with an average capital of less than $12,000 and an average total of sixteen hands. One factory manufactured satinet exclusively, and one manufactured Negro cloth. Zachariah Allen's was the only woolen factory making broadcloth. He reported to McLane's agent a total capitalization of $49,000, production of 32,000 yards of broadcloth, and employees numbering twenty-seven men, thirty women, and ten children.[84]

Connecticut: Trends toward greater specialization were clearly visible in the changes in Connecticut from 1820 to

---

[83] McLane Report, 1:66-577.

[84] Ibid., 1:927-76, 951-52.

1832. In 1820, there were forty-three factories including six satinet factories. In 1832 there were twenty-eight satinet factories, nine flannel manufactories, and fifteen manufacturing broadcloth and cassimere. Many of the latter type were small with an average capital of less than $10,000, and averaging thirteen men, nine women, and four children. Production in 1832 was about 800,000 yards of satinet and nearly 300,000 yards of broadcloth.[85]

New York: The Mclane Report compiled and tabulated figures for fifty-four woolen factories for New York in 1832. Their average capital was $19,000, and they employed over twenty-six hands each. The factories produced 274,000 yards of broadcloth, 163,000 yards cassimere, 485,000 yards flannel and bags, and 471,000 yards of satinet.[86]

New Jersey: Twenty-three woolen factories were reported in New Jersey. Their average capitalization was $23,000. Mostly satinet was manufactured.[87]

Pennsylvania: Forty-eight small woolen factories were enumerated in McLane for Pennsylvania. The average number of employees was thirteen, and capitalization averaged $6,500.[88]

---

[85]Ibid., 1:977-1050, 980-83.

[86]Ibid., 2:1-133, 60-96.

[87]Ibid., 2:134-94, 170-82.

[88]Ibid., 2:195-650, 200-6, 217-18, 221-22, 393-461, 467-70.

Delaware: There were three substantial woolen factories in Delaware. By 1832, William W. Young was manufacturing cotton and wool cloth, du Pont, as will be analyzed below, was manufacturing a wide range of woolens. The sample was too small to average.[89]

Even though the data are unwieldy and defy systematic analysis, directions and trends in the woolen industry in the decade of the 1820s are very clear. There were more factories--something in the neighborhood of 325 in 1832 as opposed to 250 in 1820; their capitalization was considerably greater. In Massachusetts, for example, capital per factory jumped from $11,000 to $37,000 in the twelve years. There were more specialized factories making satinet only, or flannel, or broadcloth and cassimere. The new factories built in the '20s were much larger and tended to be more completely mechanized. By and large, what was seen in 1820 were a number of small factories, many if not most of which were outgrowths of carding and fulling mills. Many, in fact, continued to rely on the "country" business to survive. Factory managers had added machinery such as shearing machines, billies, jennies, even water-powered spinning machines and a few powered satinet looms to older carding and fulling operations. A few of the larger, more mechanically sophisticated factories survived although

[89] Ibid., 2:651-859, 660-63, 672-74, 700-1, 707-9, 802-7.

many changed hands and changed financial structure. In 1832 many woolen factories were joint stock companies, many were incorporated; quite a few were both. By 1822 when Zachariah Allen built his factory, the definition of a woolen factory was clear, and it included the machinery described in chapter 4, except for powered broad looms. Allen very likely did install powered satinet looms. Larger factories like Middlesex in Lowell or the Somersworth factories were simply enlargements of what had become a basic mechanized woolen factory, and those mills were built late enough in the decade to include powered broad looms.

The figures in the McLane Report simply are not inclusive enough to provide a picture of profitability. The figures included were wages and payrolls, raw material costs, occasionally interest on capital, production, or more likely the value of that production without quantifying data. This last figure may be very suspect as it was normally the value the manufacturer ascribed to his finished products, but hardly the market price from say a New York city auction. Also what was missing was indebtedness and interest on that debt. Interest on debt was a large expense item that was seldom stated. Only Simon Newton Dexter of Oriskany happened to mention the $40,000 at 6 percent the firm borrowed from the Utica Bank in 1831 to pay for wool.[90] His situation was hardly likely to have been unusual.

---

[90]Ibid., 2:76.

The fact is that many manufacturers actually were not really sure whether or not their operations were profitable. This was clearly so in the early days as will be seen when the individual fatories are examined. Certain costs such as wages and raw material were obvious. Yet even wages could get fuzzy. How should the wages for running the boarding house be accounted, for example? Other accounting areas presented more glaring problems: How much should be written off for wear and tear on machinery? Was interest on capital a genuine expense? Buildings clearly became capital assets, but did expensive machinery?

Because woolen factories hired more family labor rather than single women, they tended to be _less_ paternalistic over time than the large cotton mills. Most of the large woolen factories described in _McLane_ no longer were providing board for hands in 1832. This tendency was also apparent in the case-study factories. Families working for woolen factories did very well in the decade of the '20s. As woolen weaving became more fully mechanized, those roles were taken over by women, but by the late '20s, early '30s, the provision of board often had to be supplied by the employee herself, or himself. Even the most mechanized and technically up-to-date woolen factories had a considerable need for male labor, and hence the factories continued to look for family labor. Wage costs were lowered as these factories installed machinery.

Chapter IV

A TECHNICAL REVOLUTION: MECHANIZATION OF WOOLEN MANUFACTURE

During the twenty-year period from 1813 to 1832, the entire process of the manufacture of fine woolen cloth was mechanized in the United States. Mechanical carding led off these series of machines; by 1825 all of the basic processes such as spinning and weaving, plus secondary processes such as napping and shearing, had become harnessable to inanimate waterpower.

Four and one-half yards per broad loom per twelve-hour day was considered a respectable average for the production of broadcloth with the fly-shuttle in 1820. In 1832 power looms could produce more than double that yardage--just under ten yards per twelve-hour day. Compared to the possible production speeds of the 1970s, these are not staggering speeds--thirty inches per hour, one-half inch per minute, one pick (throw of the shuttle) per two seconds.

The objectives behind mechanizing these processes were twofold. The first objective, the more obvious of the two, was to increase productivity and reduce wage costs. The hope for reducing wage costs rested on the development of machinery that did not require great skill or great strength to operate. As these were attributes thought not to exist in women, and as women were a much cheaper labor source than men, the wool factory operatives hoped to convert as many work roles in their factories as possible to jobs easily performed by women. As was seen in chapter 3, this was accomplished to a considerable extent.

The second objective was to gain much more uniformity in the finished product. It was apparent to most manufacturers by 1820 that machinery was not going to make a really superior product. What manufacturers then hoped for was a more standardized and uniform product. There seems to have been considerable success in this effort. American broadcloth manufacturers manufactured goods selling for from two to three dollars per yard in 1832 rather than the four to six dollars they often had expressed hope for ten to twelve years earlier. Machinery in no way raised the quality of goods, but it did seem to standardize quality.

How revolutionary was this mechanization? Cotton will always take the front seat in any discussion of industrialization. Yet these woolens were important too. While the scale of the manufacturing plants was smaller than those for cotton, woolen factories were by and large integrated factories producing goods by machinery from raw material to finished product in one location. So while the machinery itself was not particularly radical, the notion of having it all on one site using one power source was a fairly unique and radical notion. The rapidity of the change also can be seen as far-reaching. Carding and fulling were the only water powered processes in 1815; by 1825, spinning, weaving, and finishing were all operated by water. Also the fact that broadcloth manufacture was a very old business, very involved in England in traditional methods, adds another radical element.

This chapter will sketch the mechanical changes in the United States in the processes of manufacturing woolen cloth. By 1830 all those processes that could be mechanized were mechanized, and all the newly invented machines had the capacity to be harnessed to inanimate power, water-power by and large in the United States. The new machinery will be described following the order of the processes of the manufacture of woolen cloth.

The best single source of both English and American textile technology for the teens of the nineteenth century is Abraham Rees' forty-five volume Cyclopaedia, published in folio form in London from 1802 to 1820, and published shortly thereafter in Philadelphia also in folio form. Rees had chosen experts for the work and the section on "Woollen Manufacture" was up-to-date in 1818.[1] The second American source for technical information is William Partridge's little manual, A Practical Treatise on Dying of Woollen, Cotton, and Skein Silk with the Manufacture

---

[1]David J. Jeremy, "Innovation in American Textile Technology during the Early Nineteenth Century," Technology and Culture 14 (January 1973):37-38, whole article 40-76.

of Broadcloth and Cassimere Including the Most Improved Methods in the West of England. This source was discovered by David J. Jeremy in the not-very-dark-recesses of the Eleutherian Mills Historical Library. It was originally published in New York in 1823. Other sources include reproduced patent records from the National Archives, the 1820 Manufactures Census, and various business records. Business records did not always give detailed descriptions of machinery, but the machines were often identified by their patent-type especially if a license fee was involved. Spinning machinery invariably was identified by numbers of spindles. Power or water looms tended to be labeled as such.

Using secondary material, efforts will be made to tie in technical change in the United States with what was happening in Yorkshire and the West of England. Neither English area enjoyed more progressive woolen technology than the United States. By 1820 the direction of technical diffusion in the woolen cloth industry was transatlantic but very likely West to East. Only a few known and proven examples of this can be given without further research in English archives, but a great deal of circumstantial evidence points in this direction for spinners, power looms, and finishing machinery.[2] Unfortunately, not much is

---

[2]Cole, Wool Manufacture, 1:116-19, 126, 128-32; H(rothgar) J(ohn) Habakkuk, American and British Technology in the Nineteenth Century (Cambridge: Cambridge University Press, 1962), pp. 102-7; Mann, Cloth Industry, pp. 303-4.

known about the background of the American inventors--the Gilbert Brewsters, William H. Howards, Beriah Swifts, or William Hoveys. Still unknown are their birthplaces, education, and early work experience, and without this knowledge, the origins of the technical expertise of these men is still unknown.

The mechanization of the processes of woolen manufacture was not in itself very radical. Most of the mechanization took one of two forms: (1) application of power to existing machines, such as power looms or the early shearing machines; and (2) multiplication of existing parts of machinery--spinning was the best example, but carding as it became more sophisticated, multiplied existing processes. Certain processes defied mechanization: wool sorting was one of those.

Sorting

Wool sorters were among the highest paid hands in any woolen factory. There is no way the sorting process can be mechanized. The sorter had from four to fourteen categories in which to classify the wool: (1) general condition, (2) softness or hardness, (3) length of staple, (4) luster, (5) fineness (diameter), (6) springiness, (7) color, and (8) strength.[3] Sorters were paid by the pound. One and

[3]Allen Fannin, Handspinning: Art and Technique (New York: van Nostrand & Reinholdt, 1970), pp. 133-35; Partridge, Treatise on Dying, pp. 24-29; Rees, Cyclopaedia, 38: "Wool."

one-half to two cents per pound was a normal pay rate, 100 to 150 pounds was a normal day's work.[4]

Picking or Willowing

Wool came from the sorter in a state that ranged from filthy to dirty. It could go immediately to the wool-mill or willy or in the United States, to the picker. These are all the same machine which was basically a cylinder with spikes or teeth accompanied by other smaller rollers with spikes or teeth (see illus. 2). Its function was to shake dust and dirt out of the wool, to disentangle the wool, and in later developments of the machine, to mix the dyed wool together and to mix it with oil. After the first pass through the picker, the wool was scoured. (Not always; as Rees' writer pointed out, some Yorkshire factories dyed the wool without bothering to scour it.)[5] The scouring liquid varied, but the most common was chamber ley or sig, sometimes soap with oil. Sig is stale urine which has a very high component of ammonia. American manufacturers used a great deal of it, providing their own via the boardinghouses when they could, but buying it locally by the barrel when necessary. (Partridge would caution the manufacturer from using urine from "luxurious livers" such

---

[4]Daybooks 5-12, Dec. 3, 1825, Joseph Maltby; May 1, 1827, John Boulding, Slater, Howard & Co., Slater Coll. BL.

[5]Rees, Cycopaedia, 38: "Woollen Manufacture."

as gin drinkers; beer drinkers produced better quality.) The wool could be dyed right after it was scoured; whether or not it was dyed at this stage, the wool had to be carefully dried.[6] In the 1820 Census, there were references to dry houses, not to be confused with dye houses. The dry house usually had a stove. Bean Ing in Yorkshire had a "Drying House" that burned in the fire in 1799.[7] Most fine cloth was dyed in the wool, except apparently for black cloths.

Carding

The next step was scribbling in the scribbler, breaker, or preliminary carder. Like the picker, the scribbler can be used on the same wool two or three times. In the scribbler the wool was sprinkled with oil, olive oil or gallipoli (less pure olive oil) being the best, and the wool was mixed together, coming out of the machine in a batt or thin sheet whose color and texture were as even as possible.[8]

The next step was carding; in 1818 Rees' writer was describing single carders with as many as six workers and strippers surrounding the main cylinder, and double carders

---

[6]Partridge, Treatise on Dying, pp. 29-33.

[7]W. B. Crump, ed., Leeds Woollen Industry, pp. 33, 257, 263.

[8]Rees, Cyclopaedia, 38: "Woollen Manufacture"; Partridge, Treatise on Dying, p. 38.

with two main cylinders, workers and strippers.[9] A couple of important though small points should be noted about carding. Both cotton and woolen manufacture depend on it, although the end product is different. In cotton, the machines produce rolls whose fibers end up in an almost parallel manner. In fine wool, the roll is made up of homogenized short fibers. By 1785, there was no patent protection in England for carding machines themselves, but since it was still illegal for British machinists to emigrate, the technology was not immediately widespread. The Scholfields may have been one specific agency through which carding technology did spread to America, but by 1810, other Americans were patenting refinements to carding machines. Many too many carding machines were counted in the 1810 census to be accounted for by the Scholfields alone.

Perhaps even more important to the carding process was the Whittemore patent (1797) for a machine for bending the carding wire, piercing holes into the leather, and inserting carding staples into the leather. Whittemore was from Cambridge, Massachusetts, but the carding cloth industry concentrated in Leicester, Massachusetts where for example, Reuben Meriam perfected a device for cutting,

---

[9]Rees, Cyclopaedia, 38 and plate vol. 6: "Woollen Manufacture," plate 4, (see illus. 20).

pricking, and setting carding wire in 1831 (see illus. 21).[10]

Carding cloth did not hold up well and had to be ground repeatedly to keep the points of the wires sharp. One Gideon Drake patented a grinding and facing machine in 1817 (see illus. 25).[11] Applying the cloth to the carding cylinders evenly, and in a way that the wires would mesh easily and exactly was also difficult. A rather prolific textile machinery inventor, John Boynton of South Coventry, Connecticut, patented an ingenious pincer combined with a long screw to maintain tautness on the carding cloth while applying it to the cylinders, and while grinding the points with a second cylinder covered with emery (see illus. 26).[12]

Credit is universally given to John Goulding of Dedham, Massachusetts for the condenser device which made it possible to card and slub at the same time (see illus. 27). On early carding machines, the rolls came off the machine in pieces as wide as the machine. These literally had to

---

[10]For Amos Whittemore's machine for manufacturing sheet cards of August 5, 1797, see National Archives, Record Group 241, "Restored Patent Specifications," 1:43-4. Reuben Meriam's cut, prick, and set machine patent of May 2, 1831, "Restored Patent Specifications," 13:143-45, and Patent Drawing no. 6533. See infra, pp. 98-99 and Appendix B.

[11]Gideon Drake's machine for grinding and facing machine cards patent of Feb. 28, 1817, "Restored Patents, Specifications," 4:17 and Patent Drawing no. 2745, NA.

[12]John Boynton's machinery for straining and grinding cards, patent of Mar. 30, 1811, "Restored Patents, Specifications," 3:1-2 and Patent Drawing no. 1482, NA.

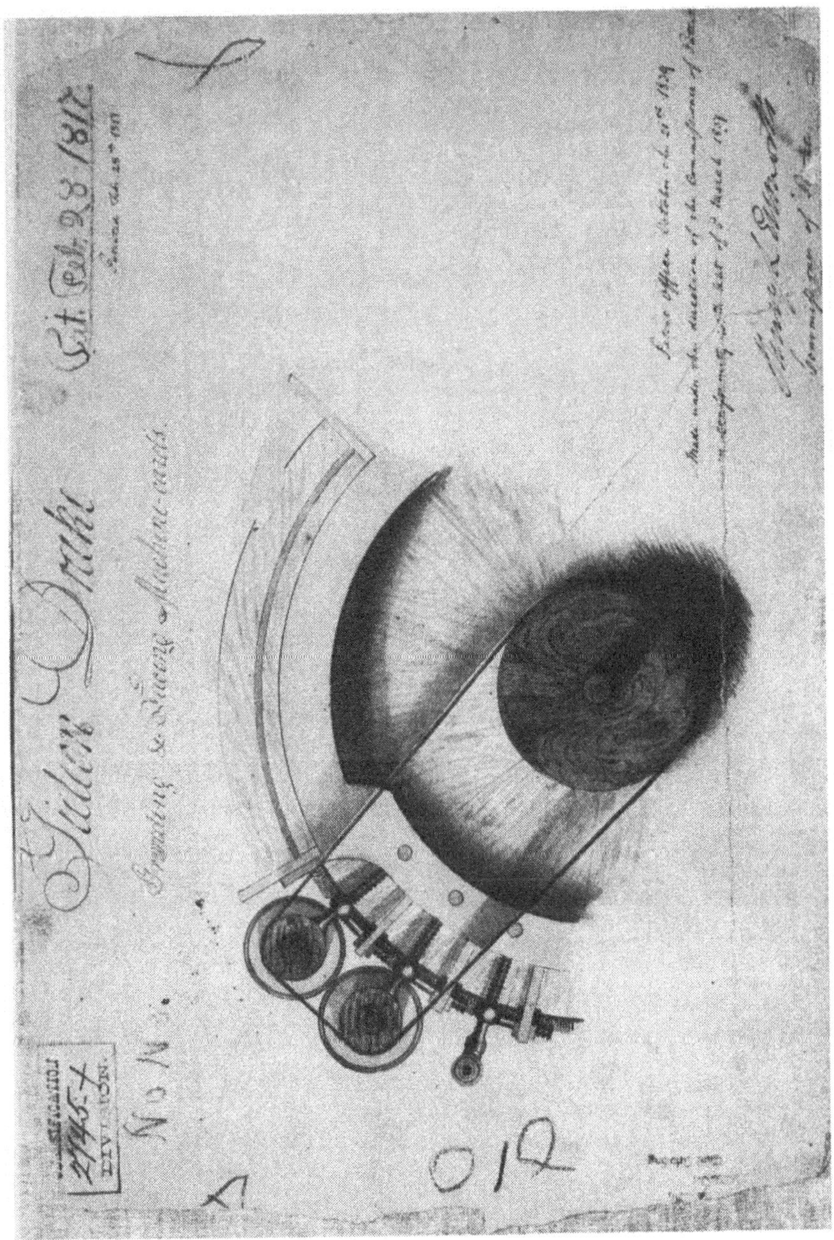

SOURCE: National Archives.

Illus. 25. Gideon Drake's Grinding and Facing Machine-Cards

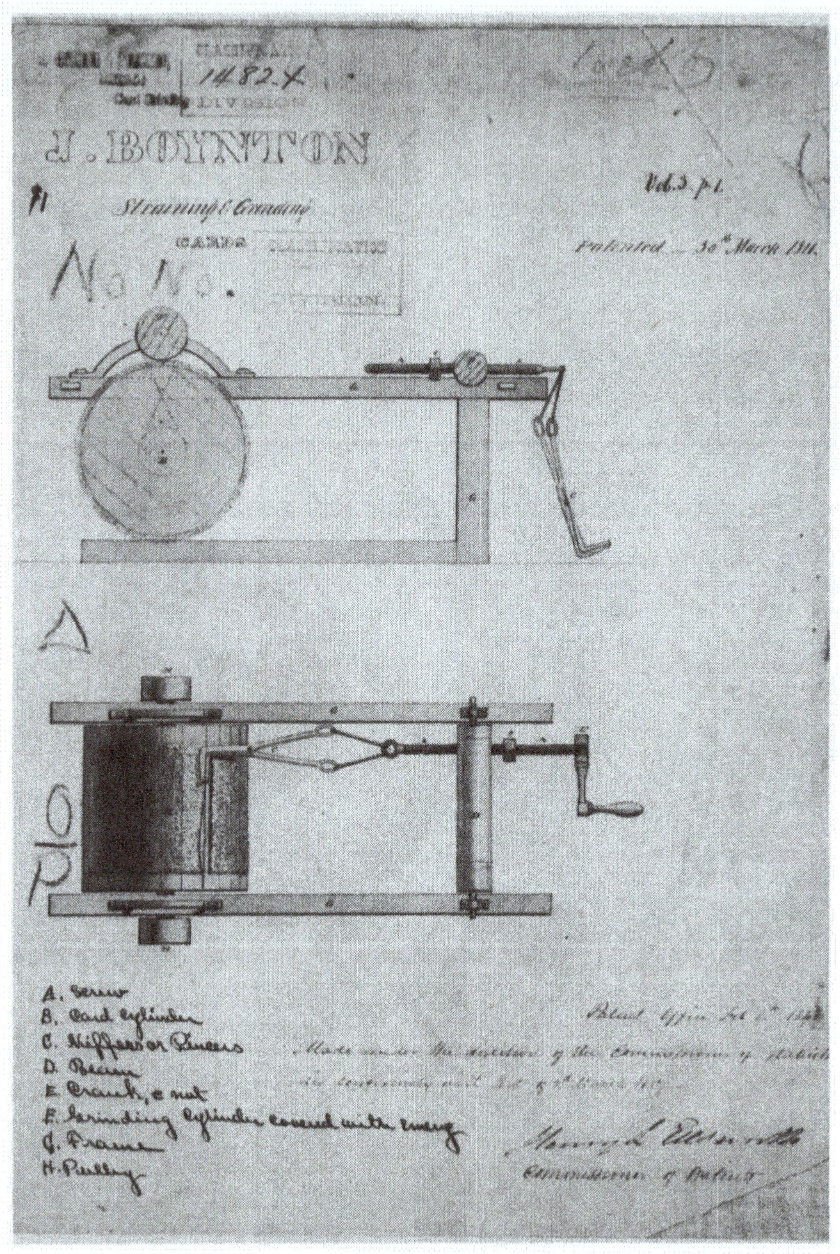

SOURCE: National Archives.

Illus. 26. John Boynton's Straining and Grinding Cards.

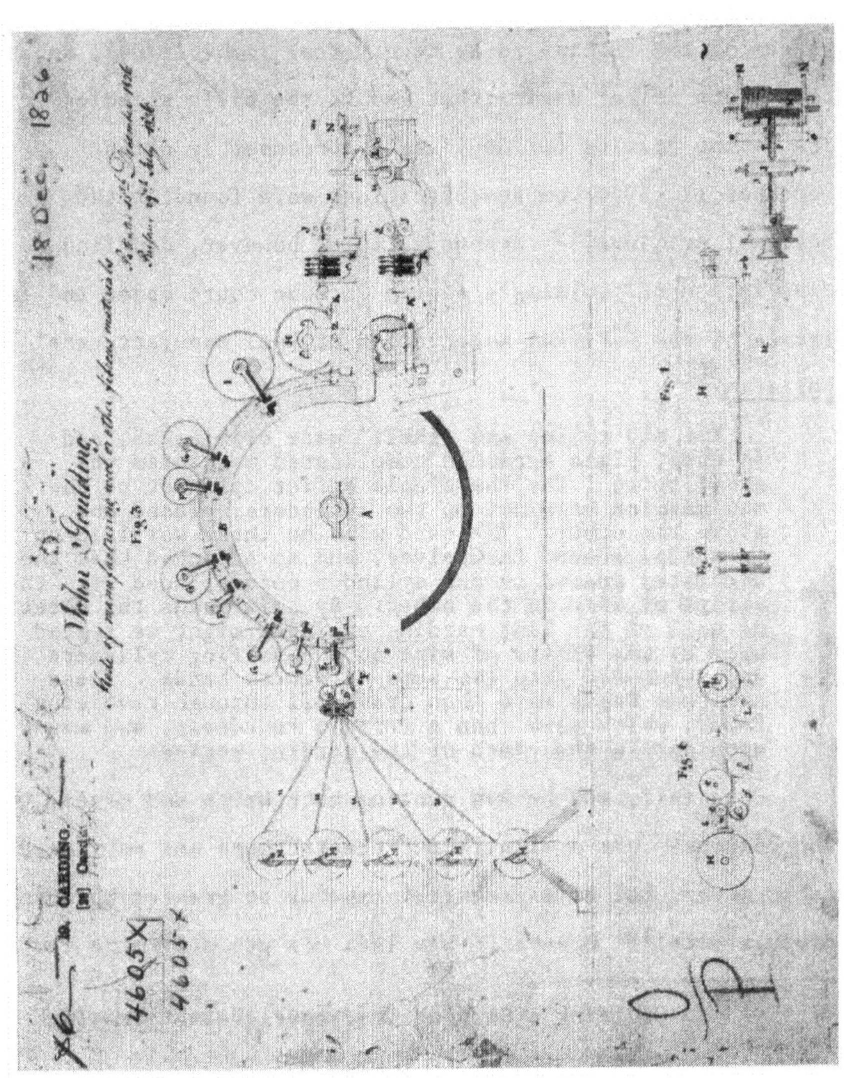

SOURCE: National Archives.

Illus. 27. John Goulding's Condenser.

be pieced or spliced together (by children generally) each twenty-four inch piece to each twenty-four inch piece (assuming the machine to be twenty-four inches wide), and fed into a roller device that led to the billy spindles. The patent drawing for Goulding's condenser is dated December 18, 1826; no specifications were found at the National Archives.[13] Arthur H. Cole, however, did find a description of Goulding's device in some court cases and in issues of the National Association of Wool Manufacturers' Bulletin:[14]

> The old roller and 'shell' were eliminated, and in their place a rather complicated mechanism was substituted. For the single doffer cylinder on the old machine were set up two cylinders, placed one above the other. The card wire on these was laid on in strips around themselves, and so arranged that the uncovered spaces on one cylinder corresponded with the strips of wire on the other. By this means the sheet of wool on the last carding cylinder might be seized upon by the strips of wire on the doffing cylinders and separated into two sets of narrow bands. These numerous bands were then drawn off through revolving tubes, which gave them a certain roundness, and wound upon spools the width of the carding engine.

Cole felt, and he was quoting both North and Hayes, that the condenser was a significant breakthrough not only as a labor saver, but as a technical impetus to greater spinning productivity.[15] However, this last was probably more

---

[13] John Goulding's Carding Condenser, Patent Drawing no. 4605, NA.

[14] Cole, Wool Manufacture, 1:103-5.

[15] Ibid.

directly related to improvements in the Brewster-type spinner.

There seems to have been a considerable lag between the invention of the condenser and its general application. Samuel Babcock of Dudley, Massachusetts was writing his agent about the potential savings of a condenser in August, 1828.[16] One was not installed in his factory until the summer of 1831 by one of Marland's (Andover, Massachusetts) machinists.[17] The du Pont's carder with a condenser came from J. and J. C. Kellog Company, New Hartford, Connecticut in January, 1831.[18] Slater, Howard and Company bought its first carder with a condenser from John Boynton of South Coventry in July, 1833 (see illus. 28).[19] The Boynton patent was dated March 11, 1833[20] and is pictured on the next page.

The condenser is one invention acknowledged by both English and American historians to have been an American breakthrough. John Goulding bought a patent for a ring

[16]Samuel H. Babcock to Nathanial Lyon, 19 August 1828, Box 21, Dudley Woollen Manufacturing Co., OSV.

[17]Samuel H. Babcock to John Brown, 21 July 1831, Box 21, Dudley Woollen Manufacturing Co., OSV.

[18]Journal 39, Ledger 57, Charles I. du Pont, & Co., Acc. 500, EMHL.

[19]Ledger 11, Dudley Manufacturing Company, Slater Coll. BL.

[20]John Boynton's wool carding and condensing patent of March 11, 1833, "Restored Patents, Specifications," 14:45-46 and Patent Drawing no. 7477, NA.

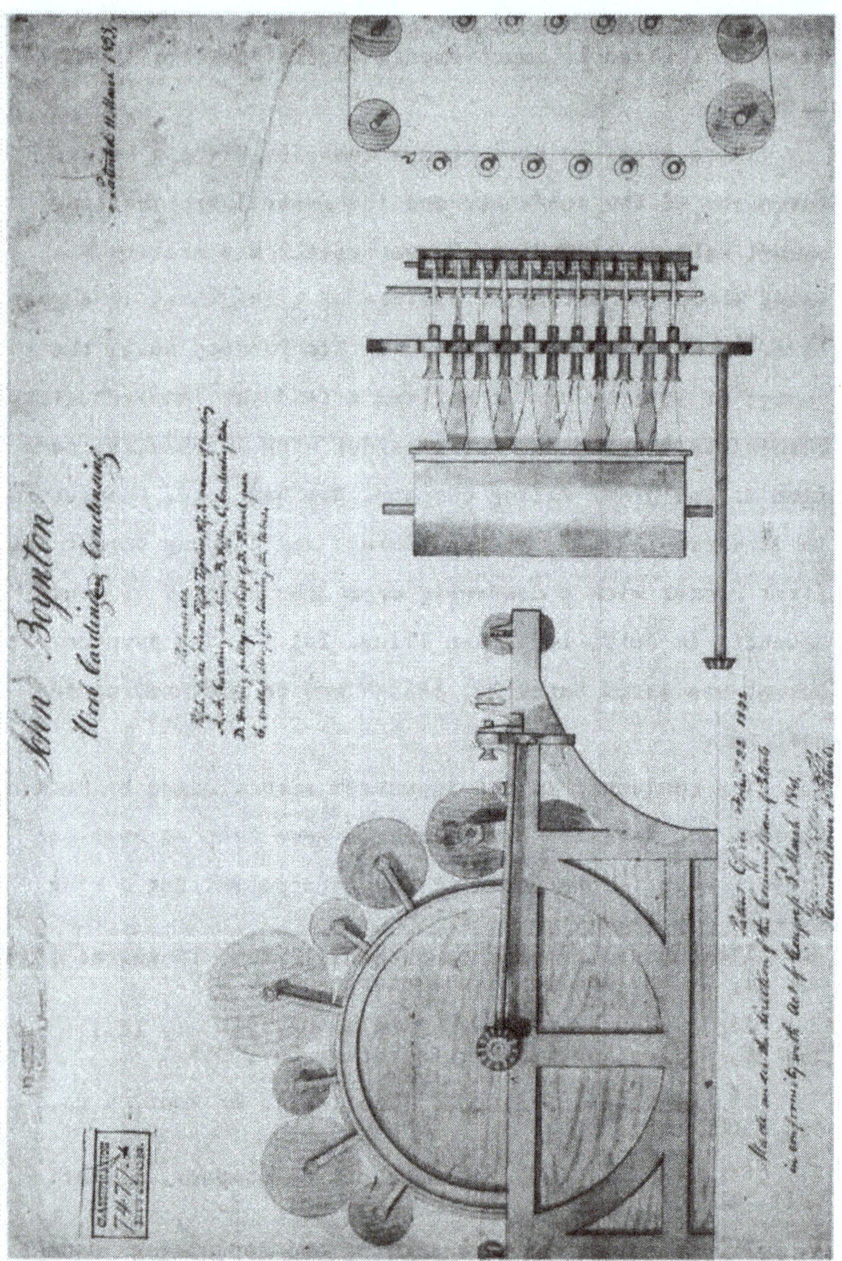

SOURCE: National Archives.

Illus. 28. John Boynton's Condenser.

doffer from Ezekial Hale of Haverill, Massachusetts in 1825. Goulding then received help from another Yankee by the name of Edward Winslow who helped Goulding perfect a method for winding the carded wool onto bobbins. The condenser was patented by Goulding in 1826 in both England and the United States.[21]

Spinning

One of the most important American inventors in the textile field was Gilbert Brewster, probably native of New England. About all that has been possible to find out about Brewster was his general whereabouts from 1812 to his death some time before 1834. He spent most of his working life in Connecticut, in the Norwich, Middletown, or New Hartford neighborhoods. He traveled to Vermont, to Providence, to the Brandywine, and he died in Poughkeepsie.[22] He invented an important spinning machine which well may have evolved into the wool jack or mule of common use in the early nineteenth century. There are two operating jacks in

---

[21] R. T. D. Richards, "The Development of the Modern Woollen Carding Machine," in *Wool Textile Industry*, ed. Jenkins, pp. 71-84, 82; Cole, *Wool Manufacture*, 1:101-105.

[22] Journal 37, Charles I, du Pont & Co. Acc. 500, EMHL; William Young Papers, HSP; Daybooks 5 and 6, Slater, Howard & Co., BL; Jeremy, "Innovation in American Textile Technology," p. 53; Daybooks 6 and 7, Letter Box 21, Dudley Woollen Manufacturing Co., OSV; *McLane Report*, 2:56; Edmund Burke, comp., *List of Patents for Inventions and Designs, Issued by the United States, from 1790 to 1847* (Washington, D.C.: 1847), p. 94.

museums in North America--one at Merrimack Valley Textile Museum, the other at Upper Canada Village. They operate very like a multi-spindled jenny. They spin intermittently, as did the old wool wheel, drafting and spinning yarn by pulling the carriage away from the spindles, winding yarn on to those same spindles by pushing the carriage toward the spindles. Like the jenny, the wool mule did not need rollers to draft the fibers. Also like the jenny, the wool jack is not necessarily self-acting. The carriage of the jack draws away from the spindles by means of power. But an operator is required to push the carriage forward as the spun yarn is wound on to the spindle.

In England William Hirst of Leeds claimed that he introduced spinning mules into woolen manufacture, but W. B. Crump felt that Hirst's machinery could not have been "earlier than 1816."[23] Since it is certain that the du Ponts possessed a Brewster 230 spindle spinning machine in 1816, at least it can be stated that the British version did not predate the American one by very much, if at all.

Rees' writer (1818) described "The Mule for Spinning of Yarn" as follows:[24]

> There is a movement in the machine that shifts the endless strap which turns the mule upon a larger pulley, as soon as the carriage is run fully out, so as to give a more rapid motion to the spindles after the stretching, or drawing out, is finished, than they

---

[23]Crump, ed., Leeds Woollen Industry, p. 25.

[24]Rees, Cyclopaedia, 38: "Woollen Manufacture."

had during the drawing back of the carriage. By this means some time is saved, because the spindles may be allowed to run very quick when it is only required to twist the threads; but whilst the extension is going on, the twisting motion must be moderate or the threads be broken.

Rees' author had reservations about the machine,

The mule has not, till lately, been in much repute for spinning woollen yarn, and the jenny is still thought to spin better yarn: but we have no doubt that when certain modifications are made, it will become a much more perfect method than the jenny, being much less dependent on the direction and dexterity of the spinner; for if the machine is once constructed so as to spin properly, it will always continue to do so.

As reported by Cole, Gilbert Brewster advertised in 1813 a "Globe-Spinner" suitable for spinning "Sheep's Wool, Cotton, Flax and Tow by Water." The spinner was already in operation in a Rhode Island factory and was supposedly manageable by women or children.[25]

David Worden, a Scottish gazeteer compiler, published the first known description of the Brewster. Worden claimed Brewster for the state of Delaware:[26]

Brewster's (Gilbert) machine for spinning wool by water power by which it is said to exceed anything of the kind known in Europe. It produces yarn of a superior quality from thirty to sixty cuts in the pound, and can be made to produce a hundred.

Brewster very likely was in Delaware at the time Worden was writing as on November 6, 1816 Gilbert Brewster

---

[25]Providence Gazette, 6 March 1813, cited in Cole, Wool Manufacture, 1:117.

[26]D(avid) B. Worden, A Statistical, Political, and Historical Account of the United States of North America, 2 vols. (Edinburgh: Archibald Constable and Co., 1819), p. 136. The term "cut" in this context is unclear.

sold a patent spinning machine to Victor and Charles du Pont and Company for $2,300. Brewster was paid in cloth and by a $500 note.[27] While in Delaware Brewster also sold three such machines to William Young, another woolen manufacturer on the Brandywine. This sale took place before 1819.[28] While in the area, Brewster apparently trained an agent in the Philadelphia region by the name of Peter Cushman. Cushman was in receipt of correspondence from both Young and the du Ponts about spinning machines from 1816 to 1819. Perhaps it was a poor choice as when William Young wrote to Cushman in 1819 asking him to come out to help repair the spinner, Cushman sent a discouraging reply,[29]

> I have no workmen at present to repair your machines. Am laid up with a lame foot, but I will be in Philadelphia soon and go down to your factory. I expect some parts will be wanting that had better be made here.

Young's son, William W., and E. I. du Pont were questioned about their use of Brewsters during the 1828

---

[27] Journal 37, Charles I. du Pont & Co., Acc. 500, EMHL.

[28] Victor & Charles du Pont & Co. to Peter Cushman, 20 November 1816 (copy), 15 March 1817 (copy), and 11 April 1817 (copy), Letter Book 27, Charles I. du Pont, & Co., Acc. 500, EMHL; Peter Cushman to William Young & Son, 24 April 1819, William Young Papers, Historical Society of Pennsylvania, Philadelphia, Pennsylvania.

[29] Peter Cushman to William Young & Son, 24 April 1819, William Young Papers, HSP.

Congressional hearings. Du Pont answered,[30] "We had one of the spinning machines, called the Brewster, but it got out of order, and we have not put it in repair. We use the jenny entirely." William W. Young answered along similar, though inconclusive lines,[31]

> We have used the jenny and the Brewster; but in 1826 and 1827, we laid aside the Brewster, because it was out of order, and used the jenny alone. I should prefer the Brewster for spinning warp, and the jenny for spinning weft.

While no patent drawings or specifications survived the 1836 patent office fire, and only the barest of information was published in the Franklin Institute Journal, there is one, albeit meager, description of the Brewster. This by Baron Klinkowstrom as he visited the du Ponts in 1818. He wrote,[32]

> Mr. DuPont has an attractive textile mill. The spinning machine is run by water and is an entirely new invention made by Mr. Brewster of Massachusetts. I did not have a chance to sketch this beautiful mechanism, but I have a sample of finely spun yarn intended for the weaving of Merino shawls . . . (Mr. du Pont) has not only readily promised me to give freely all the information needed, but in case our textile manufacturers would like a machine he would immediately order one from Brewster on which two hundred ends can be spun. He did not think it would cost over eight hundred dollars. Brewster made his

---

[30] U. S. Congress, Evidence on Woollens, 1828, pp. 123-24.

[31] Ibid., pp. 104-5.

[32] Franklin D. Scott, trans., Baron Klinkowstrom's America, 1818-1820 (Evanston, Ill.: Northwestern University Press, 1953), pp. 52-3.

> first machine for DuPont, who paid one thousand five hundred dollars for it because of the many changes made before it was perfected. The machine I saw spins two hundred thirty threads and the whole process is done by one adult and one boy.

William Partridge also knew something about the Brewster. He had left his employment at du Pont's by September 30, 1813, so he could not have seen the spinner there. Zachariah Allen's "History" claimed that there was a Brewster in Providence in 1813; Partridge worked at the Providence Steam Factory (Providence Woolen Manufacturing Company) for three years "during the late war." He must have seen the Brewster there.[33] From the Treatise, one senses that Partridge was at least au courant with developments in woolen machinery both in America and in England. About the Brewster Partridge said,[34]

> A machine has been invented by a Mr. Brewster, for spinning by mechanical motion; I have seen good work done on it, but it is said to be too expensive, both in the first purchase and in the subsequent repairs.

As was seen above, rather apt commentary.

Samuel Slater tried the Brewster and found it unsatisfactory. Slater, Howard and Company ordered a Brewster spinner on July 4, 1823. The company planned to give it a trial, and agreed to pay two dollars per spindle for the first 250 spindles, five dollars for each additional 50.

---

[33]Journal 37, Charles I. du Pont & Co., Acc. 500, EMHL; Z. Allen, "History," Allen Papers, RIHS; Partridge, Treatise on Dying, p. 10.

[34]Partridge, Treatise on Dying, p. 46.

They actually tried a 340 spindle machine which presumably would have cost $950. Slater, Howard and Company also agreed to pay transportation from Middletown, Connecticut to Dudley, Massachusetts and to put up the team of installers. The freight alone was $97.83, round trip as it turned out, and Brewster sent his man, Crane, to install the machine. It was a long job as Mr. Crane stayed at one of the boarding houses for over six weeks.[35]

While Brewster's machine was not satisfactory to Slater, Howard and Company, just down the road, the Dudley Woollen Manufacturing Company run by Major John Brown, in October of 1823, bought a 300 spindle Brewster for $2,757.[36] (This price makes the price quote from Slater, Howard and Company questionable; there may have been cost elements there that were not recorded.) John Brown, agent, and Samuel H. Babcock, Boston merchant and principal owner of the Dudley factory, must have been satisfied with their Brewster, because in June, 1827, they bought a second one.[37] In May, 1827, Babcock had written to a fellow director, Chester Clemens,[38]

---

[35]Daybooks 5 & 6, Slater, Howard & Co., Slater Coll. BL.

[36]Daybook 6, Ledger 55, Dudley Woollen Mfg. Co., OSV.

[37]Daybook 27, Ledger 56, Dudley Woollen Mfg. Co., OSV.

[38]Samuel H. Babcock to Chester Clemens, 3 May 1827, Box 21, Dudley Woollen Mfg. Co., OSV.

> If Maj. Brown purchases a wool spinner I presume we shall not want the jennys we talked about--as our old Brewster will spin as much fillng as the new would spin warp--and we shall have cards enough and billys to supply them both--have written to Mr. Howard (William H.) who will probably furnish our 8 looms very soon.

This new Brewster cost only $1,400.[39] It is important to note that pre-spinnng with a billy or slubber was still required with the water powered spinning machine until carding mechanisms were provided with condensers. Brewster also patented in 1829 an "Eclipse" speeder which according to one historian of textile machinery, John Lord Hayes, was a cheap machine for making roving (normally associated with cotton). Hayes claimed that this patent was picked up and manufactured by the Manchester, England, firm of Sharp and Roberts in 1835.[40]

It is of course Richard Roberts of Manchester who has been credited with the invention of the self-acting mule. His mule was designed to spin and draw automatically and at the same time to make automatic adjustments for the growing fatness of the cop on which the yarn was wound. While self-acting, Robert's mule was still intermittent; that is the action of the fiber--cotton or wool--included drawing and spinning or twisting, then actually stopping, and the motions reversed to wind the yarn on to the spindle itself.

---

[39] Daybook 27, Ledger 56, Dudley Woollen Mfg. Co., OSV.

[40] John Lord Hayes, American Textile Machinery (Cambridge, Mass.: University Press, 1879), p. 386.

Until ring or cap spinning was adapted for wool, wool spinning continued to be intermittent rather than constant. Now Brewster's first patent was taken out from Barre, Vermont with two other men in 1812. This must have been the "Globe-Spinner" that Cole found the advertisement for. Other Brewster patents for spinners were in 1823, two in 1824, one each for 1827, 1829, and one in 1834 for Lewis Brewster, the administrator of Gilbert Brewster's estate.[41] Harold Catling has recently stated that, "The initiative in the design of the self-actor did not come from Roberts himself . . ."[42] Unfortunately, Catling did not choose to state whom he thought the initiative did come from. Roberts applied for his mule patent in 1829 in England; is it possible this is a case of the transmission of technology in the "opposite" direction? From America to England? David Jeremy found some Brewster correspondence indicating that Brewster was working on a self-acting mule in 1824.[43] The circumstantial evidence is certainly suggestive, but unfortunately not enough is known about the Brewster spinners.

During the wool tariff hearings in the House of Representatives in 1828 some who testified were asked about the Brewster spinner. Part of the questioning was meant to

---

[41]Burke, List of Patents, pp. 93-94.

[42]Harold Catling, The Spinning Mule (Newton Abbot, Devon: David & Charles, 1970), pp. 62, 67-82.

[43]Jeremy, "Innovation in American Textile Technology," p. 53.

get at the vital question of cost of manufacture in the woolen industry, so that if such a spinning machine were deemed satisfactory, this would provide one example of how costs could be cut in a fully progressive mill. This means that some of the more negative answers may have been less than objective or disinterested. For example, Eleuthère Irénée du Pont was less than enthusiastic about the Brewster in 1828, claimed "it got out of order," and that the company used jennies exclusively.[44] There is an undated inventory in French in Victor du Pont's hand which he probably wrote about 1818. In this inventory Victor said that his spinning machine made 80 pounds of chain (warp) per day, while five jennies spun 105 pounds of fill or weft.[45] This meant that the operation lacked 25 pounds of chain to make total use of the filling. This Victor hoped to make up with two other jennies. This particular commentary from someone closer to the factory than E. I. du Pont certainly did not make the Brewster sound so useless. However, the inventory taken after Victor's death in 1827 listed no Brewster spinner, but eleven jennies.[46]

---

[44] U. S. Congress, Evidence on Woollens, 1828, pp. 122-23.

[45] Undated memorandum, Winterthur Mss., Group 3, Papers of Victor du Pont, W3-4698, EMHL.

[46] Thomas B. Hartmann, "The du Pont Woolen Venture," unpublished Resarch Report for the Eleutherian Mills Historical Library [August 1955].

Views on the Brewster were conflicting, no question about that. Simon Newton Dexter from Oriskany (Oneida County, New York) considered spinning warp on the Brewster, "a very good mode." "However," he said, "the machine is subject to get out of repair."[47] That complaint was so universal, it is impossible to dismiss, but the possibility must be posed that the fault was not only with the machine, but with the lack of skillful mechanics to fix it. James Shepherd of Northampton, Massachusetts, felt the Brewster was best for spinning third and fourth grade wools, and claimed that their own spinning costs at Northampton were cut 50 percent or more, probably, although his statement is not entirely clear on this point, because he could use women instead of men to spin.[48] It also was possible that his cost decreased because the large numbers of spindles employed by Brewsters simply increased the productivity per man. When Samuel Slater and Edward Howard tried their Brewster in 1823, they tried a young woman as "tender."[49] Possibly, the premise of using cheaper female labor to spin was the rationale for the experiment. When that proved unfeasible, Slater, Howard and Company returned their Brewster spinner to its builder.

---

[47]U. S. Congress, Evidence on Woollens, 1828, p. 80.

[48]Ibid., pp. 88-89.

[49]Daybook 6, 16 March 1824, "Susan Moffatt tending Brewster frame, 23 1/2 ds @ 14/ per wk, ($) 9.13 1/2." Slater, Howard & Co., Slater Coll., BL.

At Babcock's carding and roping was subcontracted to a team of two men and nine or ten children. In 1830 three women were listed as spinning on the Brewster and four men simply as spinning. It is a distinct possibility that girls had been tending the Brewster since October 1823, but as they earned weekly wages rather than being paid by the pound or run, they were not identified until 1830.[50]

At du Pont in 1818 there were four male spinners and three females. Presumably it was the latter that spun on "the machine." By 1822 all six spinners were men, and while one or two of the men may have operated billies, no one was recorded as spinning on a Brewster.[51]

Aaron Tufts, another Dudley, Massachusetts manufacturer testified that jennies were considered preferable to Brewsters so the Tuft's factory had never used one.[52] On the other hand, William W. Young testified that he "should prefer the Brewster for spinning warp, the jenny for spinning weft," even though his own machine was out of order.[53] Of the others who testified, James Wolcott, Jr., and Joshua Clapp had Brewsters in their factories in 1820, but were not asked to comment on them at the hearings.

---

[50]Journals 45-49; Ledgers 55-57, Labor Account, Dudley Woollen Mfg. Co., OSV.

[51]Journals 37-39; Daybook 46, Ledger 56, Charles I. du Pont Co., Acc. 500, EMHL.

[52]U. S. Congress, Evidence on Woollens, 1828, p. 23.

[53]Ibid., pp. 104-5.

Abraham Marland, Abraham Schenck, Joshua W. Pierce, and Jonas B. Brown probably had some form of power spinning in their factories, but did not testify on the subject; William Phillips from Wallkill, New York did not own one, and so did not know whether or not it was preferable; William R. Dickinson from Steubenville, Ohio was not asked. Both Benjamin Poor and Theodore Chase were Boston merchants and investors in woolen factories. Neither claimed knowledge of the manufacturing processes. Out of twelve woolen agents who testified in 1828, six definitely used Brewster spinners at one time, and three more very likely did.[54]

Out of 250 woolen factories in an area from Maine to Maryland whose manuscripts survived from the 1820 Census, there were reported twenty-one water powered spinning machines in fifteen factories. Fifteen out of twenty-one machines were definitely Brewsters, and very likely so were the other six.[55] Six factories in Connecticut (out of 43) used water power for spinning. The other nine factories were well scattered: two in Massachusetts, two in New York, one each in Rhode Island and New Hampshire, two in New Jersey, two in Pennsylvania, and two in Delaware. In 1832 Gilbert Brewster was listed as owner of a cotton mill in Poughkeepsie.[56] By 1834, he was no longer alive as

[54]Ibid., passim.

[55]1820 Manufactures Census, passim.

[56]_McLane Report_, 2:56.

Lewis Brewster was listed in Burke as the administrator for G. Brewster's final spinning patent dated December 17, 1834.[57]

In the three factories studied in depth jenny spinning continued alongside Brewster spinning. Even at Babcock's the spinners continued to use jennies along with the two Brewsters. One reason for this may have been that warp and filling yarns had to be spun in opposite directions--open band or closed band (S or Z twist).[58] In theory jennies or Brewsters could spin in either direction, but Brewsters seem to have been used mostly for coarser warp yarns and the jennies were probably adapted accordingly.

It is unfortunate that Gilbert Brewster has proven to be so elusive. In a heroic account of invention, Brewster surely would have been a star. But perhaps the fact that a Gilbert Brewster left only vague traces says something about the whole genre of American inventiveness. It was commonplace, or at least deemed so in the early nineteenth century. Economics played both a superficial role and a deeper one. Machinery was looked to by American manufacturers as a means to save labor and therefore reduce costs. What matters in this instance is not just British competition; in woolens, labor costs were not that much cheaper in

---

[57]Burke, List of Patents, p. 91.

[58]Partridge, Treatise on Dying, p. 43.

England than the United States. Although they were not very articulate about it, American manufacturers were certainly aware that cheaper products found broader markets. But woolen broadcloth can in no way be construed as a cheap product. What could make it less expensive to manufacture was machinery--machinery would reduce labor costs and standardize the quality of the finished product. That finished product would never have the quality of the finest imported broadcloth, but ultimately it would serve most American needs. As it turned out, this is not exactly what happened. American broadcloth did become cheaper, but even more significant were the substitutes for superfine cloth--satinet and cassimeres. As production for these woolens was mechanized, a whole new industry developed, but this is a story for a later time frame.

Gilbert Brewster and the commonplaceness of American inventiveness had economic roots in the very richness of the country. Natural resources including land and power provided the economic base that allowed American sons (and daughters to a limited extent) to go to school, to become literate and skilled in basic arithmetic. Knowledge of letters and numbers--this was the basis for widespread skill in mechanics among Americans.

Warping and Sizing

After the wool was spun into warp or chain yarn, it was wound from the spindle cop on to spools on a simple spooling machine manned by children. In the process broken yarns were joined together. Spools of yarn were placed on wooden pins from which the yarn was drawn off and measured by winding on pegs or on to a warping mill. The yarn was wound on to the warping mill in units of one-half beers or half porties, nineteen to twenty-one yarns each. Every effort was made to keep an even tension on the warper and to keep the yarns from tangling. The yarn was measured--so many revolutions on the warper to the skein, then removed to be sized in glue.[59]

Fineness of the yarn determined the width of the cloth and the density of the warp yarns (numbers of warp yarns per measure of width). This, in turn, determined the fineness and therefore weight of the fill. The fill or weft yarns were spun coarser than the warp, and they were given less twist. William Partridge included a complex table from which one could make calculations starting from the degree of fineness that the warp yarns had been spun.[60] This

---

[59]Duhamel du Monceau, "Art de la Draperie," pp. 131-32, Planche V and VI; Herman Freudenberger, _The Waldstein Woolen Mill_ (Cambridge: Harvard University Press, 1963), pp. 26-27, plates 12 and 13 (see illus 5 & 6).

[60]Partridge, _Treatise on Dying_, between pp. 52 and 53.

degree of fineness related directly to the quality of the raw wool and the nature and quality of the dyes used on it. The finer the wool could be spun, the finer became the finished woolen cloth. The quality of the wool itself was the first variable, but the skills of the spinner and the capacity of the machines, also determined the fineness of the warp yarns and ultimately the fineness of the cloth.

Before the warp was turned on to the loom, it was scoured (according to Rees) and sized in a glue mix to give it strength (according to all authorities). Sizing was simply a matter of soaking the beers (or porties) of yarn in a thin glue solution and carefully drying the yarn--outside in good weather, or in wool drying houses with stoves.

In August 1826 Zachariah Allen went on a short trip to visit woolen mills and machine shops "to notice improvements in machinery &c." One objective of his tour was to look at the warper and dresser invented and built by Baily Ammidon of Dover, New Hampshire. Allen saw the machine at Shepherd's in Northampton and described it thus in his journal.[61]

> His machine for warping & sizing broad cloth first attracted our attention, it being the immediate object of our visit to his mill. The yarn is first run from the cops upon bobbins, which are placed in a creel like the cotton bobbins. The thread passes from the bobbins under calendar rollers like those for the operation in warping and sizing cotton warps, except the substitution of glue for starch. After passing

[61]Zachariah Allen, "Diary," Allen Papers, RIHS.

> twice back & forth a distance of about 6 feet over cylinders made open with wire like drums to allow the air to come to the thread it is wound upon a large reel about nine feet long and two feet 6 inches diameter, which as a slight traversing movement to lay the thread regularly, and a spiral gearing to give the count of the length of the warp. From this reel the yarn is wound hard upon the yarn beam (of the loom) by hand.

Allen was not hugely impressed by Ammidon's dresser and warper. He himself had developed a type of rack or frame for drying the warps and felt that his was a better technique than Ammidon's wire drums which wound the yarn in layers, subjecting it to potential sticking.[62]

In September 1827 Samuel H. Babcock wrote to Chester Clemens to inquire if the Ammidon warper and dresser could be used in the Dudley factory.[63] In the next few months Babcock, Major Brown, and Clemens investigated the machine. At one point they were assured by William H. Howard, the Worcester machinist, that a machine could be built without danger of patent infringement and that indeed Mr. Hurd had had one made at Lowell.[64] By April the following year, Babcock had determined to buy one from Ammidon himself.[65]

---

[62]Ibid.

[63]Samuel H. Babcock to Chester Clemens, 5 October 1827, Box 21, Dudley Woollen Mfg. Co., OSV.

[64]Samuel H. Babcock to John Brown, 29 February 1828, Box 21, Dudley Woollen Mfg. Co., OSV.

[65]Samuel H. Babcock to John Brown, 18 April 1828, Box 21, Dudley Woollen Mfg. Co., OSV.

By August 15, 1828, the machine had been installed and $300 paid for it.[66].

The machine did not function flawlessly. In March 1829 Babcock wrote to Brown,[67]

> The warper and dresser will certainly do well when understood by Mr. Knap--it has been successfully try'd in several places and I hope you will not give up but persevere till it works well.

Four years later Babcock wrote Clemens, "Keep Mr. Ammidon with you till the dresser is in order and get a good man upon it."[68]

In 1829 the Charles I. du Pont Company bought an Ammidon warper and dresser. In the same year the du Ponts made their first contact with William H. Howard.[69] He may have been the link for transmitting this particular bit of technical advice.

Weaving

Applying inanimate power to the loom was a critical aspect of textile mechanization. Yet the development of this mechanization is somewhat obscure. The main reason the development is hard to follow probably has to do with

---

[66]Daybook 30, Ledger 56, Dudley Woollen Mfg. Co., OSV.

[67]Samuel H. Babock to John Brown, 24 March 1829, Box 21, Dudley Woollen Mfg. Co., OSV.

[68]Samuel H. Babcock to Chester Clemens, 13 September 1833, Box 21, Dudley Woollen Mfg. Co., OSV.

[69]Daybook 48, Ledger 57, Charles I. du Pont Co., EMHL.

the commonplaceness of weaving and the difficulty of making patentable improvements. The Singer History of Technology gives considerable credit for a "first" power loom to Edward Cartwright in 1787 but acknowledges that his was a "very imperfect machine."[70]

The loom pictured in Rees (see illus. 29) is the Scotch type wiper or cam loom developed at almost the same time by two Englishmen, Robert Miller and John Austin. These essentially were mechanized fly-shuttles using cam shafts to raise and lower warp yarns, and another set of cams to throw the shuttle back and forth. This second cam set was a substitute for the springs of the fly-shuttle, but this loom still used springs and weights to beat the cloth.

The problem with mechanizing looms was that of timing the various mechanical operations: the raising of the heddles and forming of the shed, the passage of the shuttle, beating with the beater or reeds, and the continued winding on of the finished cloth to the cloth beam. This last was particularly troublesome, because as weaving proceeded, the thickness of the cloth wound on the beam required the revolving movement to be slowed down.

William Radcliffe of Stockport, Lancashire devised a series of weights and ratchets to take up the woven cloth,

---

[70] T. K. Derry and Trevor I. Williams, A Short History of Technology (Oxford: Oxford University Press, 1960), pp. 564-66.

SOURCE: Rees's Cyclopaedia, 1814.

Illus. 29. Austin's Loom.

but automatic changes in speed came later with the application of various cranks and gears.[71] Power loom weaving had to be interrupted every four to six inches by the need to regulate the speed of the winding on of cloth, and until the invention of the self-acting temple, by the need to prevent the woven cloth from "drawing in" or narrowing on the far side of the reeds.[72]

William Horrocks was given credit by Radcliffe in collaborating with him in developing the crank to wind on cloth to the cloth beam, but Horrocks' main contribution to textile technology was the adoption of cranks instead of springs to operate the reed or batten (see illus. 30).[73]

Another significant innovation by Radcliffe was the separation of the sizing process from weaving. In cotton, mechanized sizing was perfected by Francis Cabot Lowell and Paul Moody before Lowell's death in 1817, and this was most important in accelerating the pace of cotton weaving. As was seen above, glue sizing was not mechanized for woolens until the mid-1820s. Woolen cloth productivity was not nearly so dependent on mechanized sizing, because even with

---

[71] Richard L. Hills, Power in the Industrial Revolution (Manchester: University of Manchester Press, 1970), pp. 221-24.

[72] P. Ellis, "The Techniques of Weaving," in Wool Textile Industry, ed. Jenkins, pp. 129-30; Jeremy, "Innovation in American Textile Technology," pp. 59-60.

[73] Hills, Power in the Industrial Revolution, p. 224.

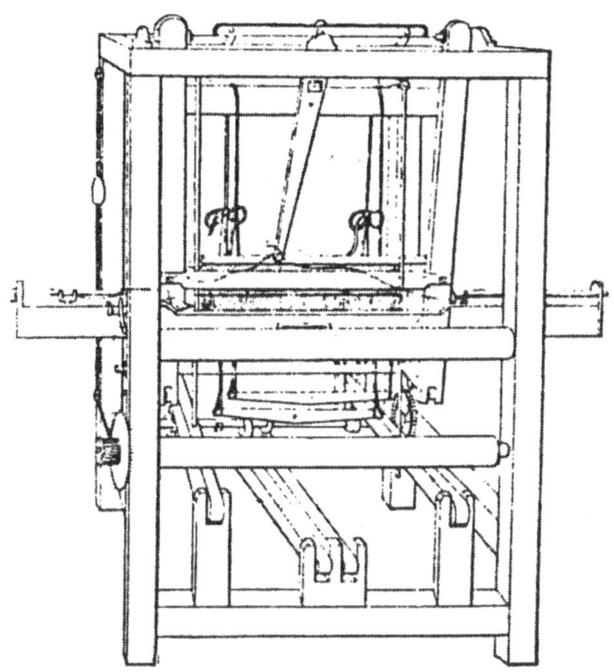

SOURCE: J. Geraint Jenkins, <u>The Wool Textile Industry in Great Britain</u>.

Illus. 30. Horrocks' or Scotch Loom.

power looms, the weaving pace continued to be slow compared to cotton.[74]

What Lowell had seen in England in the winter of 1810-11 was very likely Radcliffe-Horrocks' type of cloth production. Yet the looms that Lowell and Moody built were cam looms (see illus. 31 & 32)[75]--one would have to say more like John Austin's pictured in Rees than William Horrocks' loom. Horrocks' Scotch loom apparently was used in this country; it was introduced by William Gilmour or Gilmore in about 1814. John Slater was among the first to see it, and according to George S. White, John Slater was unable to prevail among his other partners, including brother Samuel, to launch into the manufacture of cotton cloth at that time.[76] Gilmore patented a power loom in 1820, but nothing about a Gilmore loom was found in the National Archives. Through the agency of such machinists as David Wilkinson (Slater's brother-in-law), according to White, the loom proliferated in Rhode Island.[77]

---

[74]Jeremy, "Innovation in American Textile Technology," p. 55.

[75]George S. White, Memoir of Samuel Slater (Philadelphia, 1836; repr. New York: A. M. Kelley, 1967), p. 387; Spalding, "Boston Mercantile Community," p. 23; Ware, New England Cotton Manufacture, ch. 5.

[76]White, Memoirs of Slater, p. 387; Bagnall, Textile Industries, pp. 546-48.

[77]Bagnall, Textile Industries, pp. 546-48.

SOURCE. Richard L. Hills, Power in the Industrial Revolution.

Illus. 31. Cam or Wiper Loom (front view).

SOURCE: Richard L. Hills, Power in the Industrial Revolution.

Illus. 32. Cam or Wiper Loom (side view).

Power looms came to the woolen industry in New England in the mid to late 1820s, and apparently came primarily through the agency of one man--William H. Howard of Worcester and later, Philadelphia. This particular Mr. Howard has proven more elusive than Gilbert Brewster. Thomas R. Navin traced one William Howard, "machine maker," from a Slater owned spinning mill in Warwick, Rhode Island to the Natick Manufacturing Company where he formed a partnership with another "Slater alumnus," William Potter. Navin claimed it was William Howard who taught Paul Whitin all of Slater's secrets so that Whitin could go on to be one of New England's more important machinery manufacturers.[78] It is not known whether or not this was the same Howard since so little is known of him. Charles G. Washburn one of Worcester's local historians had William H. Howard firmly placed in Worcester by at least 1820. (None of this contradicts the above, of course.) At one point, Howard was a partner of William Hovey who made his name inventing and manufacturing shearing machines. According to Washburn, Hovey and Howard began making power looms modeled on the common Scotch type. Washburn claimed that Howard looms were sold to Goodell in Millbury, Massachusetts, Colonel Shepherd in Northampton, to Pameacha in Middletown, Connecticut, to Wolcottville in Litchfield County, and to

---

[78]Thomas R. Navin, The Whitin Machine Works since 1831: A Textile Machinery Company in an Industrial Village, (Cambridge: Harvard University Press, 1950), p. 17.

Zachariah Allen in Providence. All were well-known woolen factories as were their proprietors. Howard definitely sold looms both to Slater, Howard and Company and to Babcock's in Dudley; these sales were recorded in account books from 1825 to 1829. One William H. Howard moved to Philadelphia in 1830 or 1831; he was likely the same. In 1832 Phelps and Bickford of Worcester became licensed to sell "Howard Improved Patent Broadlooms."[79]

There clearly was such a patent dated February 12, 1830 (see illus. 33, & app. C).[80] Careful examination of the specifications and drawing of Howard's loom show that Howard had substituted cams and a pendular movement for the crank that would regulate the movement of the reeds or beater. As Richard L. Hills said of Horrocks' cranks,[81]

> They gave positive movement in both directions, but their disadvantages were that the weft was not given a sharp enough blow and the reed advanced too soon so that it caught the shuttle in the shed.

Horrocks solved the problem with levers, but Howard's solution seems simpler and nicer, and seemingly not very different from Richard Roberts' patent of 1823 with "two driving shafts, one for driving the treadles, and the other

---

79Charles G. Washburn, "Worcester--Manufacturing and Mechanical Industries," in *History of Worcester County*, comp. H. Hamilton Hurd, 2:1605-16.

80William H. Howard's vibrating cam loom, "Restored Patent Specifications," 10:139-40 and Patent Drawing no. 5826, NA.

81Hills, *Power in the Industrial Revolution*, p. 224.

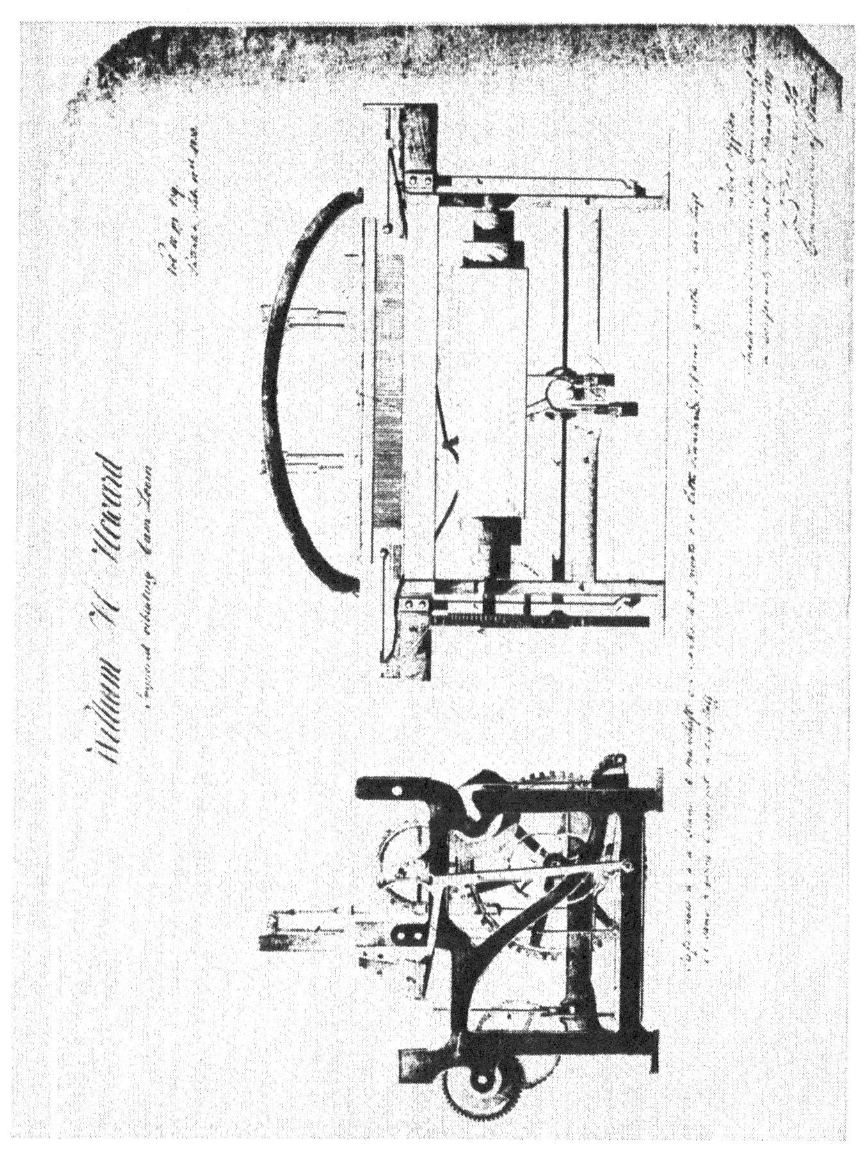

SOURCE: National Archives.

Illus. 33. William Howard's Power Loom.

for the batten--the former also provided the striking power for throwing the shuttles."[82]

Stop-action for broken yarns, either in the warp or in the shuttle, did not seem to be an American development in woolen weaving technology before 1830. It is doubtful that broad woolen looms needed stop-action as their speed was probably only a little more than twenty picks per minute based on production of seven yards per twelve-hour day. As productivity reached ten yards per day per loom,[83] picks per minute reached the rate of nearly thirty. This, of course, was for broadcloth; cassimere was something

---

[82]Ellis, "Techniques of Weaving," p. 129.

[83]From Slater, Howard and Company records fly-shuttle broadcloth weaving averaged about 4 1/2 to five yards in 1824. Power broad looms in the first years (Slater, Howard & Co. 1828) produced about seven yards per day. By 1832 this production was nearly ten yards. This comes to .225 inches per minute for the fly shuttle, based on a twelve-hour work day, or thirteen to fourteen picks per minute at sixty picks to the inch. For the early power looms .35 inches per minute or twenty-one picks could be produced, and .5 inches per minute or thirty picks for the 1832 weavers.

Partridge's specifications show the finest cloth at:

$$\frac{4.75 \text{ Runs} \times 1600 \text{ yd.} \times 51 \text{ lb.} \times 36''}{(12/4 \text{ qr. width} \times 36'')(36'' \times 54'')}$$

$$= \frac{387{,}000}{5832} = 66.5 \text{ picks/inch}$$

Third quality cloth:

$$\frac{3.75 \text{ Runs} \times 1600 \text{ yd.} \times 50 \text{ lb.} \times 36''}{(11.5/4 \times 36'')(36'' \times 54'')}$$

$$= \frac{300{,}000}{5589} = 53.7 \text{ picks/inch}$$

else. By 1829 power looms for these narrow cloths were operating at a level between fifty and sixty picks per minute.[84] Satinet was surely faster; on a per inch basis it was nearly two times faster than cassimere, but since no yarn specifications for satinet were uncovered, it is impossible to be more precise.[85] By 1830, 120 picks per minute in cotton was not uncommon so it would not be illogical to assume satinet with its cotton warps at say 100 picks per minute.[86] By 1830 satinet was woven at a rate of twenty yards per day; for a twelve-hour day, this comes to sixty inches per hour.

William Partridge saw power looms at Shepherd's factory in Northampton before he published his <u>Treatise on Dying</u> in

---

[84]Single milled cassimere according to Partridge:

$$\frac{7.6 \text{ Runs} \times 1600 \text{ yd.} \times 16.5 \text{ lb.} \times 36''}{(4.25/4 \times 36'')(45'' \times 36'')}$$

$$= \frac{200,640}{1721.25} = 116.5 \text{ picks/inch}$$

9 to 9.5 yards per day in twelve hours:

$$\frac{9.25 \times 36''}{(12 \text{ hr})(60)} = \frac{333}{720} = .46'' \text{ per minute or}$$

$$.46 \times 116.5 = 54 \text{ picks/minute}$$

[85]Satinet weaving was over twenty yards per day per loom in 1830 at Slater, Howard & Co..

[86]Hills, <u>Power in the Industrial Revolution</u>, p. 227. In 1826 one twenty-four yard piece of cotton could be woven in a day of probably twelve hours, 9/8 width. At 100 shoots to the inch, this would come to 120 picks per minute. (Seventy-two inches per hour.) Also, Jeremy, "Innovation in American Textile Technology," p. 59.

1823. The reference by Charles Washburn that William H. Howard had sold looms to Shepherd is corroborated by Zachariah Allen who described Shepherd's looms in August, 1825, as having "the cam motion instead of the crank motion."[87] Partridge described the cloth he saw woven on Shepherd's power looms as follows, "(It) appeared to be very passable, quite as good as that which was done by hand in the same factory."[88]

This statement reflected a very common sentiment among early nineteenth-century manufacturers. Mechanization not only would increase productivity, save labor and costs, but increase the overall standards of workmanship. These standards are not yet related to precision instruments whose measurements and calibrations are far more perfect than human eyesight or movement. But a point-of-view is represented--that quantity and speed often outweighed quality in many a value system, and yet overall quality actually could be improved or at least standardized by machinery. As Partridge put it,[89]

> weaving is seldom well done in this country, and the greater part of it is wretchedly performed, and it would be a great advantage to the woollen manufacturer, could a machine be invented to perform the work.

---

[87]Z. Allen, "Diary," Allen Papers, RIHS.

[88]Partridge, Treatise on Dying, p. 60.

[89]Ibid. James Shepherd manufactured wool from 42 picks to the inch to 56 picks in 1825 on the power loom, Allen's "Diary," Allen Papers, RIHS.

Finishing and Dressing

Finishing and dressing the cloth were the final steps in the manufacture of fine woolen cloth. These processes seemed to be a rich combination of traditional technology mixed with up-to-date mechanization. Traditional technology was perhaps most tenacious in the chemistry of scouring and fulling. Soap, sig, and pig dung (the last two for their ammonia content) were age-old detergents, the latter two a good deal cheaper than soap. Fullers earth was known and recommended by such as Partridge, but it too was expensive, and little evidence of regular use was found in this country before 1832.[90]

Scouring

Scouring was what Rees' writer called the first process after the cloth was taken from the loom; Partridge called it braying.[91] The cloth was thoroughly wetted down, the alkali (ammonium hydroxide) mix of urine and dung entered into combination with the grease and oils in order to remove them from the cloth. Pounding stocks were used, but they were supposed to pound only on layers of cloth. Care was taken not to allow the process to go on too long or to

---

[90] Partridge, *Treatise on Dying*, pp. 61, 85.

[91] Rees, *Cyclopaedia*, 38: "Woolen Manufacture;" Partridge, *Treatise on Dying*, pp. 60-64.

get too hot. At this stage the clothier did not want the woolen fibers to felt.[92]

Steam scouring with fullers earth was recommended for trial by Partridge, but his brief discussion of it was more theoretical than practical.[93] Since fullers earth was so seldom referred to among American manufacturers, it is doubtful Partridge's techniques were given much trial.

Fulling

Next the cloth was dried on the tenters, and then burled. In burling women removed knots and double yarns from the cloth. The women needed a good north light, a long bench to stretch the cloth on, and something to keep the cloth from slipping such as emery. They burled with burling irons, then perched the cloth with linting irons.[94] Finally, the cloth was ready to be fulled. Partridge here mentioned a poacher as a substitute for fulling stocks, but he recommended that it be used mainly for satinets. The essence of what happened in the fulling mill was that the cloth was pounded and pounded in soapy water with very heavy wooden mallets for from fourteen to eighteen hours. Finally, the cloth was rinsed, preferably in fullers earth.[95]

---

[92]Partridge, <u>Treatise on Dying</u>, p. 61.

[93]Ibid., pp. 62-63. [94]Ibid., pp. 65-66.

[95]Ibid. It will be recalled that the Hollingworths had a poacher at the Woodstock mill.

Partridge described the process of steam fulling. Rees' writer in 1818 did not mention this technique. Steam fulling did not work well where Partridge saw it in Bloomfield, New Jersey. Partridge felt that there was considerable potential in the process, but that the lack of controlled experimentation with the temperature of the steam meant that inexperienced workmen would produce defective cloth.[96]

Steam fulling was observed by Zachariah Allen in Yorkshire in 1825, particularly at William Hirst's in Leeds. Hirst claimed both English and American patents for this process. It seems to have been a matter of introducing steam right into the fulling mill itself, the idea being to save on soap which was so expensive.[97] Babcock may have tried something like it in 1830, but without much success.[98]

Gigging

The final finishing processes were more modernized by mechanization. The first process was raising the nap while the cloth was still wet. The level of mechanization of

---

[96]Ibid., pp. 71-73.

[97]Zachariah Allen, "Travel Journal," pp. 5-8, 45-46, Allen Papers, RIHS. Hirst's patent was reported in the Franklin Journal and American Mechanic's Magazine, 2:90 (August 1826).

[98]Samuel H. Babcock to Nathanial Lyon, 13 September 1830, and 30 September 1830, Box 21, Dudley Woollen Mfg. Co., OSV.

raising, dubbing, timming, or gigging is a matter about which today there is some dispute. The gig-mill (see illus. 34) is only slightly younger than the fulling mill, meaning that it went back to medieval times. But it had been the subject of Luddite protests in the eighteenth and nineteenth centuries in English woolen manufacturing centers, because it was a type of labor-saving and time-saving device that could eliminate jobs. Yet even using a gig-mill, the raising operation could take, according to Partridge, eight to sixteen hours.[99] The mill was uncomplicated, consisting of rollers for the cloth and a set of hoops on which frames of teasels were attached, forming cylinders about the diameter of a medium-sized barrel. Partridge described a "course" as six runnings of the cloth in one direction, six in the other, and recommended ten to twelve courses per each forty-two yard piece. After each course, the teasels had to be removed and cleaned, usually by a small boy with an iron comb. Teasels required special care; they were expensive, and did not last long given the work required of them. Partridge's view of American gig-mills was that they were "miserably deficient."[100]

The current dispute both here and in England revolves around the question of whether or not gig-mills were

---

[99]Partridge, Treatise on Dying, pp. 77-78.

[100]Ibid., p. 81.

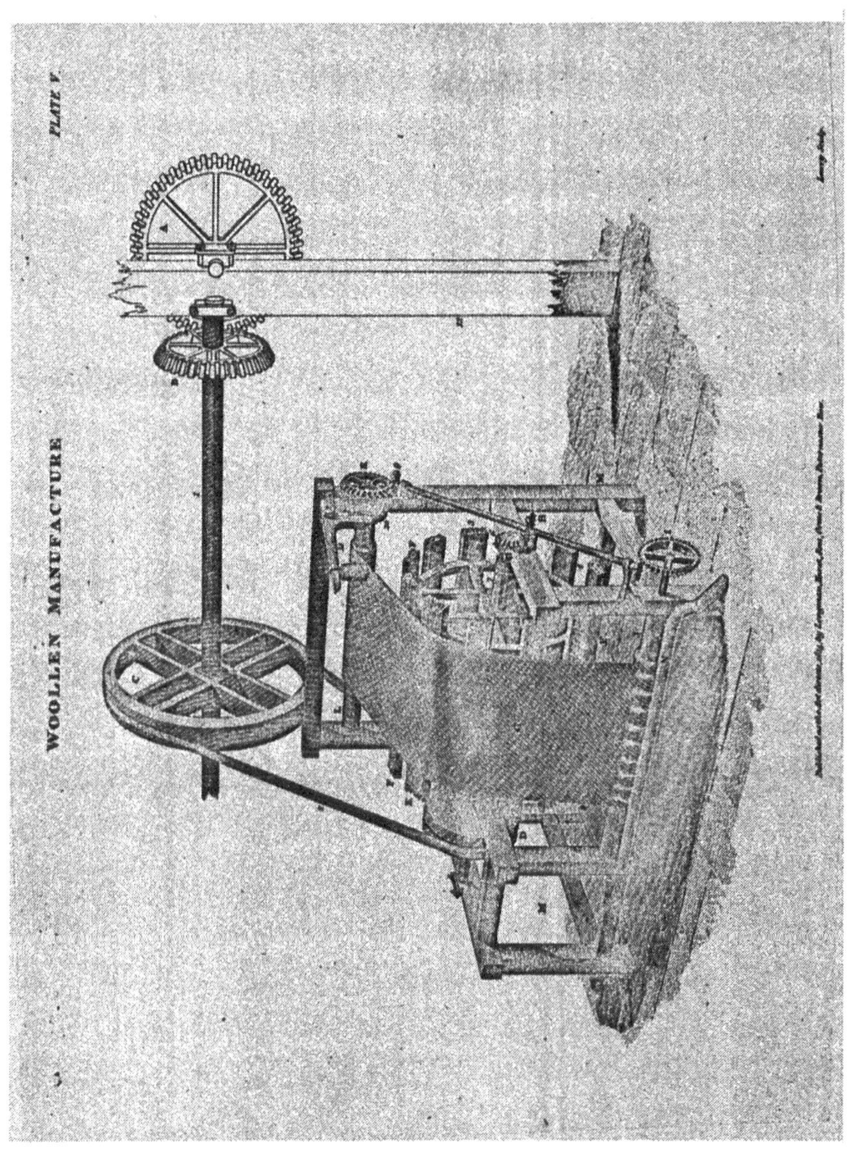

SOURCE: Rees' Cyclopaedia, 1815.

Illus. 34. Gig Mill, or Nap Raising Machine.

commonplace. Not many were listed in the 1820 Manufacturers Census, but it is possible they were so common, they were assumed to be a part of the most ordinary woolen mill. The problem in England is not quite the same; there it is a question of whether or not manufacturers genuinely were intimidated by Luddite behavior to the extent that they did not use gig-mills, and how late in time the English continued to use old-fashioned hand-held teasel frames.[101] Certainly Zachariah Allen saw any number of gig-mills in England in 1825.[102]

Partridge's views were very clear; since "wages are full 40 percent higher (in the United States) than in England," the gig-mill was an important labor-saving and money-saving machine. Well-managed he figured that one machine should be able to raise the nap of sixty yards of broadcloth per day.[103]

When Zachariah Allen visited Yorkshire in 1825, he saw some nap raising machines that particularly appealed to him (see illus. 35). It is not possible to say what parts of these machines were new to him. He made a series of drawings which are very similar to the drawings that exist

---

[101]Ponting, Woollen Industry of South-west England, pp. 71-74.

[102]Z. Allen, "Travel Journal," passim, Allen Papers, RIHS.

[103]Partridge, Treatise on Dying, pp. 73-74.

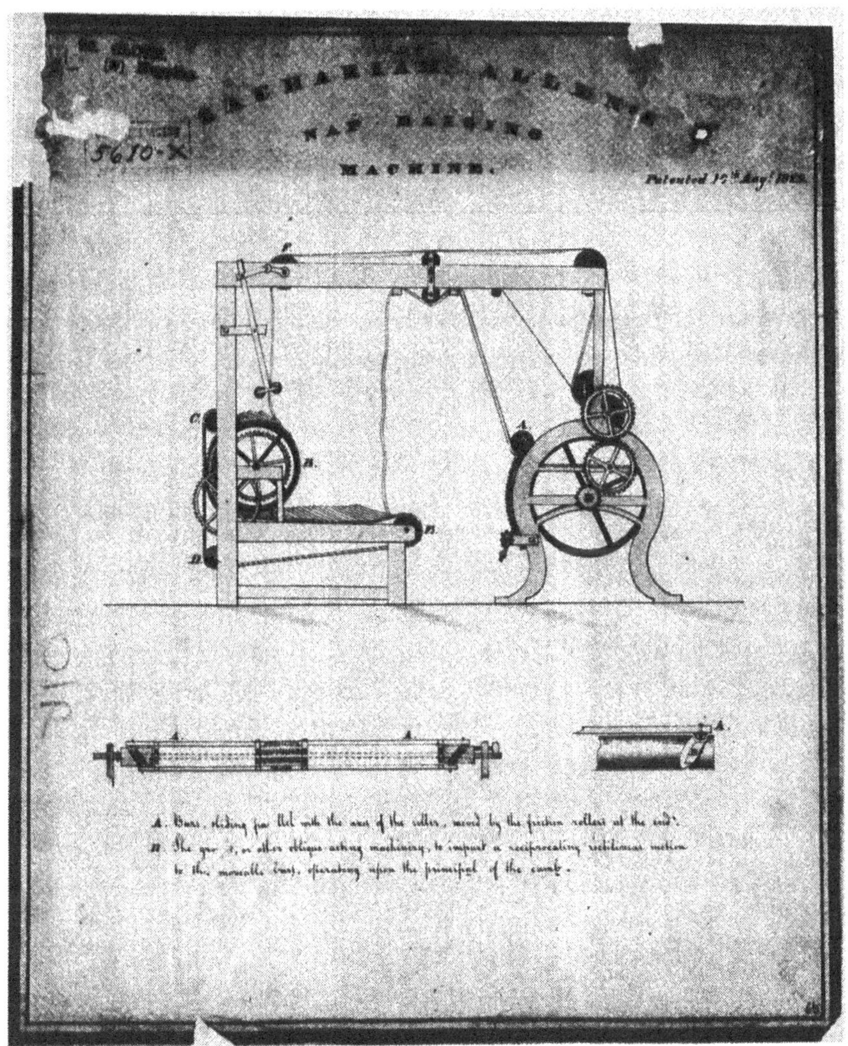

SOURCE: National Archives.

Illus. 35. Allen's Nap Raising Machine.

for his 1829 patent.[104] What he claimed was new in 1829 were two things: a roller device and bar for keeping the cloth smooth before the nap was raised, and a technique for compactly folding the piece of cloth after each run-through in the machine. Within less than a year, Allen had improved on the above system with a very compact rack and pinion geared system to stretch the cloth around and between rollers, raising a small surface of cloth with wire gigs.[105]

Tentering

During the napping process, the cloth was kept constantly wet. The next step was to block and to dry the cloth on the tenter hooks. Partridge's prescription was the following:[106]

> A cloth intended for seven quarters, being fulled into six and a half within the lists, is stretched to seven in the tenters, and is pulled in length, one yard in twenty beyond what it measured when it came from the stocks.

Care was taken not to allow the cloth to become hardened by heat or by sunlight.

---

[104] Z. Allen, "Travel Journal," pp. 34-35, Allen papers, RIHS; Z. Allen's Nap Raising Machine patent of 10 August 1829, "Restored Patents, Specifications," 8:393-94 and Patent Drawing no. 5610, NA.

[105] Z. Allen's Napping machine patent of 2 February 1830, "Restored Patent, Specifications," 10:411, Patent Drawing no. 5811, NA.

[106] Partridge, <u>Treatise on Dying</u>, pp. 82-83.

Shearing

The process of shearing would seem to have been the tinkerer's dream. Many, many patents were issued in England and America for shearing machines from 1787 in England, from 1792 in the United States. Traditional shearers used those great iron shears that weighed fifty or so pounds plus weights. Various levers were manipulated to open and close the shears. Cropping and napping were considered highly skilled, and the whole process was very cumbersome and slow (see illus. 14). Even the new gigs and shearing machines of the nineteenth century were slow. One of the early shearing machines was advertised as shearing one yard per minute. What the broadside neglected to state was that one had to put the cloth through the machine a half dozen times or more to achieve the desired effect.[107]

Rees' Cyclopaedia described John Harmer's mechanized shearing machine (see illus. 36) patented for woolen cloth in 1794, for fustian a few years earlier. As with many of these early machines, the mechanization consisted of providing inanimate power by means of endless belts and in cam shafts; this case, moving the cloth by power, and opening and closing the shears with a very simple cam shaft.[108] In 1823 Partridge was still more favorably

---

[107]Broadside from Hall & Weld, Boston, Oct. 3, 1810, Charles I. du Pont Co., Acc. 500, EMHL.

[108]Rees, Cyclopaedia, 38: "Woollen Manufacture."

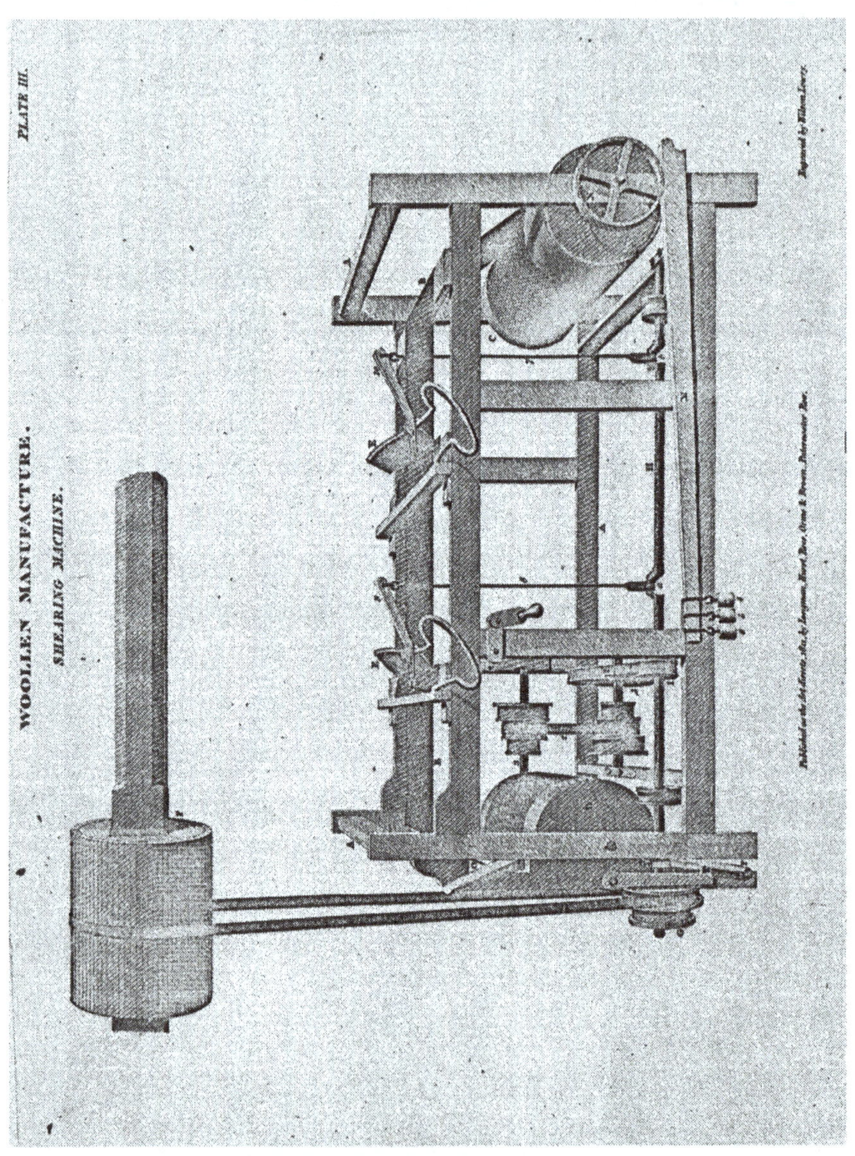

SOURCE: Rees' Cyclopaedia, 1811.

Illus. 36. Harmer's Shearing Machine.

disposed toward Harmer's frame than any of the new machines. By 1825, however, Zachariah Allen was recording in his "Travel Journal" that the old shears with or without power would shortly be displaced by the more efficient "new spiral knives."[109]

Samuel G. Dorr of Albany is the person most often given credit for inventing spiral shears. There is no patent drawing of Dorr's machine, but there is a written specification for what he called his "wheel of knives":[110]

> . . . A wheel having twelve spring knives regulated by two metal wheels in a metal frame consisting of three metal posts placed within a wooden frame, and encompassed by two brass rings having four tangent knives so as that in its revolution the edges of each coming in contact operate in the manner of shears. In the said brass rings are also placed four rollers having sliders, which bring the cloth up to the said tangent knives, and twelve other rollers to protect the cloth from the injury of the wheel of knives. A revolving shaft having a brush thereon is placed at the bottom of the third wheel, so as on the one side to raise the knap of the cloth for shearing and on the other to brush off the flocks . . .

An advertisement from Boston dated 1810 was found in the du Pont papers (see illus. 37-38). The machine clearly shows spiral knives. It may have been Dorr's machine, or possibly Beriah Swift's 1814 patent, or even possibly William Hovey's "Ontario Machine."[111]

---

[109] Z. Allen, "Travel Journal," p. 18, Allan Papers, RIHS.

[110] Samuel G. Dorr's patent for a "wheel of knives," 20 October, 1792, "Restored Patent, Specifications," 1:42-43, NA.

[111] Broadside from Hall and Weld, Winterflur Mss. Group 3, Papers of Victor du Pont, W3-2715, EMHL.

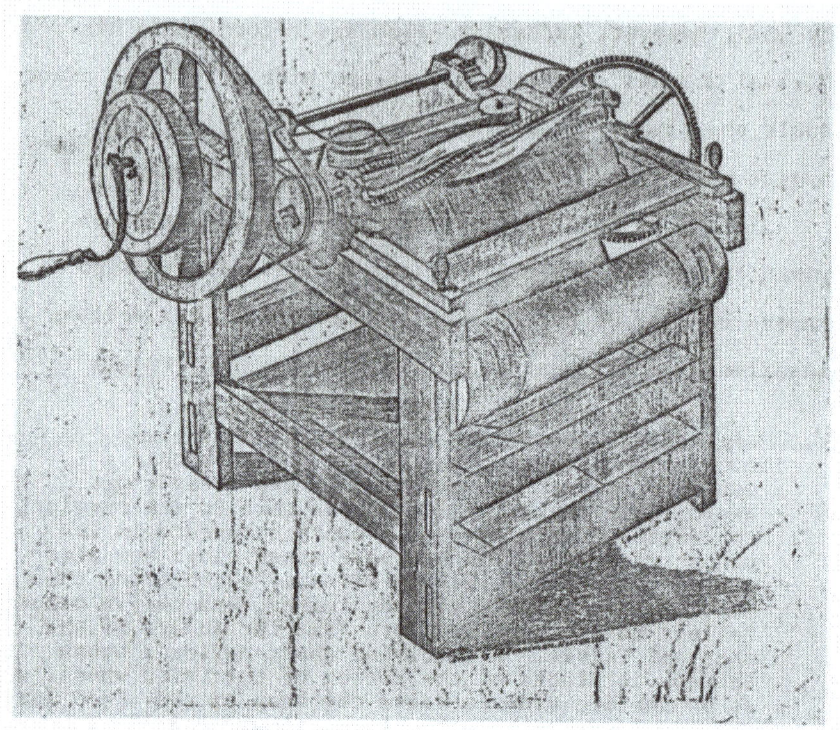

SOURCE: Courtesy of the Eleutherian Mills Historical Library.

Illus. 37. Unknown 1810 Shearing Machine.

DEAR SIR,

In a country like that of the United States, where the number of inhabitants are small in proportion to the quantity of land fit for cultivation, most of its members must be immediately or remotely interested in the encouragement and success of labour saving Machines, according to their relative situations, and the importance of the branches they may be designed to promote. Influenced by the correctness of this principle, we take the liberty of recommending to your inspection and patronage, a MACHINE FOR SHEARING WOOLEN CLOTHS, which has lately been completed and secured to the inventor by patent. The simplicity of this machine, in design and construction, has obtained the decided approbation of many of the best judges in the United States, and experience (the best proof of machinery) hath fully demonstrated in shearing upwards of twenty thousand yards, that it is not less to be admired for accuracy of performance, and dispatch of business. The difficulties heretofore complained of in shearing machines, such as cutting the edges of long selvage cloth, the inequality of the feed between the beginning and ending of the piece, the liability of cutting kockled cloth, &c. are entirely obviated. This machine, for cloth of common width, occupies a space equal to about four feet square, and may be put in operation either by water or by means of a crank, which a boy fourteen years old may turn without much fatigue, to shear from fifty to sixty yards an hour; where it is convenient to put it in operation by water, no further attention is necessary after putting on the piece until it is completed, when by the most simple process the gate is shut and all motion ceases. On the safety of this principle, so full confidence may be rested, that the business of the day may be closed by putting in a piece for shearing, and leaving the machine to finish it after the workmen have retired for the night. It may not be improper to inform you that this invention is the result of nearly seven years experiment, by a man well acquainted with the process of dressing cloth. It is unnecessary to enlarge upon the growing importance of the woolen business, in the Northern and Middle States, as that must be sufficiently obvious to every person acquainted with the great encouragement given (in premiums and otherwise) by men of the first standing in this country, for the importation and growth of the best breed of sheep.

THIS machine may be seen at the store of HALL & WELD, No. 1, *Union Street*, near the Market, where after a few weeks they will be kept for sale, and warranted with proper management to fulfil the above statement.

HALL & WELD have constantly on hand a large and general assortment of Dye-woods, Clothiers' Tools and Implements, Drugs and Medicines, Oils, Paints, &c. &c. which they offer to sell on reasonable terms.

BOSTON, *Oct. 3*, 1810.

SOURCE: Courtesy of the Eleutherian Mills Historical Library.

Illus. 38. Hall & Weld 1810 Broadside

There is a shearing machine patent by a Russel Dorr, who may have been Samuel's son, dated May 8, 1807.[112] It did not have spiral knives, but a "flying shear" suspended by bars on a hanging frame. The frame and shear had an "oscillating or pendulum like motion when in the act of cutting."[113] Seth Parsons (see illus. 39) in March 1819 a machine he claimed as an improvement of Dorr's "wheel of knives." This machine had a set of spiral blades which sheared against a bed shear, and another set of spiral brushes. This machine also had a three piece "spreader" consisting of two end pieces, cone shaped, then a smaller central cylinder with hooks to hold and spread the cloth.[114] Only one reference was found to Parson's machine; Shearwood & Goreham, woolen manufacturers from Renssalaer County, New York, owned one in 1820.[115]

The two outstanding names in the development of an American shearing machine were Beriah Swift and William Hovey. Both of their machines were patented in England, the first by

---

[112]Mann, Cloth Industry, p. 303.

[113]Russel Dorr's shearing machine patent of 8 May 1807, "Restored Patent, Specifications," 2:157-60, Patent Drawing no. 763, NA.

[114]Seth Parson's Improvement on a machine for shearing cloth called a "wheel of knives," of 2 March 1819, "Restored Patent, Specifications," 4:289-94, Patent Drawing no. 3082, NA.

[115]1820 Manufactures Census: New York, 1055.

SOURCE: National Archives.

Illus. 39. Parson's Shearing Machine.

Thomas Miles, the second by John Lewis. The Lewis machines were so important in Yorkshire that they became known as "lewises."[116] Partridge mentioned both; Zachariah Allen commented on them both; all three of the case-study factories ordered shearing machines from Swift and/or Hovey.

Beriah Swift was a Quaker from Washington, New York (Dutchess County, near Poughkeepsie) who patented his first shearing machine in May 1806 (see illus. 40, 41, 42). It was clearly <u>not</u> one with spiral cutting knives. In fact, it was imitative of the old hand shears, although the blades were much lighter in weight.[117] Swift's second shearing machine of July 1, 1814, did refer to[118]

> the spiral vibrating shear which thereby performs the operation of shearing the cloth cross ways equal to the hand shears and a Youth fourteen or fifteen years of age can with the improved machine perform four times the quantity of shearing that a good and experienced work man can turn out of hands by means of hand shears . . .

No drawing of this machine has survived unless it is the one from the Victor and Charles du Pont and company papers (see illus. 37 & 38).

Swift's February 7, 1824 (see illus. 43) was most likely his machine that was so well known. In this patent,

---

116 Mann, <u>Cloth Industry</u>, p. 305.

117 Beriah Swift's shearing machine patent of 28 May 1806, "Restored Patent, Specifications,"2:109-12, Patent Drawing no. 693, NA.

118 Beriah Swift's shearing machine of 1 July 1814, "Restored Patent, Specifications," 3:289-91, NA.

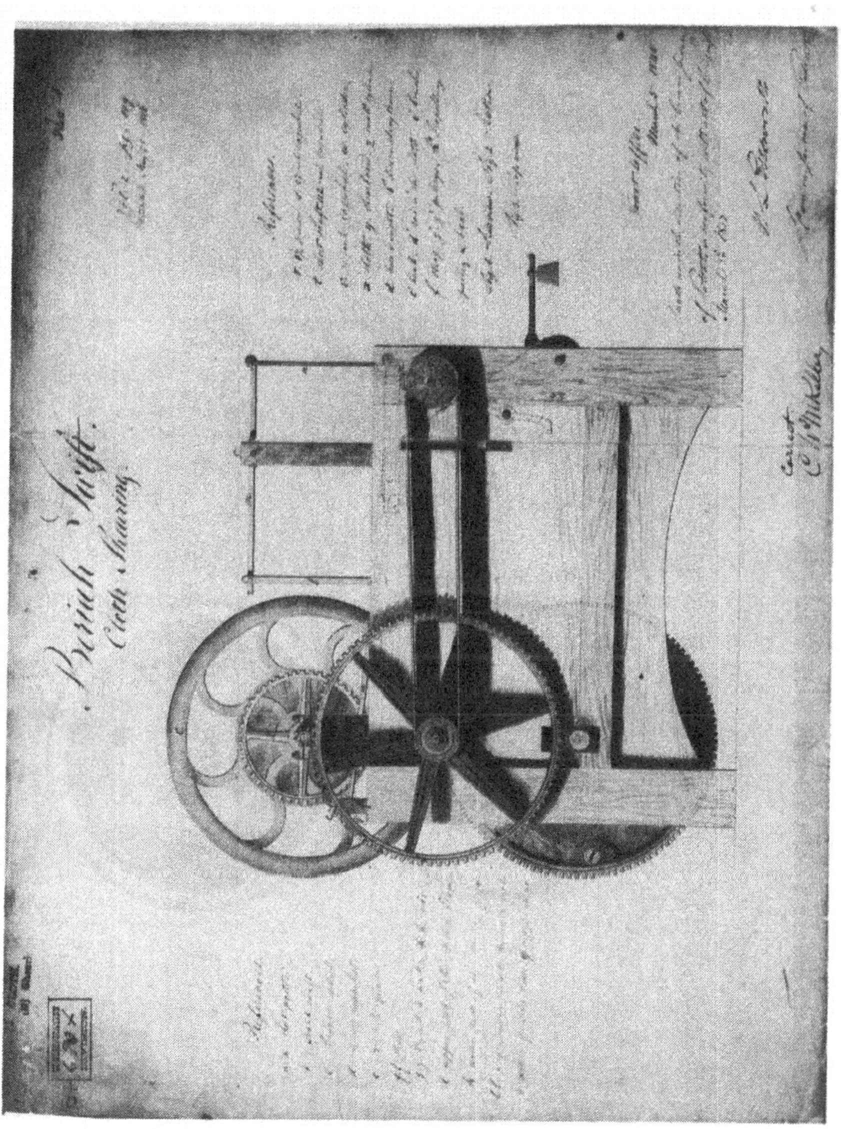

SOURCE: National Archives.

Illus. 40. Swift's 1806 Shearing Machine (side view).

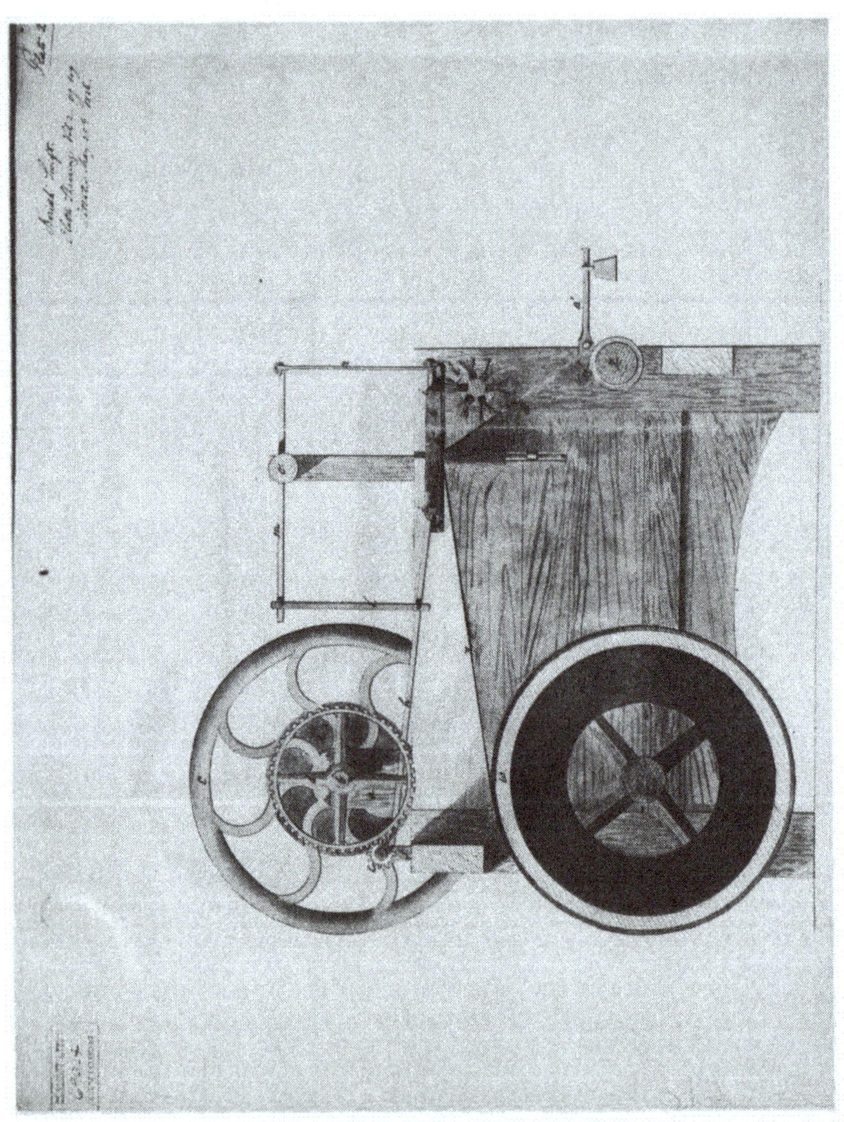

SOURCE: National Archives.

Illus. 41. Swift's 1806 Shearing Machine (side view).

SOURCE: National Archives.

Illus. 42. Swift's 1806 Shearing Machine (top view).

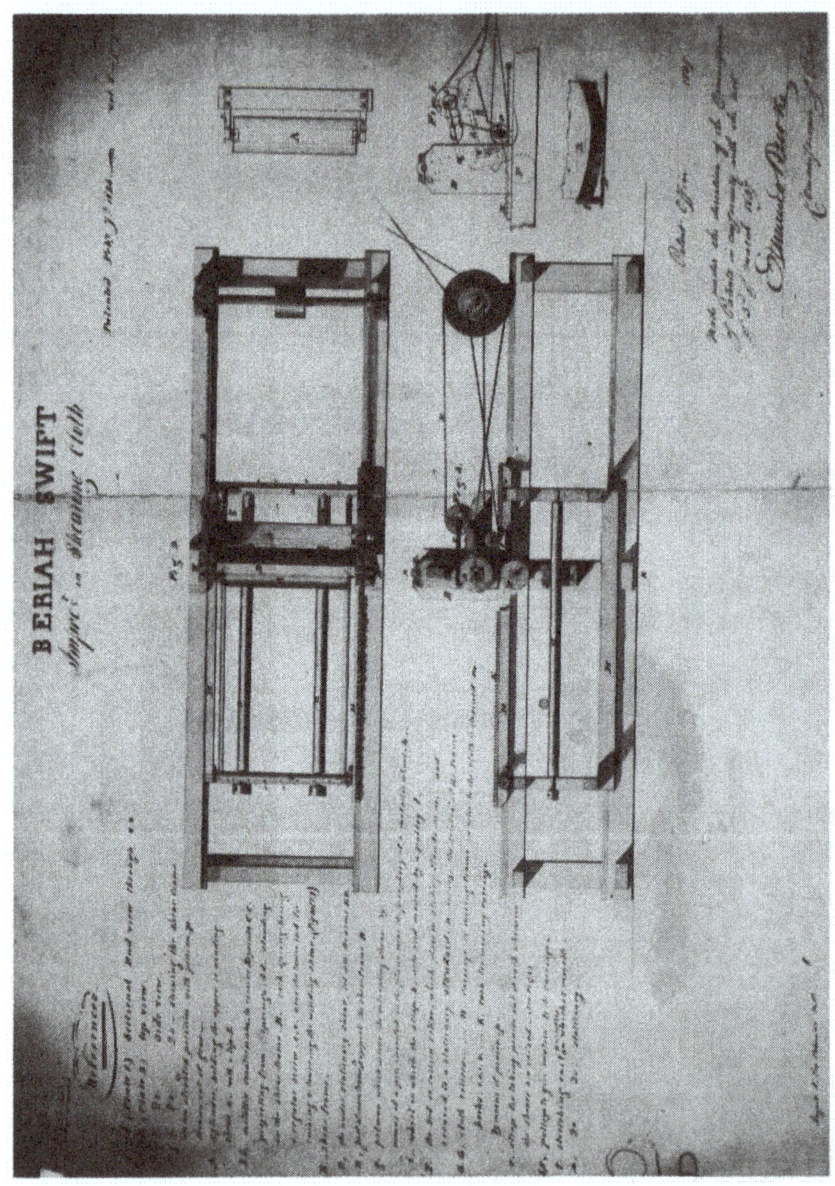

SOURCE: National Archives.

Illus. 43. Swift's 1824 Shearing Machine.

Swift claimed, "The essential principle of this improvement consists of a winding upper shear having a vibratory instead of revolving motion."[119] The vibration was apparently accomplished with springs and a pitman which revolved and vibrated at the same time while simultaneously the blade joined with a permanent bed shear to do the cutting.[120]

Partridge said,[121]

> It cuts more cleanly than any other shearer I have seen, and when worked with a motion sufficiently rapid and regular, and the edges of the working and ledger blades are in good order, it performs what may be called good work.

In 1825 Zachariah Allen saw some Swift's (Miles patent) in the West of England, but described them as "very roughly built.--Not so handsomely as those in operation in the United States."[122]

William Hovey returns this monograph to that center of woolen machinery technology--Worcester, Massachusetts. Hovey had been experimenting with a spiral shear from 1810 when he advertised an "Ontario Machine" which, it was claimed, could facilitate the work of shearing some ten

---

[119]Beriah Swift's shearing machine of 7 February 1824, "Restored Patent, Specifications," 5:157-60, Patent Drawing no. 3812, NA.

[120]Ibid.

[121]Partridge, Treatise on Dying, p. 83.

[122]Z. Allen, "Travel Journal," p. 124, Allen Papers, RIHS.

times.[123] No further description of the machine was found. Hovey, somewhat in the fashion of William H. Howard, who was his partner at one time, was involved in many phases of machinery building. He built double carders, and by 1822 he was using iron for carding cylinders as well as the frames. He built power looms with Howard. In 1824 he patented a shearing machine which was the one most often referred to in both England and American (see illus. 44).[124] This particular machine (like Swift's of 1824) was designed to shear from list to list. The shearing frame was separated from the cloth rollers and moved across the cloth on a rack and pinion rail. Between the rollers was an adjustable cushion which brought the cloth in contact with the shears.[125]

Partridge described an improvement of Hovey's machine by John Lewis (of Gloucestershire): namely, supplying extra blades with the machine so that the shear blades could be sharpened without long-term interruptions to work.[126] Keeping the blades of a shearing machine sharp was one of the common problems of manufacturers.

After shearing the cloth was brushed either by hand or by machine. The machine described by Partridge was similar

---

[123]Cole, Wool Manufacture, 1:121.

[124]Washburn, "Worcester Manufacturing," 2:1609-15; William Hovey's cloth shearing machine of 17 December 1824, "Restored Patents, Specifications," 5:165-70, Patent Drawing no. 3984, NA.

[125]Hovey's shearing machine patent 17 December 1824.

[126]Partridge, Treatise on Dying, p. 84.

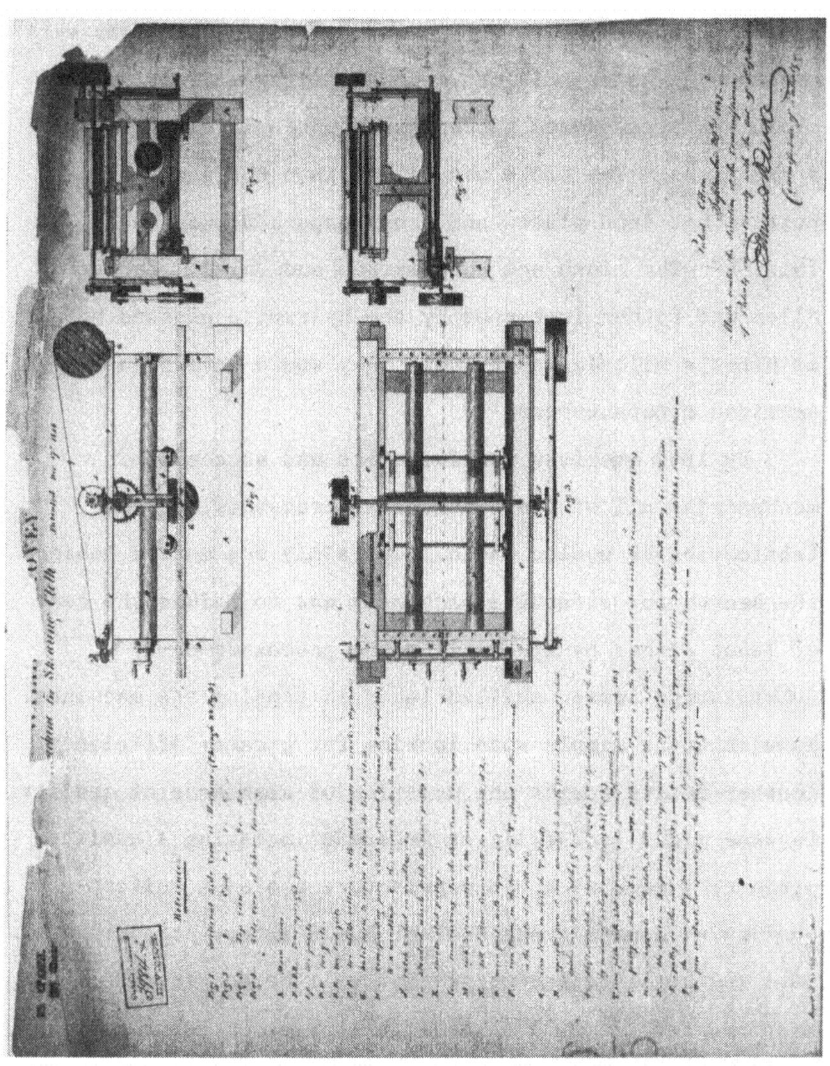

SOURCE: National Archives.

Illus. 44. Hovey's 1824 Shearing Machine.

to a gig-mill but with brushes instead of teasels or wires. Partridge went on to describe oiling the cloth, a practice Kenneth Ponting in his notes to the *Treatise* said was very uncommon.[127] Rees did not mention oiling. Finally the cloth was pressed and packed, most often in an ordinary screw press. The cloth was folded into the press by putting hot iron plates and press papers between each fold.[128] The cloth was then marked and baled. Zachariah Allen was rather impressed by the hydraulic presses he saw at Hirst's mill in Yorkshire. They would have been new to American manufacturers.[129]

By 1832 American manufacturers had succeeded in mechanizing all of the fundamental processes for the fabrication of woolen cloth. Certainly one motive behind the search for effective machinery was to reduce the cost of labor either by speeding up the processes or by substituting lesser skilled labor in tending the machines. Manufacturers simply were looking for greater efficiency. Another motive sought the creation of standards of quality. Persons might lack skill or interest in making a quality product; a machine could manufacture goods of uniform quality without a great deal of human intervention.

In the three factories that will be considered in the next chapter, it will be seen that wages or labor costs with machinery were not as critical in reducing the cost of

---

[127]Ibid., pp. 84-85, 237. [128]Ibid., p. 85.

[129]Z. Allen, "Travel Journal," pp. 50-51, Allen Papers, RIHS.

production of cloth as raw material costs. Yet wages were _thought_ to be critical, or very important, at least. Otherwise it would not be possible to explain why woolen manufacturers spent moneys buying the most up-to-date equipment or why invention was so encouraged. Competition was everywhere, not only from Americans, but mostly from English imports even after the prohibitive tariffs of 1828. Modernizing machinery was the most obvious and most visible way to increase productivity. Americans did increase their productivity, and technically, their wool factories were superior to the English. In trying to maintain competitive positions many manufacturers from the 1820 Census failed; many others found themselves forced to modernize not only the workings of the factory, but management, marketing, financing, and their methods for distribution of goods.

The argument for the technical superiority of American woolen manufactories is not a new one. Arthur H. Cole believed it although at times his arguments seem more intuitive than concrete.[130] A stronger set of arguments came from W. Paul Strassmann in the 1950s. His emphasis was on the absence of risk because initial capital investment was small, and because there was little reason for Luddite type behavior in the American labor force. In woolens, in the 1820s the normal investments in machinery were less than $10,000 even among substantial manufacturers. Since these

[130] Cole, _Wool Manufacture_, 1:86-136,120.

factories tended to create jobs where none had existed before, it would be difficult to imagine any large group of early nineteenth-century American woolen laborers intent on destroying machines.[131] When men were displaced by women, there was anger, but no action as the groups involved were so small, and the displacement process so gradual.[132] Habakkuk's "labor scarcity" arguments do not work well for woolens, because it is doubtful that wages were significantly more in America than in England.[133] More to the point, wage costs were not nearly as important a cost item as raw material cost. Yet as Nathan Rosenberg has pointed out, borrowing from W. E. G. Salter, if price was a factor, as it was for American finished woolens competing against each other and British imports, _any_ saving would be important.[134]

Zachariah Allen may well have been an early Yankee chauvinist. Nevertheless, his observations about the state of the art of woolen manufacture in New England and Old England buttress nicely the view that American technology in woolen

---

[131] W. Paul Strassmann, _Risk and Technological Innovation: American Manufacturing Methods during the Nineteenth Century_ (Ithaca: Cornell University press, 1959), pp. 106-114.

[132] Leavitt, ed., _Hollingworth Letters_, p. 66.

[133] Nathan Rosenberg, "Anglo-American Wage Differences in the 1820's," in _Perspectives on Technology_ (Cambridge: Cambridge University Press, 1976), pp. 50-58.

[134] Nathan Rosenberg, _Technology and American Economic Growth_ (New York: Harper Torchbooks, 1972), p. 56.

manufacture was superior. In a little book on mechanics published in 1829, Allen expressed it this way:[135]

> From the habits of early life and the diffusion of knowledge by means of free schools, there exists generally among the mechanics of New England a vivacity in enquiring into the first principles of science to which they are practically devoted. They thus frequently acquire a theoretical knowledge of the processes of the useful arts, which the English labourers may commonly be found to possess after a long apprenticeship and life of patient toil. For this reason the American mechanic appears generally more prone to invent new plans and machines than to operate upon old ones in the most perfect manner. The English mechanic on the contrary, confining his attention simply to the immediate performance of the process of art to which he is habituated from early youth, acquires wonderful dexterity and skill.

In 1825 Zachariah Allen and Abraham S. Schenck of the Glenham Company, Dutchess County, New York, made a trip to Europe to visit woolen manufactories. On the trip Allen kept a journal that has never been published. In it he said,[136]

> From the various mills and machinery I have yet seen, and the manner of their use, I am convinced that in making cloth in America we fail more from the hurry & want of care & attention - with which the processes are completed - than from want of skill & good machinery.

On the trip it became patently clear to Allen that the Americans had surpassed Europeans, including even those in Yorkshire, in technical and mechanical improvements in the methods of making broadcloth and its woolen relatives.

---

[135]Zachariah Allen, _The Science of Mechanics as Applied to the Present Improvement in the Useful Arts_ (1829), cited in Strassmann, _Risk and Technological Innovation_, p. 186; White, _Memoirs of Slater_, p. 342.

[136]Allen, "Travel Journal," p. 16, Allen Papers, RIHS.

Francis Cabot Lowell universally has been given credit for creating the first integrated factory--in 1814, the Boston Manufacturing Company began, and by 1816 it was producing cotton cloth from the raw material. The entire process was accomplished at the Waltham plant. Whether by accident or design, American woolen manufacturers almost all operated integrated factories fabricating cloth and finishing it from the raw material in one location. But by Boston Manufacturing Company standards, the scale of these woolen mills was very small. Yet in 1825 Allen commented on the separation of these processes among English factories, and the waste of time involved because the processes within English mills was so specialized that raw materials and goods continually had to be transported from place to place, sometimes quite a distance.[137]

By and large, Allen seemed to have been impressed with British workmanship, both in terms of the fabrication of woolen cloth and in terms of the building of the machinery itself, some of which he felt was made more solidly than American-made machinery. It was the level of technology that Allen found inferior in England. While there were a multitude of power looms in the cotton industry, not only in the Manchester region, but in Scotland as well, he and Schenck saw no power looms for woolens. They did see advanced gig-mills with high velocities, carding machines with greater breadth than most American

---

[137]Ibid., p. 4.

carders, but few of the "new" spiral shearing machines, and much shearing with the powered hand shears that had appeared in the Rees Cyclopaedia in 1811. They saw steam brushing that was apparently novel to them, and steam fulling that Benjamin Gott himself told them was not satisfactory. They saw hydraulic cloth presses and were impressed by them.[138] Of course, they visited two of the largest woolen manufactories in the world--Benjamin Gott's Bean Ing in Leeds which employed 750 persons and William Hirst's, also near Leeds, with 500 employees. Gott's mill manufactured and finished broadcloth Allen felt to be "equal in quantity to all the broad cloth manufactured in all the various mills in New England."[139] It was the extensiveness of these mills that really made an impression on the two Americans. In America in 1825, the only factory with these kinds of numbers would have been the Merrimack Cotton Manufacturing Company of Lowell. This scale required a type of labor management probably not possible in American woolens in the 1820s. As will be seen in the next chapter, the three manufacturers studied closely tried to modernize in other important ways besides modernizing their machinery. While judgments about labor supervision are difficult, it was probably in that general area that Allen and Schenck would have felt the most inexperienced.

[138]Ibid., pp. 12-14, 18, 27-29, 33, 46-47, 65, 72-73.

[139]Ibid., pp. 22, 41-63.

Chapter V

A BUSINESS REVOLUTION: TOWARD MORE RATIONAL BUSINESS PRACTICES

Within a span of eighteen to twenty years the American woolen industry had revolutionized its manufacturing processes by harnessing its machinery to inanimate power. Carding and spinning to weaving and finishing were by 1832 run by gears, cam shafts, springs and levers propelled by endless belt systems attached to revolving shafts. At the primary end of the power train was a water wheel forced to revolve by that most ancient and universal source of kinetic energy--falling water. Newly invented and newly mechanized machinery had increased the production potential of woolen broadcloth by about 125 percent per each broad loom. By some standards perhaps this was not so revolutionary; yet the fact that an entire set of processes had been mechanized did represent major change. The fact that this change took place in an industry whose "correct" hand processes had been well-known for years, even centuries, added another revolutionary element. Further, virtually all of these woolen factories including the smallest ones, were integrated factories producing on their sites a finished product from raw materials. This technical revolution had important consequences in labor saving and wage costs themselves. The implications for industrial organization were far-reaching.

By tracing various aspects of the development of three companies, some insight can be gained into some of the reasons one company became more efficient and productive than the others. Technology was paramount as it was technology that enabled Slater, Howard and Company, for example, to replace a large proportion of its male working force with women. That replacement was probably the essential breakthrough in reducing labor costs.

Machinery/Wage Costs

On July 31, 1813, Victor du Pont entered an amount into the company ledger that he felt was the total cost of the du Pont woolen establishment. It came to $53,599.94, but it included $22,888 in wool and $7,215 in dye stuffs and warps leaving $23,497 for buildings and machinery. By February 14, 1815 another $11,612 had been invested in buildings and another $1,293 in machinery. All of the machinery was purchased or built locally in Philadelphia, Germantown, or Wilmington.[1]

The first years of the Victor and Charles I. du Pont and Company[2] were beset with personal tragedies. The

---

[1]Journal 37, Ledger 56, Chas. I. du Pont & Co., Acc. 500, EMHL.

[2]The company was Du Pont, Bauduy & Company until February, 1815.

son of one of the original partners, Ferdinand Bauduy, died within a few weeks after his marriage to one of the du Pont daughters. The senior Bauduy withdrew from the firm. William Clifford who probably supervised the original building and machinery purchases, first alienated another partner, and then was discovered as a bigamist. His marriage to another du Pont daughter was annulled.[3] Yet the company seemingly did well crediting nearly $113,000 to the cloth account, debiting but $98,000 in 1813 and 1814. However, these figures require considerable caution. Assuming that the factory produced about 11,000 broad yards, each of the two years, this would come to a price of about six dollars per yard.[4] This would not have been an unreal price for those inflationary war years, but it does assume that this was the price received by the du Ponts, an assumption that cannot be proven.

Until the end of 1815, the company employed the following:

---

[3]Riggs, Guide to the Manuscripts, pp. 14-18.

[4]Journal 37, Ledger 56, Papers of Chas. I. du Pont & Co., Acc. 500, EMHL.

10 weavers	15 women*
3 millwrights and mechanics	8 children
2 overseers	5 male apprentices
1 shearer	28
1 spinner	
1 fuller	50% men
2 dyers	27% women
1 scourer	23% children including apprentices
1 sorter	
2 laborers	
2 team drivers	*6 spinners
1 invalid	6 burlers
1 boys' master	
28 men	

The payroll for this group amounted to $895 per month. Wages averaged $26.00 per month for weavers, $34.00 for mechanics, $11.75 for women and $4.50 for the children. In December of 1815 nearly half the work force was laid off. Thirty-one persons remained employed, and the payroll was reduced to $446.50 per month. One overseer, all three of the mechanics, eight women, and five of the children were dismissed, and those who remained took reductions of pay so that their new pay averaged $20.00 per month for weavers, $10.00 for the women.[5]

Machinery at Du Pont, Bauduy and Company[6] in July of 1814 consisted of the following:

---

[5]Letter to hands, 29 December 1815, Winterthur Mss., Group 3, Papers of Victor du Pont, W3-4652-4, EMHL.

[6]Prior name of Victor and Charles I. du Pont & Company, changed when Peter Bauduy withdrew from the firm in February 1815.

3 carding machines, 2 fine and 1 coarse[7]
2 billies
6 jennies--1 of 50 spindles, 4 of 60, 1 of 70 spindles

8 wide looms
4 narrow looms
1 water powered gig
6 hand shears

Labor costs per yard amounted to about 98¢ per yard before the lay-offs, about $1.24 afterwards. While efficiency was clearly not improved, annual labor costs went from $10,740 to $5,358.[8]

The major machinery commitment by the du Ponts before 1827 was the investment in the Brewster spinning machine. Brewster was paid $1,727.57 in cloth plus a company note for $500.[9] The spinning machine was purchased on November 6, 1816, but seems to have been out of commission by 1822.

In 1818 the payroll was greater in numbers of personnel, but not a great deal larger in money wages paid than in 1815:[10]

---

[7]"Du Pont, Bauduy & Company, Manufactory at Brandywine, Delaware, July 15, 1814," Antietam Woolen Manufacturing Company Papers, Acc. 1422, EMHL.

[8]Letter to hands, 29 December 1815, Papers of Victor du Pont, EMHL.

[9]Petit ledger 62 (Petit ledgers 61-65 are actually daybooks or journals.), Chas. I. du Pont & Co., Acc. 500, EMHL.

[10]Petit ledger 63, Chas. I. du Pont & Co., Acc. 500, EMHL.

20 weavers (12 full-time, 8 part-year)
1 mechanician
2 overseers
4 spinners (male)
3 spinners (female)
1 fuller
2 dyers
1 scourer
2 sorters
3 laborers
1 driver
37 men

11 women, spinning, warping, burling
28 children
3 apprentices
42

47% men
14% women
39% children including apprentices

The du Ponts tried to reduce their labor costs by hiring more children, but since children did not work that regularly, labor costs were not lessened materially by that means.

Production in 1818 was about 25,084 yards of what must have been narrow cloth as the weaving prices were fourteen and fifteen cents per yard. Reducing that to finished broad yards comes to 10,662 broad yards which cost in wages $9,708, not including board.[11] This came to ninety-one cents per broad yard.

During 1822 accounts were kept for wages, wool, other raw materials, and machinery. A daily record of sales was also kept. By the use of a pocket computer and painstakingly going through these records, it was possible to come up with a set of figures that represent a fairly accurate picture of operating costs and sales, and therefore profits, or in this case, losses.

The 1822 payroll is included in the appendix. In summary form, Victor and Charles du Pont and Company

[11] Ibid.

employed the following:[12]

22	weavers (22 full time, 14 part year)		
5	spinners and slubbers (5 full time, 5 part year)		
1	scourer		
3	dyers		
3	fullers and finishers		
1	sorter		
1	mechanician		
8	laborers		
45	men	48% men	48% men
15	women	16% women	28% women & girls
21	boys	36% children	24% "children" (boys only)
2	apprentices		
11	girls		
94	+ 3 agents or salaried officers		

Exact machinery for 1822 could not be ascertained, but there is an inventory probably taken after Victor du Pont's death in January 1827 that lists machines and their value at that time. Except for looms, which do not correspond with weavers in 1822, the list may not be very different from the machinery that was in the du Pont factory in 1822:[13]

12	carding machines, complete @ $250	$ 3,000
4	billys @ $2 per spindle	400
11	jennies @ $1 per spindle	660
2	wool pickers	100
	pressing utensils and presses	1,000
5	shearing machines and 1 brushing machine	600
5	power looms	
22	broad looms and gears complete @ $30	660
12	narrow looms	165
6	pairs hand shears @ $20	120
	copper vats, kettles, & dyeing apparatus, turning lathe, tools, machinery, blacksmith shop and 40 bags unopened wool	200
		$10,900

[12] Ibid.

[13] Thomas B. Hartmann, "The Du Pont Woolen Venture."

Weaving production in 1822 was 6,332 3/4 yards of broadcloth costing sixteen to thirty-one cents per yard to weave, and 39,121 yards of what was probably narrower cloths costing from eight to fourteen cents to weave. Reducing this for shrinkage and putting it into broad yards brought the production to 21,693 broad yards.[14]

The total for wages came to $17,310.64 including the three large salaries of Louis Sacriste and the two du Ponts. Labor costs per broad yard came to eighty cents per broad yard in 1822.

About 40,000 pounds of wool was purchased for $20,739; dyes, lumber, firewood, candles, reeds, and other raw materials and machinery maintenance cost $10,002.46. Machinery itself cost another $2,784.68.[15] Most of the machinery was replacement for worn out machinery. The du Ponts were not as interested in updating with newly developed machines as Samuel H. Babcock in Massachusetts. Perhaps they had felt stung by their experience with the Brewster spinner which apparently was so difficult to repair that it was no longer functioning in 1822.

A summary of the costs in 1822 showed the following:[16]

---

[14]Petit ledger 63, Chas. I. du Pont & Co., Acc. 500, EMHL.

[15]Ibid.

[16]Ibid.

<u>1822</u> (estimated)

Machinery	$ 2,784.68
Sundries (factory?)	7,889.78
Drugs (dyes)	2,112.68
Wool	20,739.00
Wages (incl. mill race)	17,532.50
Interest on debt (estimated)	5,004.79
	$56,063.43

Ten different types of cloth were manufactured in at least five colors. Each cloth type had at least a dozen grades at different prices. Much of the cloth was sold in retail lots of 1 1/4 yards to 3 1/2 yards, although of course some of it was sold in pieces of twenty or so yards. This was one area that begged for greater organization and better management. It is not possible to measure the inefficiency that these practices produced, but a sense of chaos is conveyed just by the huge variety in the sales record. Selling in pieces in more standard cloth types surely would have given greater rationality to the factory operation.

The following is a summary of 1822 sales:[17]

Broadcloth	449 3/8 yds	@ $3.00 to	6.50/yd
Cassimere	1,711 1/2	1.00	2.75
Cassinet	4,552 1/2	.70	1.50
Satinet	9,036	.75	1.375
Fine Kersey	843 1/8	1.50	1.75
Linsey	1,292	.45	.625
Negro cloth	4,197	.65	1.25
Army kersey	14,509 1/2	1.59	1.60
Army broadcloth	604 3/4	2.35/yd	
Kerseynet	543	.60 to 1.00	
	37,738 3/4 yds (19,396 1/2 broad yds)		

Colors included blue, brown black, grey, drab, and olive.

16,317 1/4 yds were sold to the army for	$26,561.55
21,421 1/2 yds were sold to regular commercial customers	22,233.64
	$48,975.20

[17]Production and sales 161, Chas. I. du Pont & Co., Acc. 500, EMHL.

This made the losses for the Victor and Charles I. du Pont and Company $7,088.23 in 1822. This was a considerably higher loss than was posted on the average during the five-year period from 1827 to 1832. One problem surely related to the range of products and the small lot sales. At eighty cents per broad yard labor costs were less than Zachariah Allen's computation of one dollar, less than the early costs for Babcock's woolen factory, and less than Slater, Howard's costs in 1825. This eighty cents did not include board for hands; there were some payments for board. It certainly was not as efficient a labor force as it became in 1827 to 1832 for the newly named Charles I. du Pont and Company, but labor costs were not as significant as the cost of raw wool.

Technically, the du Pont woolen mill was much slower to change than the two Dudley, Massachusetts companies. There were no radical machinery purchases after the Brewster spinner in 1816 until 1832; in that year Charles I. du Pont and Company bought two broad power looms and a new carder with a condenser from New England. The labor force was not becoming more female. While payrolls were not found for the late twenties and thirties, one was found for 1842.[18] While no ages were given, clearly women were little more important in numbers than they were in 1822. Out of seventy-eight hands in 1842, twenty-five persons or 32 percent were women, but 68 percent were men and boys. While this does represent a small increase from 28 to

---

[18] Payroll account, Box 26, Chas. I. du Pont & Co., Acc. 500, EMHL.

32 percent, it is no where near the degree of change that New England factories accomplished.

Throughout most of its history the du Pont woolen company was a supplier of woolen cloth to the United States Army. In the earlier years from 1816 to 1823 deliveries to the Commissary tended to be erratic and inconsistent, and overall, du Pont supplied between one-half and three-quarters of what was contracted for. During this period the Army contracted for 119,100 yards of mostly six-quarter cloth and kersey for $219,285. Over the eight-year period Victor and Charles du Pont and Company delivered 73,685 yards for which the company was paid $142,726.[19]

Sometime during this period one of the du ponts, probably Victor, analyzed the cost for producing forty-six yards of black cloth for gaiters for the Army:[20]

75 lbs. wool @ 50/100	$37.50
Sorting @ 2/100, picking @ 2 1/2¢	3.375
Oil, pints (6 ?)	1.75
Carding and slubbing @ 6¢	4.50
Spinning chain @ 6 1/2¢	2.145
Spinning filling @ 5¢	2.10
Warping 61 yards @ 2 1/4¢	1.37
Glue for chain	.50
Winding and spooling	.60
Fulling and scouring	2.75
Dying black and rinsing	4.60
Drilling teasels and tentering	1.35
Shearing	2.00
Weaving 61 yards @ .18 3/4	11.44
Finishing, brushing and pressing	.75
Wear and tear of machinery ($8,000 ?)	3.00
Interest on capital ($70,000)	8.40
	$88.13

[19] Winterthur Mss., Grp. 3, Papers of Victor du Pont, W3-4660, 4664, 4666, 4667; Petit ledger 62, Chas. I. du Pont & Co., Acc. 500, EMHL.

[20] Hartman, "The du Pont Woolen Venture."

This comes to $1.92 per yard total cost, eighty cents for labor alone, and the du Ponts sold this batch of cloth, or hoped to, for $2.333 per yard.[21] Theoretically at least, according to this traditional method of cost accounting, the Army deals were profitable. But the dependence on the Army for business cannot have been entirely healthy.

After Victor du Pont's death in 1827, a new bookkeeping system was established for Charles I. du Pont and Company. As will be shown in the second part of this chapter, this new system was much clearer for determining profits and/or losses. However, sales and production must have been recorded in other types of account books, account books that are no longer extant. Without these records, only approximations can be made.

By dividing the amount credited in the "woolen goods" account by $1.25, a rough guess at yardage has been reached (see table 7). (In 1822, the average price per yard of du Pont cloth was $1.30.) Dividing yardage into wage costs gives an approximate value of wages per yard. Because of the various estimates, considerable caution should be exercised in comparing these figures with wage costs reached with firmer data in other companies. Yet the figures are probably accurate relative to each other, and

---

[21]Petit ledger 62, Chas. I. du Pont & Co., Acc. 500, EMHL.

TABLE 7

RELATIVE WAGE COSTS PER YARD,
CHARLES I. DUPONT & COMPANY

Year	Approximate Yardage	Wage Costs Per Yard	Broad Yardage*	Wage Costs Per Broad Yard
1827	25,271	36¢	13,015	70¢
1828	36,858	32¢	18,982	63¢
1829	33,413	28¢	17,207	54¢
1830	35,173	25¢	18,114	49¢
1831	43,368	23¢	22,334	44¢
1832	36,026	26¢	18,554	50¢

*Note that broadcloth was 3 percent of production in 1822. That was subtracted from total yardage, the remaining yardage was divided by two and broadcloth yardage added again.

despite the estimations, the amounts are fairly consistent with similar amounts calculated from harder data collected from Slater, Howard and the Dudley Woollen Manufacturing Company.[22]

Edward Howard may have been an inadequate bookkeeper, and he must have been an extravagant manager, but he seems to have had a sound grasp of what a woolen factory should consist of. He oversaw an elaborate building program, bought machinery, updated that machinery, and hired hands who had perhaps less wanderlust than most textile workers. At the end of 1824, after about two years of Howard's management, the factory had purchased the following machinery:[23]

2 teasel breakers (single carding machines) from William Stowell of Worcester	$ 560.00
2 double carding machines from John Boynton of Coventry, Connecticut	1,420.00
1 fifty spindle billy) by Rowland Perry	100.00
2 eighty spindle jennies) of Dudley	192.00
1 sixty spindle jenny repaired by Stowell	-
7 broad looms) built by various local men	140.00
6 kersey looms)	
1 gig, built by Nathan Cody, local smith; repaired by Stowell	291.43
1 shearing machine, Hovey patent	100.00
fulling stocks, possibly milling machine	-
	$2,803.43

---

22 Journals 38, 39, Ledger 57, 58, Chas. I. du Pont & Co., Acc. 500, EMHL.

23 Blotters 1-4, Daybook 5, Slater, Howard & Co., Slater Coll., BL.

In 1823 Slater, Howard and Company <u>tried</u> a 350 spindle Brewster spinning machine. The contract with Brewster spelled out procedure, and it was tried in the factory with a young girl tending it. For reasons never recorded, the machine was returned to Middletown, Connecticut. The price given was a good one, favorable to Slater, Howard and Company; in fact, it was so much less than known prices for other Brewsters, there may have been other costs not disclosed in the contract.[24] Although Slater, Howard and Company did not keep the Brewster, the company was certainly abreast of machinery innovations. Howard's cloth won important prizes at fairs in Massachusetts; he may have determined that he could not get the necessary quality of spinning from the machine. Early in 1826, Slater, Howard bought two 100 spindle jennies built by Rowland Perry.[25]

In the next few years, Slater, Howard and Company expanded by building new buildings and buying the following machinery:[26]

<u>1825</u>

2 wool presses by Israel Sibley, local machinist	$ 35.00
8 broad power looms by William H. Howard of Worcester	1,000.00

---

[24]Box 23, Folder 1, Slater, Howard, & Co., Slater Coll., BL.

[25]Daybook 8, Slater, Howard, & Co., Slater Coll., BL.

[26]Daybooks 5-12, Slater, Howard, & Co., Slater Coll., BL.

1826

press plates by Shepherd Leach of Easton,	
Massachusetts	$ 54.25
1 fifty spindle billy)by	125.00
2 one-hundred spindle jennies)Rowland Perry	240.00
1 narrow shearing machine from William	
H. Howard, probably a Hovey patent	75.00
1 shear grinding machine by William Hovey	
of Worcester	77.62

1827

8 kersey power looms from William H.	
Howard	736.00
1 broad shearing machine from White and	
Boyden of Worcester	100.00
1 broad shearing machine from Beriah Swift	
of Washington, New York	110.00

1828

1 each breaker and finisher, and 1 picker	
from John Boynton of Coventry,	1,695.00
Connecticut	150.00
2 carding machines, 1 picker, 4 gigs from	850.00
John Field, local machinist	150.00
	350.00
1 each breaker and finisher, and 2 power	875.00
broad looms from William H. Howard	250.00
1 fifty spindle billy by William Stowell	125.00
1 fifty spindle billy) by Rowland Perry	125.00
3 eighty spindle jennies)	264.00
4 broad shearing machines from William Hovey	
of Worcester	500.00
2 broad shearing machines from Beriah Swift	210.00

1829

1 eighty spindle jenny from R. Perry	80.00
10 satinet power looms from David Wilkinson	
of Providence (bankrupt)	800.00
2 broad shearing machines from White and	
Boyden	200.00
2 straight shears for Hovey's machine,	
6 straight shears for Swift's, from	65.00
White and Boyden	42.00
	$9,283.87

During this same period, 1822 to 1829, Slater, Howard and Company built a town (see illus. 43). The factory consisted of one stone factory building with a hewn stone basement that Zachariah Allen called "a costly bit of folly."[27] There was a long narrow weaving shop with a carpenter's shop attached at the end, a dye house, a tiny building for sizing yarn, and a large drying building.[28] There was also the company store that was sold to J. and J. E. Day in 1826[29] but whose transactions still continued as the vehicle for the overall accounting system. Mr. Howard kept one boarding house, Willard Davis another. Howard kept the boarding house for the single men; as many as ten boarded with him at two dollars a week. The women and boys boarded with Davis. The little wool storage house was in back of the Howard's house, and the property also included a large garden and barn, and probably the use of Wakefield's orchard. By 1827 there were three one-family dwellings in the town, six for two families, one house for four and another for five families.[30] During the course of 1826 a tavern was built.[31]

---

[27] Z. Allen's "Diary," entry for 19 March 1824, Allen Papers, RIHS.

[28] "Ground Plan of Slater & Howard's Factory Village," Box 26, Slater, Howard, & Co., Slater Coll., BL.

[29] Box 23, Folder 1, Slater, Howard, & Co., Slater Coll., BL.

[30] "Ground Plan of Slater & Howard's Factory Village."

[31] Daybooks 7 and 8, Slater, Howard, & Co., Slater Coll., BL.

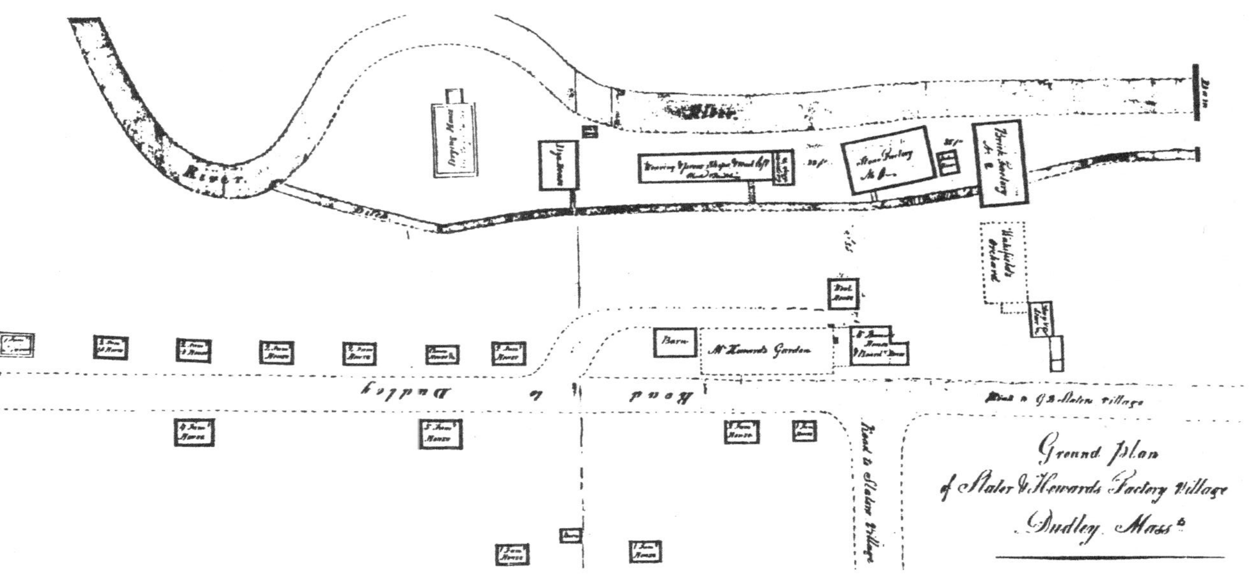

SOURCE: Baker Library, Harvard Business School.

Illus. 45. Ground Plan of Slater and Howard's Factory Village.

The factory went through a major expansion in 1827-28. A new "Brick Factory Number 2" was built adding 7,140 square feet to the 4,884 that existed in the old stone factory.[32] Shepherd Leach of Easton, Massachusetts (also Chelmsford and Foxboro) furnished the castings for shafts, gudgeons, power wheels, gearing, and a crown wheel.[33] Israel Sibley, local machinist, did most of the installation and rigging of machinery to power.[34] This did not seem to be an elaborate power system, and it was no doubt installed to power the looms and other equipment purchased in 1828. Those looms were not fully operational until 1829, after Edward Howard left the company.

During Edward Howard's tenure, modern up-to-date equipment was at least tried and often purchased and implemented. Yet Howard himself may not have eagerly endorsed the new mechanization. He rejected the Brewster spinner, or someone did.[35] Power looms were not installed when purchased, although some were in use in 1828. In June of that year ten male weavers wove an average of 5.6 yards of broadcloth per day on hand-powered looms. Three women wove 8.6 yards of kersey on hand-powered looms, and eight

---

[32]"Ground Plan of Slater & Howard's Factory Village," assuming the stone factory to have had two usable stories, the brick factory three.

[33]Box 23, Folder 2, Box 25, Folder 3, Slater, Howard, & Co., Slater Coll., BL.

[34]Box 23, Folder 2, Slater, Howard & Co., Slater Coll., BL.

[35]Blotter 4, Slater, Howard & Co., Slater Coll., BL.

women wove 6.7 yards per day on the average of broadcloth on power looms.[36] By 1830 the men still using hand-looms were averaging less than five yards per day, but the women were manufacturing 7.7 yards of broadcloth on power looms and 20.5 yards per day of satinet. In 1832 all the weaving was done by women on power looms. They averaged 9.8 yards of broadcloth per day, 16.5 yards of cassimere, and 21.5 yards of satinet.[37] The factory's labor costs per yard continually decreased not only as processes were mechanized, but as employees learned more efficient ways of operating them.

The following figures show that by 1832 efficiency had been greatly increased. From 1822/1823 labor costs relative to production had been reduced over 70 percent. Since 1829 many of the men had been replaced by women who by 1832 had become the majority of the work force.

1823[38]

26 men	57%	8,845 broad yards broadcloth & kersey
10 women (4 girls)	22%	$7,584 labor cost
10 boys	22%	86¢ labor cost per yard
46		Estimated sales: $19,274.

1824

30 men	59%	11,827 broad yards
9 women (5 girls)	18%	$13,093 labor cost
12 boys	24%	$1.11 labor per yard
		Estimated sales: $19,752.

[36] Daybook 11, Slater, Howard & Co., Slater Coll., BL.

[37] Wastebook 7, Ledgers 11 and 12, Dudley Mfg. Co., Slater Coll., BL.

[38] Blotters 1-4, Daybooks 5-12, Ledgers 13-14, Slater, Howard & Co., Slater Coll., BL.

Combine 1823 and 1824

		20,672 broad yards $20,577 labor costs $1.00 labor per yard

1825

33 men	53%	13,509
13 women (2 girls)	21%	$13,362 labor cost
16 boys	26%	97¢ labor per yard
62		Estimated sales: $25,609

1826

41 men	56%	19,572 broad yards broadcloth & kersey
22 women (5 girls)	30%	$13,352 labor cost
10 boys	14%	68¢ labor per yard
73		Estimated sales: $46,398.

1827

48 men	53%	30,420 broad yards*
24 women (6 girls)	27%	$18,800 labor cost
18 boys	18%	62¢ labor per yard
90		Estimated sales: $52,287.

1828

59 men	59%	34,068 broad yards
24 women (8 girls)	24%	$18,920 labor cost
16 boys	16%	63¢ labor per yard
99		Estimated sales: $47,263 (to Sept. 30)

1829

64 men	52%	48,060 broad yards
40 women (14 girls)	32%	$19,763 labor cost
20 boys	16%	44¢ labor per yard
124		

1830

47 men	47%	41,970 broad yards
37 women (12 girls)	37%	$13,984 labor cost
16 boys	16%	37¢ labor per yard
100		

---

*Yardage estimated from June weaving production from 1827-32.

<u>1831</u>

33 men	38%	36,850 broad yards
37 women (14 girls)	42%	$13,951 labor cost
18 boys	16%	37¢ labor per yard
88		

<u>1832</u>

32 men	31%	61,550 broad yards
55 women (16 girls)	53%	$17,764 labor cost
18 boys	16%	29¢ labor per yard
105		

As the new management came to feel more confident, it too invested in modern machinery. In 1831 they bought four new broad power looms. In 1833 some of the latest machinery was purchased: two finishers (carding machines) with condensers from John Boynton of Worcester (see p. 202) and two warp and two filling mules from the Schenck owned Matteawan Company of Dutchess County New York. Expansion continued with further purchases of power looms, gigs, a brushing machine, and more finishers with condensers from Boynton.[39]

Other aspects of Samuel Slater and Sons showed the trend toward more modern methods, most especially the bookkeeping system, but nothing more significantly reveals how these new machines wrought change than these declining cost per yard figures. From 1829 to 1832 half the men were let go, yet only half of those were replaced by women.

---

[39]Waste books 7-8, Dudley Manufacturing Co., Slater Coll., BL.

Since generally women's wages were roughly half those of men, this could and did result in considerable savings.

As reported for the McLane Report in 1832, the Dudley Woollen Manufacturing Company and S. Slater and Sons of Webster, Massachusetts had much in common or at least much of their operations were broadly similar (see table 8). This included capital assets, production, wages, and the labor force.

As the two payrolls are compared (see Appendix A) from Slater, Howard and Company in 1828 and from Dudley Woollen Manufacturing Company in 1830 the apparent discrepancies in the labor force become smaller. Many of the men on the Slater payroll were not working in the factory, but as farm or other type of day labor. If Dudley Woollen had these laborers, their accounts were kept separately.

Yet there were significant differences in the way each company arrived at their position in 1832. The Dudley Woollen Manufacturing Company did not start from scratch in 1823. The old Merino Wool Factory Company had existed in Dudley from 1811 to 1818. It had manufactured some woolen cloth and had spun cotton yarn which had been put out to be woven. That company was purchased by John Brown and Company in 1818 and transferred the following assets:

1 factory building
1 store
1 dry house
1 dye house
1 blacksmith shop
5 dwellings, one of which was a boarding house
1 fulling mill

TABLE 8

COMPARISON OF SLATER, HOWARD & COMPANY TO DUDLEY WOOLLEN MANUFACTURING COMPANY TAKEN FROM THE MCLANE REPORT, 1832

	S. Slater & Sons	Dudley Woollen Mfg. Co.
Real estate	$55,000	$50,000
Machinery	45,000	30,000
Stock	57,500	50,000
Wool	114,000 lb. @ $73,840	105,000 lb. @ $60,000
Raw material	$13,628	$17,638
Production	27,750 yds broadcloth 14,000 " cassimere 37,850 " satinet 53,675 broad yards	30,000 yds broadcloth 37,500 " cassimere 48,750 broad yards
Value	$110,762	$109,687
Labor	57 men @ 83¢ 55 women @ 32¢ 16 children @ 21¢ 128 @ $21,163.70 45% men 43% women 12% children	42 men @ 83¢ 56 women @ 46¢ 10 children @ 25¢ 108 @ $19,567.20 39% men 52% women 9% children

SOURCE: *McLane Report* 1:484-85, 576-77.

1 Humphrey Ville spinster, water-powered, 72 spindles
3 jennies
1 billy
1 picker
2 sets carding machinery plus 1 old set (1812)
2 Hovey shearing machines, 1 broad, 1 narrow
fulling stocks
5 narrow looms
5 broad looms
1 set warping bars[40]

In 1823, the company still called itself John Brown and Company (John Brown, and three others had purchased the factory in 1818, but there are no records from this company.) and purchased the following machinery in 1823:[41]

1	water powered wool spinning machine by Gilbert Brewster, 300 spindles	$2,750
1	shearing machine by White and Boyden of Worcester	100

In 1824, 98 of 100 shares of this company were transferred to Samuel H. Babcock for an unrecorded price. He and his fellow officers incorporated the company in that year; the name of the company was changed to the Dudley Woollen Manufacturing Company, and this company proceeded to buy the following machinery in the next five years:[42]

<u>1825</u>

2	broad looms, 1 jenny by Rowland Perry, local machinist	$117.00
5	broad power looms by A. & G. Spalding from Greenfield, Massachusetts (Franklin County)	450.00

---

[40]Account Book, Merino Wool Factory Company Papers, Merrimack Valley Textile Museum, North Andover, Massachusetts.

[41]Journal 45, Ledger 55, Dudley Woollen Mfg. Co., OSV.

[42]Clerk's book, Merino Wool Factory Co., MVTM; Journals 45-49, Ledgers 55-57, Dudley Woollen Mfg. Co., OSV.

1827	
Cassimere looms (probably 10) by William H. Howard of Worcester	$ 984.25
Broad looms (probably 3) by Howard	360.00
Brewster spinner bought through Samuel D. Hubbard of Sanseer, Middletown, Connecticut	1,400.00
Carding machine and probably 2 narrow looms by William H. Howard	1,000.00
1828	
1 50 spindle billy) Rowland Perry	110.00
1 120 spindle jenny) Rowland Perry	120.00
1 turning engine by John Field, local mechanic	100.00
1 press screw by David Wilkinson of Providence	43.80
1 billy by William Stowell, Worcester	125.00
1 carding machine by William Boynton, Coventry, Connecticut	830.00
1 warper and dresser by Baily Ammidon of Middletown, Connecticut	300.00
Looms by William H. Howard (3 broad, 2 narrow, probably)*	564.10*
1829	
1 shearing machiner, broad, William Hovey	125.00
1 shearing machine, broad, Stephen R. Tenny of Worcester	230.00
1830	
5 shear blades) White & Boyden, Worcester	27.00
1 narrow shearing machine) White & Boyden, Worcester	65.00
1 shear grinder) White & Boyden, Worcester	?
1831	
1 shearing machine from H. Waldo & Co., Worcester	190.00
	$ 9,991.15
	480.00
	$10,471.15

---

*By 1829, the Dudley Woollen Manufacturing Company was using fourteen cassimere power looms and ten broad. The five Spalding's were presumably given to Howard in trade, according to correspondence. Four broad power looms from Howard were not found in the accounts, but there is correspondence indicating they were purchased. This would add $480.00 to the above.

Samuel H. Babcock was a Boston merchant who throughout his ownership of the Dudley Woollen Manufacturing Company operated his wholesale and retail dry goods business in Boston. It was he who furnished market intelligence to his agents in Dudley, and who kept them up-to-date on the latest in technical developments. He apparently knew many of the southern Worcester County, northern Connecticut woolen operatives and machinery manufacturers. There seemed to be little of the type of industrial secrecy that prevailed in England in the early nineteenth century.[43] It is not clear that there was much awareness among woolen manufacturers of the substantial profits to be made from machinery building; possibly Zachariah Allen had such a glimmer and that glimmer may have been gained by his association with Abraham Schenck from the Matteawan Manufacturing Company (and Glenham) in Dutchess County, New York.[44] It was common for local smiths and machinists to manufacture carding or spinning machinery whose processes were basically unpatentable. There were such local machinery builders in Dudley, Massachusetts, but none was on the payrolls of the three woolen manufacturers. From Babcock's corresondence one senses that he was more eager

[43]Letters of Samuel H. Babcock, passim, Box 21, Dudley Woollen Mfg. Co. Papers, OSV.

[44]One of the major stockholders in Matteawan was Philip Hone, one time mayor of New York. In 1828 Hone received a 17% dividend from Matteawan. Allan Nevins, ed., The Diary of Philip Hone, 2 vols. (New York: Dodd, Mead, 1927), 1:3.

to innovate and try new methods than his agents or superintendents were. Often the factory experimented, and at least occasionally, the experiments were not successful. Some of the lack of success was not from inferior machinery but from personnel who were not committed to changing traditional technology.[45] Babcock and his fellow operatives saw technical improvement as leading not only to greater productivity, but also in promoting a work force requiring less and less skill and strength and costing less and less for wages. The most obvious types of change emulated the cotton mills in working with fewer and fewer men, and employing more and more women. Factory managers tended to be defensive about children; Americans, in fact, viewed English textile mills with misgivings, because the English did employ so many children. From the two Dudley companies and du Pont, the demands made on children had little in common with the "dark Satanic mills" of Manchester. In only a very few cases did children work year-round, every day.

From 1824 to 1830, the productivity of the weavers in Babcock's factory went from 4.1 yards of broadcloth per day on the hand loom to 6.7 yards on the broad power loom. Cassimere production increased from 6.8 yards to 11.7 yards per day on the narrow power loom.[46] Wages went from

---

[45]Samuel H. Babcock to Maj. Brown, 13 November 1824; Babcock to Chester Clemens, 3 May 1827; Babcock to Maj. Brown, 19 May 1828; Babcock to Dudley Woollen Mfg. Co., 24 May 1828; Brown to Nathaniel Lyon, 19 August 1828; Box 21, Dudley Woollen Mfg. Co., OSV.

[46]Factory goods 91-93, Dudley Woollen Mfg. Co., OSV.

twenty to twenty-seven cents per yard in 1824 to six cents in 1830 for broadcloth; eight to twelve cents in 1824 for cassimere, to 3 1/2 cents in 1830. In 1830 all the weavers were women except for Joseph Scholfield. Productivity did not leap forward with the introduction of power looms. Spalding looms were installed in the last months of 1825, but weaving production did not show a significant increase until 1827.[47] Learning the new techniques was obviously an aspect of increased productivity. Besides, there is some evidence to indicate that the Spalding looms were not satisfactory. There were only limited references to them in the correspondence while there were many references to Howard looms by Babcock to Brown and others. At one point Babcock suggested that they trade in the Spalding looms to William H. Howard. Also, there are letters from the Spalding brothers that picture them as very hard up, and with no means to hire decent help.[48]

Labor-saving machinery was the most obvious and visible way to cut costs. Yet it very likely was not the most rational means for saving, and it was hardly the most prudent considering how little could have been known of its

[47] Journals 45-49, Dudley Woollen Mfg. Co., OSV.

[48] A. & G. Spalding Co. to Dudley Woollen Mfg. Co., 12 June 1825, 12 November 1825, 7 December 1825, Box 20; Babcock to Clemens, 5 October 1827, Box 21, Dudley Woollen Mfg. Co., OSV.

rate of obsolescence or deterioration. Someone like Samuel H. Babcock was aware of the risks, but also responsive to the competition. In February 1828, in a letter to Major Brown, Babcock complained of poor business conditions and added,

> I cannot agree to making any further addition to our establishment after this under any consideration whatever. We both agree that our woollen business is bad enough and unless we can go without sinking more money we shall be compel'd to stop it. I consider the present time is critical with us; from appearances in Washington we shall get no relief and must depend on ourselves for success.[49]

A few months later he admonished Brown about the saving of money by attaching condensers to the carding machines,

> Mr. Hurd of Lowell uses them altogether and says he saves one half the cost of our principle. Tufts is doing the same thing in Dudley. We must not (be) in the background. I wish you to make yourself acquainted with the improvements going on.[50]

It is arguable that a greater concentration on the reduction of resource costs might have been a more reliable way of saving. The prices of imported dyes, particularly the expensive indigo, was probably out of anyone's control although one might have hoped to see some interest in developing cheaper alternatives. But wool itself should have been the obvious material whose cost could have been

---

[49]Babcock to Maj. Brown, 29 February 1828, Box 21, Dudley Woollen Mfg. Co., OSV.

[50]Babcock to Nathaniel Lyon, 19 August 1828, Box 21, Dudley Woollen Mfg. Co., OSV.

lowered with greater production. While interest was not totally lacking in wool and sheep husbandry in New England, manufacturers seemed completely divorced from agricultural persuits. Complaints were made about the tariff on raw wool, but by and large woolen manufacturers were passive in the face of a very high raw material cost. It was as if once the invisible hand had made its determination, manufacturers were content to pass those costs on to consumers.

In the area of labor costs, reductions were made. Most came from the introduction of machinery, especially, or most visibly, from power weaving. But skilled labor itself must have been more readily available. Even such a skill as sorting went from eight shillings and six ($1.42) per hundred pounds in 1824 to six and six ($1.08) at the end of 1829.[51] A good sorter could sort 130 pounds per day, 3,500 pounds in a month, so even at the reduced pay rate was able to earn thirty-seven dollars per month.

A summary of production, the labor force and costs, and labor productivity for the Dudley Woollen Manufacturing company is below:[52]

---

[51]Journals 45 and 49, Dudley Woollen Mfg. Co., OSV.

[52]Journals 45, 49, Ledgers 55 and 56, Factory goods 91-93, Dudley Woollen Mfg. Co., OSV.

<u>1823-1824</u> (15 months)

25 men	50%	16,471 broad yards broadcloth and cassimere
12 women	36%	$13,936 labor cost
<u>13</u> children (6 girls)	26%	85¢ labor cost per yard
47		Estimated sales: $14,163.

<u>1825</u> (6 months)

22 men	45%	6,270 broad yards
14 women	29%	$21,689 labor cost
<u>13</u> children (4 girls)	27%	$3.46 labor per yard
49		Estimated sale: $32,908.

<u>1823-1825</u> (21 months)

$22,751 broad yards
$35,625 labor costs
$ 1.57 labor per yard.

<u>1826</u>

23 men	41%	19,537 broad yards
22 women	39%	$13,476 labor cost
<u>11</u> children	20%	69¢ labor per yard
56		Estimated sales: $34,788.

<u>1827</u>

25 men	45%	18,270 broad yards
17 women	31%	$10,413 labor cost
<u>13</u> children	24%	57¢ labor per yard
55		Estimated sales: $50,495.

<u>1828</u>

27 men	39%	27,300 broad yards
28 women	40%	$13,474 labor cost
<u>15</u> children	21%	49¢ labor per yard
70		Estimated sales: $53,421.

<u>1829</u> (9 months)

26 men	36%	19,215 broad yards
28 women	39%	$11,119 labor cost
<u>18</u> children	25%	58¢ labor per yard
72		Estimated sales: $45,292.

1830

25 men	32%	31,333 broad yards
27 women	35%	$14,906 labor cost
24 children (17 girls)	32%	48¢ labor per yard
77		Estimated sales: $68,810.

1831

21 men	28%	36,079 broad yards
28 women	37%	$13,753 labor cost
26 children	35%	38¢ labor per yard
75		Estimated sales: $85,833.

1832

42 men*	39%	38,344 broad yards
56 women	52%	$16,561 labor cost
10 children	9%	43¢ labor per yard
108		Estimated sales: $105,651.

*Labor force in 1832 taken from the McLane Reoprt. The group was obviously larger than in the previous year as cost was greater, but for publication, the Dudley factory probably submitted all the girls under "women," and the children were probably all boys.

There were problems in the Babcock operation. While sales and production showed a fairly normal growth, many costs besides wool were unsteady and erratic; the building and repair account was the most wildly fluctuating of all. There was a problem with the initial debt; after five years of operating, the Dudley company showed a deficit of more than $30,000. Considerable efforts were made to pay off the debt, but about the same time that interest payments reached a reasonable sum, the building and repair account rose by three times. This was partly a result of company expansion, partly because it was necessary to replace worn machinery. Money had to be borrowed to pay for that.[53]

[53] Ledgers 55-58, Dudley Woollen Mfg. Co., OSV.

This was a logical result of the newness of the industry and machinery, and the general and overall inexperience of factory management. Bezelael Taft from nearby Uxbridge Massachusetts delineated the problem for McLane's marshalls:

> Machinery, slightly constructed, has been frequently nursed with all the attention required by ricketty children--a continual tax on the business for which it was designed. In other cases, the use of expensive and well constructed machinery has been entirely superseded by the introduction of new improvements, by which a saving in labor was to be obtained beyond the value of the old machinery, or the expense of the new. In this way, the garrets and out-houses of most of our manufactories have been crowded with discarded machinery, to make room for that of more approved character. The expenses incident to such a course of operations has been a charge on the business, sometimes sustained by its profits, and occasionally by new assessments on the owner, but, in most instances, without that precision in the accounts, that could enable the owners to ascertain, with any thing like precision, how much of the profits of the business, or rather how much of their funds have been absorbed in outfits, improvements, or repairs.[54]

There could be no escaping the problem of estimating machinery replacement costs until more experience could be accrued, and possibly shared, by factory managers and machinists. At this point in time the progressive factory manager replaced and up-dated his machinery as necessary, and hopefully kept records carefully enough for himself or his successors to make appropriate judgments in the future. American machinery developed a reputation for flimsiness in the nineteenth century. In the 1820s this flimsiness was necessary to keep the machinery inexpensive enough to

---

[54]<u>McLane Report</u>, 1:80.

allow inexperienced factory managers to take the risk of investing in it in the first place.[55]

Bookkeeping, Cost Accounting

The industry also went through less tangible but no less important changes in the realm of business practices and procedures. Central to these changes were the introduction of various systems of accounting that allowed for cost analysis. American merchants, even backcountry storekeepers, seem to have been up-to-date when it came to setting up and using modern double-entry accounting systems. Merchandise accounting systems were not difficult to understand and the basics were often taught in the common schools in the nineteenth century. One had a daybook in which to enter *all* daily transactions. Unless one operated an exceptionally busy enterprise, a half-dozen to a dozen entries was a normal day's business. They were entered in the daybook as debits *to* or credits *by* an individual. At his leisure, the merchant posted his daybook entries into his ledger. The ledger was organized on an individual account basis. A debit or credit was entered under the individual's account on the left or right of the page. Usually the entry included the date, the purchase or

---

[55] Habakkuk, *American and British Technology*, pp. 86-87; Strassmann, *Risk and Technological Innovation*, pp. 108-9.

payment, and a cross-reference page number to the daybook. New accounts were entered into the ledger as they were opened, and a good bookkeeper kept an up-to-date alphabetized index of his accounts in the front of the ledger. He had some type of system for indicating that he had posted in his ledger to a certain point in time in the daybook.

This system worked fine for establishing the status of an individual account at a glance, but a merchant was required to go through his entire ledger painstakingly to determine his income or costs for a given span of time. Many a small merchant never bothered, but lived from day to day knowing his mark-up was 50 to 100 percent so that he had to make a profit if he made any sales at all. After all, he was not dealing in perishable merchandise, so his business just went on.

The entire mercantile system involved an elaborate credit network. Merchants extended credit to their customers for as long as a year--a period of time required because of the agricultural base of the economy. There was some debt payment in every community "in kind"--in goods and services, but even the "in kind" payments were based on price currents and entered into the books as money amounts based on those prices. The merchant bought from jobbers--other larger merchants located in cities often on the coast. The credit from large merchant to smaller merchant was often extended for eight months to a year. The city merchant, in turn, obtained credit from even larger merchants or importers, or after the 1790s American banks. Credit from banks was created by issuing notes as loans. By 1820 notes were as much a part of American currency as pennies and dimes.

Manufacturers had no difficulty at all working within this credit system. Hands were credited wages and their accounts were debited for rents or for goods purchased from the company store. The manufacturers used city merchants as their credit base receiving raw materials through the merchant on credit and shipping finished goods to the merchant to be sold by him and credited to the manufacturer's account. When the manufacturer himself was a merchant--Samuel H. Babcock, for example, the goods were received and sold by him and he in turn arranged shipments of raw materials through a third party.[56] Banks played a critical role providing notes in times of special need or in the case of possible expansion of plant facilities. All three companies studied relied on banks for what was ostensibly short-term credits, which actually were loans that were rolled over again and again, and for all practical purposes became long-term credits.

Most manufacturers in nineteenth-century America--those that were manufacturing beyond the stage of one or

---

[56] Samuel H. Babcock to Asa Chapman, various letters 1830-32, Box 22, Dudley Woollen Mfg. Co., OSV.

two-man workshops--were in a series of peripheral businesses besides that of manufacturing. They ran general stores, rented dwellings, managed boarding houses, operated taverns, leased farm land besides making goods. But that was not the principal problem. The principal problem seems to have been a conceptual one--just what were the elements that went into costs? Obviously raw materials were key; no manufacturer had trouble with those. Wages also were obvious, but not so simple. One could figure a given quantity of wool for a yard of broadcloth. Simon Newton Dexter figured two pounds per yard of broadcloth; Colonel Shepherd figured 2 1/4 pounds per yard.[57] Wages could not be conceived so precisely. Yet thinking in terms of labor costs per yard was exactly the tradition represented by Justice Hale in the seventeenth century, the Trowbridge clothier of 1798, and Zachariah Allen and Frederick Wolcott in the United States in 1823.[58] These analyses became fairly sophisticated as they included amounts of the wages of clerks and overseers besides the machine labor, but a great deal was left out. Depreciation or wear and tear on machinery was known to be costly. In the McLane Report, some wool manufacturers allowed 8 to 10 percent of machinery cost for machinery depreciation,[59] but where to enter it

[57] U. S. Congress, Evidence on Woollens, 1828, pp. 75, 89.

[58] Infra.

[59] McLane Report, 2:79.

in the account books? Even labor tended to be accounted in individual accounts, not as one overall labor or wage account. Commission payments, insurance, above all interest payments on debts were all significant cost items, but the bookkeeping systems in the early days had no way to include them. One could estimate "interest on capital," but where to include it? Furthermore, debt interest was often more real and immediate, than "interest on capital" and involved more in the quantity of money. There were questions about fixed versus liquid capital. Should machinery be considered an operating expense or did it become part of the company's capital investment with a resale value of its own, albeit a depreciating resale value? There was simply no one with experience in these matters.

Manufacturers succeeded in reducing their costs per yard considerably in the 1820s. This can be determined from existing ledgers. While manufacturers were surely aware that they were reducing their labor costs, no series of figures was found to indicate that they saw how much less per yard these costs became. Yet, the information was there.

The general area of business practice varied notably from factory to factory. While one senses a sizeable amount of intercommunication on technical matters from agent to agent, on matters of bookkeeping and accounting procedures, there seems to have been less interchange.

The Dudley Woollen Manufacturing Company had a sound accounting system from its inception in 1824. But its predecessor, the Merino Wool Factory Company did not keep systematic books. Slater, Howard and Company went through a major accounting change after Edward Howard left in 1829, and Victor and Charles I. du Pont and Company went through two major changes: the first when Bauduy left the firm in 1815, the second after Victor du Pont's death in 1827.

On Christmas Day, 1828 Samuel H. Babcock wrote from Boston to his agent, Major John Brown at the Dudley Woollen Manufacturing Company,

> Payments for the m$^{o.}$ of January are very large (for raw materials). You must therefore make arrangements with the Oxford Bank for what may be wanted during the ensuing month. In the meantime forward steel mixed broad which are the only kind in demand. We must appropriate all our power looms for them--grade 3 and 4 will bring 2 1/4 (dollars) in New York; the cassimeres same grade will bring 92-95 cts. I hope you will discharge the wheel-wrights, carpenters, masons, and others who are not absolutely wanted as I fear our expenses are too great for profit.
>
> P.S. Cannot you agree with Sibley and the other mechanics to wait for their money till we have a chance to get our machinery fully in operation say 6 or 8 months in order that we may pay the wool notes.
>
> *I hope you will look into our manufacturing business and see whether we are making money or whether we are losing--*
>
> If such an establishment as Hurd's (at Lowell) cannot make money, I tremble for the small ones.
>
> I believe *we* have done well the last season--but should have *done* better if more goods had been sent to market and we must now rely on our sales to pay our debts and it will be necessary to hurry our goods into market with all expedition. (Italics added.)[60]

---

[60]Samuel H. Babcock to Major John Brown, 25 December 1828, Box 21, Dudley Woollen Mfg. Co., OSV.

If Samuel H. Babcock and his agent were unable to determine the profitability of their woolen manufacture, how indeed can anyone else?

There is enough information in the daybooks and ledgers to indicate that the factory flourished, annually increasing sales, production, and productivity. Yet, except for four profitable years out of thirteen, the company lost money. One year (1831) profits were over $19,000, but this was not enough to overcome the losses of the prior six years.[61]

The factory account was the key account. It debited costs, and credited the value of production that was either sold or put away into stock. Through 1837 the factory account always showed a surplus ranging from $5,000 in leaner years to highs of $32,722 in 1831 and $37,679 in 1835.[62] The merchandise account from the company store also regularly brought in a profit usually in the neighborhood of $1,700 to $1,900 per year. And so too did the boarding house make money; not much in this case, but it did post a small credit for profit and loss. What ate up the profits for the Dudley Woollen Manufacturing Company? Expense account which included freight, advertising if there was any and some salaries was one important debit, and commissions took a few thousand dollars. But by far

---

[61]Ledgers 55-58, Dudley Woollen Mfg. Co., OSV.

[62]Ledgers 55 and 56, Dudley Woollen Mfg. Co., OSV.

the two biggest items were building and repair and the interest account.[63] As building and repair became a large item, so too did the debt and outstanding notes, and therefore interest payments. In a very good year, debt and interest could be reduced, but interest then increased as the building and repair account went up again. Most of building and repair was maintenance; new machinery purchases were nowhere near the amount debited from the building and repair account. Some of building and repair may have been capital spending, spending for buildings for example that ultimately became assets of the company. A more sophisticated accounting system would have put those expenditures in a real estate account. As accounted for at Dudley, however, they became profit and loss debits.

The Dudley Woollen Manufacturing Company's bookkeeping system was by far the most up-to-date of the three systems. It was somewhat imperfect in its lack of real estate and stock accounts, but it did separate factory costs from others. Most importantly, it did have a profit and loss account which unfortunately was not consistently balanced. It is the most human behavior to postpone the accounting of losses, and that by and large was what was done at the Dudley factory. Losses were simply forwarded to the following year, no doubt with some hopes that they somehow would be made up. After all, there was only one stockholder,

---

[63]Ibid.

and Samuel H. Babcock certainly did not need a publishable annual report. As stated above, total losses for the Dudley Woollen Manufacturing Company through 1837 were about $52,000.[64]

While in many ways the Dudley Woollen Manufacturing company was the most progressive and up-to-date of the three studied here, it alone failed in the panic of 1837. One reason is obvious: it simply lacked the resources of a du Pont or a Slater company to hold on during a protracted slow period. Aside from the macro-economics of such an economic depression--the underlying causes of the panic, for instance--individuals and companies, particularly small ones, found that their credit collapsed. They received short or no payments for goods, and creditors hounded them. The most solidly financed institutions could ride out the period and survive; many others could not, and the Dudley Woollen Manufacturing Company was one of these. Dudley was well-managed, and apparently in time was able to satisfy its creditors. The Dudley factory borrowed heavily, and like du Pont and Slater, Howard and Company included their own hands among their note holders. Jacob Oaks, one of the overseers, was a major note holder; in 1827 he accepted one for $927.29. Isaac A. Newell, another overseer, accepted a note for $2,000 March 31, 1831.[65]

---

[64]Ibid.

[65]Notes and bills 67, Dudley Woollen Mfg. Co., OSV. It should be kept in mind that the placement of

That was an auspicious year, and one can hope the note was redeemed at face value before the company stopped. The records do not show the disposition of the final debt. It is perfectly possible that all the notes were finally honored at face value. An accounting done in February 1842 showed credits greater than debits by $24,814.28.

The key to the following figures lies in the factory account. In this system that account posted as debits raw materials including wool, wages, and sundry operating expenses such as candles, firewood, belt leather, dyes, and other material required to run the factory. As can be seen, the factory had more credits than debits every year, but in some years such as 1828 or 1831 it did much better than other years. The cost of wool played a role in that. But these figures are more significant because they show with terrible clarity how much machinery maintenance, interest, and commissions cut into any potential profit. As the building and repair costs increased, the company was required to borrow more money and so increased interest debits. The best hope was that interest costs could be offset by lower factory costs, whose most likely form was cheaper wool prices.

---

certain types of debits in a given account was, and is today, a matter of personal judgment. If, for example, some of the larger building and repair account debit had been posted in a real estate account, the losses as posted in the profit and loss account would not have been so large. But one might pay the piper for such a practice; if at the time the assets of the company were sold, if those building and repair credits did not come out as assets, the loss would show up at that point.

SUMMARY OF PROFIT AND LOSS ACCOUNT, DUDLEY WOOLLEN MANUFACTURING COMPANY

Year / Item	Dr	Item	Cr	Profit or (loss)
1825 (June 30)				
Bldg & repair	$ 9,401.11	Factory	$13,704.22	($ 1,377.25)
Expense	2,068.46	Mdse	2,078.96	
Interest	2,702.39	Bdg Hse	8.91	
Commission	2,347.07			
	$17,171.40		$15,794.15	
1826				
Bldg & repair	$ 4,002.31	Factory	$ 5,281.12	($ 5,051.28)
Expense	2,031.99	Mdse	1,309.46	
Interest	2,341.94	Bdg Hse	139.26	
Commission	2,289.80			
	$11,785.03		$ 6,733.75	
1827				
Bldg & repair	$ 9,533.59	Factory	$ 5,206.05	($10,912.70)
Expense	2,240.40	Mdse	1,754.72	
Interest	3,671.93	Bdg Hse	390.93	
Commission	2,442.22			
	$18,400.58		$ 7,487.88	
1828				
Bldg & repair	$ 9,456.57	Factory	$17,750.73	$ 2,471.96
Expense	2,316.55	Mdse	1,744.64	
Interest	2,673.43	Bdg Hse	797.73	
Commission	3,030.45			
	$17,823.21		$20,295.17	

SUMMARY OF PROFIT AND LOSS ACCOUNT, DUDLEY WOOLLEN MANUFACTURING COMPANY--(Continued)

1829	Dr		Cr	Profit or (loss)
Bldg & repair	$14,419.76	Factory	$ 5,943.46	($16,123.53)
Expense	1,803.21	Mdse	1,394.00	
Interest	4,862.97	Bdg Hse	1,187.39	
Commission	2,906.18			
	$24,915.42		$ 8,791.89	

1830	Dr		Cr	Profit or (loss)
Bldg & repair	$ 4,132.37	Factory	$11,074.42	($ 1,778.01)
Expense	2,558.34	Mdse	2,525.73	
Interest	5,740.37	Bdg Hse	922.79	
Commission	3,617.22			
	$16,337.12		$14,778.01	

1831	Dr		Cr	Profit or (loss)
Bldg & repair	$ 2,324.50	Factory	$32,722.39	$19,011.77
Expense	2,128.94	Mdse	2,525.73	
Interest	5,349.81	Bdg Hse	840.78	
Commission	3,850.67			
	$15,357.98		$34,369.75	

1832	Dr		Cr	Profit or (loss)
Bldg & repair	$ 7,072.32	Factory	$18,254.07	($ 639.81)
Expense	2,225.89	Mdse	1,442.12	
Interest	6,756.04	Bdg Hse	1,783.96	
Commission	4,553.93			
	$22,138.44		$21,498.63	

SUMMARY OF PROFIT AND LOSS ACCOUNT, DUDLEY WOOLLEN MANUFACTURING COMPANY--(Continued)

	Dr		Cr	Profit or (loss)
1833				
Bldg & repair	$ 7,633.25	Factory	$15,055.21	($ 5,421.02)
Expense	3,246.27	Mdse	1,928.75	
Interest	8,159.40	Bdg Hse	1,591.67	
Commission	4,957.63			
	$23,966.55		$18,545.53	
1834				
Bldg & repair	$ 6,557.52	Factory	$23,220.14	$ 1,787.06
Expense	3,065.90	Mdse	1,924.94	
Interest	8,958.65	Bdg Hse	860.55	
Commission	5,951.06			
	$24,533.70		$26,320.76	
1835				
Bldg & repair	$ 7,249.78	Factory	$37.678.65	$ 5,441.76
Expense	3,443.84	Mdse	723.61	
Interest	12,436.84	Bdg Hse	993.52	
Commission	10,540.39			
	$34,141.01		$39,582.77	
1836				
Bldg & repair	$20,535.25	Factory	$22,569.30	($16,021.91)
Expense	3,298.15	Mdse	1,754.88	
Interest	9,924.86	Bdg Hse	700.93	
Commission	6,677.44			
	$41,047.81		$25,025.90	

SUMMARY OF PROFIT AND LOSS ACCOUNT, DUDLEY WOOLLEN MANUFACTURING COMPANY--(Continued)

1837	Dr		Cr	Profit or (loss)
Bldg & repair	$14,997.02	Factory	$14,789.70	($23,365.31)
Expense	4,112.26	Bdg Hse	210.97	
Interest	12,317.43			
Commission	6,593.30			
	$38,365.98		$15,000.67	

Total profit or (loss) from 1824 through 1837: ($51,978.27).

Whether Samuel H. Babcock himself actually lost money is difficult to say. Presumably most, if not all, the sale of fabric went through him. (These account books, like Slater, Howard and Company and Charles I. du Pont and Company lack a sales record.) If the sales did go through Babcock, he would have received the commission payments carefully posted each year in the commission account, amounting to $57,413.86 through 1837.[66] That sum plus the $11,900 dividend payments to Babcock would have made up for the company losses of $51,978.37 through March 31, 1837.[67] If these sums did accrue to Babcock, his total gain over thirteen years amounted to $17,336. The crucial piece of information that is missing is the amount of Babcock's own initial capital investment and the amount he was able to salvage after the factory closed in 1837. Even though he may have made up some of his manufacturing losses on the retail sales, it seems unlikely that he could have made up for them in their entirety. However, if $20,000 is an accurate estimate of Babcock's initial investment, and if he was able to retrieve all or most of it, an income of about $1,300 per year or 6 1/2 percent of $20,000 would seem a reasonable rate of return. ($17,336 divided by thirteen years equals $1,333.)

---

[66]Ledgers 55-58, Dudley Woollen Mfg. Co., OSV.

[67]Ibid.; Stock shares 2, Papers of Mr. and Mrs. H. Willis Babcock, OSV.

In its early years from 1822 until Edward Howard left in 1828, Slater, Howard and Company was a fine illustration of a factory with very up-to-date technology, combined with a business not well versed in advanced practices. Like most of the firms described, there was a mixture of the traditional with the more progressive. The most visible backward practice was the accounting system itself. In this case, Edward Howard used the company store, not only as a way to pay his hands in goods, but to provide the vehicle for the bookkeeping system for the entire factory village. As Sidney Pollard has shown, bookkeeping systems were rooted in merchandising, estate management, or in the old "putting out" system.[68] In the case of Slater, Howard and Company all of the factory purchases, sales, wages, insurance and commission payments, building payments, board, rents, and interest were recorded in the store daybook and posted in the ledger under the corresponding name. There was no itemization of separate accounts for say, the factory, or wool, or building and repair. Until 1829, all sales went through the commission agents, Tiffany, Sayles, and Hitchcock. This happenstance meant that the sales account went under one head.

Unless at some point costs are pulled together and broken down into fixed capital and operating expenses,

---

[68]Sidney Pollard, The Genesis of Modern Management. pp. 126, 212-13, 222-23.

there is really no way to determine profits. With each entry personalized and posted under the person who transacted the business, virtually no costs can be isolated. The only advantage the ledger has is in the determination of the status of a given personal account. Is the person owing, or is the company owing the person? Furthermore, farm labor, building labor and materials, were separated more than one logically would like. Eldridge Mason did all the masonry; Asa Wood most of the building; Alvin Wood blew stones. All of this labor was posted in the daybook among factory purchases, wages owed, purchases of groceries by hands, boarding bills and the like. To determine building costs, one had to know who built or sold what.

What is further visible from these account books is how completely the entire operation depended on credit. Samuel Slater himself provided the initial credits. Soon Slater, Howard and Company became a Boston related firm, and as soon as major sales were made by Tiffany, Sayles, and Hitchcock by May of 1823, the commission agents handled the bulk of the credit.[69] The agents paid Slater and Howard bills with Boston bank drafts, then charged the wool factory. By 1820 Boston had become a wool jobbing center, and Slater Howard and Company used as a sales agent, a firm that either could job the wool itself or be easily accessible

[69]Ledger 13, Slater, Howard & Co., Slater Coll., BL.

to companies that could. Tiffany, Sayles, and Hitchcock handled the vast bulk of the factory's raw materials, most of which came from Boston.

Wages and other costs were duly posted in the Slater, Howard and Company ledgers under the individual. Employees bought merchandise, owed rent or board, all of which were debited against their accounts. Balances were struck, apparently when there was some need, rather than on a set schedule, and payment in the early days was usually in the form of a company note, payable on demand. This varied though; some payments were in cash, specie, provided by Slater, himself. In March, 1823, William Stowell, who had built the first carding machines for Slater, Howard and Company, was paid $300 in cash, in this case, specie.[70] Payments could and were made in cloth, although this was not common locally except to Edward Howard, himself, and occasionally to Almy, Brown and Slater. Some payments were with bank notes; in July, 1823, William Stowell was paid again in cash, but now represented as a note from the Oxford Bank.[71] By 1825 Slater, Howard and Company used checks occasionally, and had accounts in the Oxford Bank locally, and one in the New England Bank of Boston.[72]

---

[70]Blotter 1, Slater, Howard & Co., Slater Coll., BL.

[71]Blotter 2, Slater, Howard & Co., Slater Coll., BL.

[72]Daybooks 5 and 6, Slater, Howard & Co., Slater Coll., BL.

Samuel Slater's major banking needs were no doubt answered by the Manufacturers Bank of North Providence, Rhode Island, of which he was President.

Edward Howard came to Dudley, Massachusetts in 1812. The French River site at Dudley had been described to Samuel Slater in 1811 by a friend and business associate as "the most benighted part of the globe," yet as a convenient and secure water power source with sufficient water fall to erect a sizeable mill.[73] Howard, too, must have seen something he liked as he stayed in the area working for Merino Wool Factory Company and probably others until he began his association with Samuel Slater in 1822. Slater's biographers have described his association with Edward Howard as that "rare instance of his (Slater's) selection of a partner who proved lacking in integrity and business judgment."[74] It is certainly true that Slater was dissatisfied with Howard's performance. A letter written February 3, 1829, stated with some clarity the dissatisfaction with Howard's operation, but unfortunately sheds no light on specific onerous acts:

---

[73]Bela Tiffany to Samuel Slater, 27 May 1811, cited by Holmes Ammidown, Historical Collections, 2 vols. (New York: By the Author, 1874), 1:464-65.

[74]Edward H. Cameron, Samuel Slater, Father of American Manufactures (Portland, Me.: Bond, Wheelwright, 1960), p. 136.

Messrs.--

North Providence, Feb. 3, 1829

Gentlemen,--S. Slater & Sons have come to a to place that ignoble establishment in Dudley, called Slater & Howard's woollen factory, in a state of respectability. Whether or not it was got up in iniquity I cannot say; but I fear some things during the life of it, are mysterious. It is the united wish of S. Slater & Sons to sink into oblivion the past inroads that have been made, one way or another, on that establishment. They are very anxious to place the business, in future, on a fair mutual ground, so as to pay about six thousand dollars a year for extra stock, raising the wind, bad debts, and too liberal commissions...Yours, &c

Samuel Slater[75]

It seems most likely that Edward Howard was extravagant and dissolute rather than dishonest. He made fine cloth and both the Massachusetts Agricultural Society and the Franklin Institute had awarded Slater, Howard and Company broadcloth first premiums.[76] One local antiquarian described Howard as,

> This big Yorkshireman, of good mental capacity, was a very giant in size, rotund, rosy, and jolly to a remarkable degree. It is impossible for the 'milksops' of our degenerate age to conceive of the grand fashion in which Howard and his boon companions drank rum and sung songs, making these hills and valleys vocal with their carousals.[77]

The record of the daybooks and ledgers do bear out extravagances. After Howard left the firm, for example,

---

[75]White, Memoir of Slater, pp. 245-46.

[76]Manufacturer's and Farmer's Journal, 11 November 1824, 27 October 1826.

[77]Ammidown, Historical Collections, 1:477.

the average monthly wage costs dropped $300 to $1,489 per month in 1829.[78] After the company was reorganized in October, 1829, a profit and loss account was established. The entire company debt was renegotiated, tabulated, and posted. One hundred-ninety notes were drawn for a total debt of $105,480.74.[79] Most notes were written to suppliers and dealers, including Sayles and Hitchcock with whom the bulk of the business had been carried. Some of the debt was negotiated with the Oxford Bank. Other notes were made payable to hands and to local Dudley residents from whom Slater, Howard and Company had purchased land and water rights. At this point a new clerk was employed, and now while cost accounting may have been less than adequate by contemporary standards, there was a very great improvement.

Howard's personal debt to the company was sizeable--he left a note to the company for $18,318.34. How this sum was reached is not clear, and it was paid off by 1836.[80]

Since sales after 1829 were dispersed under a variety of accounts in the ledgers, there can be no clear sense of how well the company was doing from that viewpoint. There was an interest account, and that may serve as a reference point for profit and loss:

---

[78] Daybooks 9-12, Slater, Howard & Co.; Labor account, Ledgers 11 and 12, Dudley Manufacturing Company Papers, Slater Coll., BL.

[79] Ledger 11, Dudley Mfg. Co., Slater Coll., BL.

[80] Ibid.

Interest debit, Slater, Howard[81]	
1829	$ 5,162.15
1830	3,040.49
1831	7,971.60
1832	10,611.90
1833	7,209.20
1834	11,141.40

Indebtedness must have increased as losses increased. Assuming that most of the debt was carried at the legal Massachusetts rate of 6 percent, the 1834 debt was $185,690. While sales of cloth may be estimated at more than $90,000 by 1832 ($1.50 x yardage), indebtedness increased $39,000 from 1831 to 1832; decreased $57,000 from 1832 to 1833; but increased again by over $65,000 from 1833 to 1834. This represents not only highly fluctuating losses and gains, but just plain high losses for a small manufacturing institution. It also should be borne in mind that this was debt on notes, not simply credit debt. The ratio of note debt to credit debt was probably very, very high for S. Slater and Sons' woolen factory, as management sought to get good credit ratings from raw material dealers after Edward Howard left. What allowed the woolen factory to stay in business was Samuel Slater himself.

In 1829, Dan Munyan, a home grown product who with his family owed all to Slater, Howard and Company, was made a supervisor. A new clerk brought modern bookkeeping

[81]Interest account, Ledgers 11 and 12, Dudley Mfg. Co., Slater Coll., BL.

methods with labor accounts, wool accounts, and interest accounts, enabling management to get some quick overviews of how moneys were being spent. The company debt was itemized and provisions made to deal with it systematically and through appropriate banking agencies if necessary. In short, while it could never in those early years count on a decent price for raw wool, and while the Slater assets provided a considerable cushion for the business to fall back on, one small factory found its business practices catching up to its technological expertise. By 1832 they would seem on a par with each other.

Edward Howard clearly was no classic entrepreneur. If anything, he symbolized the attitude of Saint Monday, the lack of discipline and time sense that New Englanders, and Americans generally, were rooting out of their efficient factories. Local historians describe Edward Howard dying impoverished in his native Yorkshire, a fitting end, some must have felt, for this jovial, inefficient non-Yankee.

The accounting system used by Victor and Charles I. du Pont and Company consisted of journals used as daybooks and a ledger. Most transactions in the ledger were listed under the given names of the account. This, of course, is very similar to standard merchandising bookkeeping. Some attempts were made to isolate types of accounts to obtain a clearer notion of specific gains or losses--there was a wool account, one for the dye house and most importantly, one for cloth. The cloth account credited the value of factory production and debited wages, wool, and the dye house, but this ledger stopped in February, 1815, and whoever took over the bookkeeping after that was a less sophisticated or less interested accountant.

A record was kept for bills payable. Most of these were short term notes for thirty days to four months, and most were owed to commission merchants for wool and other raw materials. Some were for machinery. Most of the notes were renewed as they came due. That particular type of indebtedness went from $4,200 in January, 1811, to $40,408 by the end of 1815 plus the drafts on the Philadelphia agents, Garische and Ravesies, of $21,600. Twenty-seven thousand, five hundred dollars of the debt was a mortgage held by Peter Bauduy for his share of the business.[82]

The du Ponts were certainly no strangers to modern financial institutions. As early as 1802 E. I. du Pont de Nemours & Company was writing checks on the Bank of Delaware. In 1814 Victor and Charles I. du Pont and Company were paying some employees by check.[83] The woolen factory did not get involved financially with local banks until after the War of 1812. It probably

---

[82]Bills payable 72, Chas. I. du Pont & Co., Acc. 500, EMHL.

[83]Check stub book 131, Bank of Wilmington & Brandywine, Charles I. du Pont & Co., Acc. 500, EMHL.

did not need to. This situation existed not because the company did not need credit and loans, but because the parent gunpowder company provided all the credit support the woolen company needed.

From February 16, 1815 to April 1, 1827, the records for the Victor and Charles I. du Pont Company are scattered and uneven. Judging by the accounts, there was no consuming interest on anyone's part in running the business. If Charles du Pont was running the company, the change in bookkeeping practices that took place after his father's death indicate a complete reorientation or renaissance on his part. Most likely, Victor du Pont was in charge until he died in January 1827. Perhaps, Charles du Pont, like a proper eighteenth-century French lad of the upper classes deferred to his father, and interfered with the record keeping as little as possible.

Starting April 1, 1827, the newly created Charles I. du Pont and Company began a new era. The most visible aspect of the new organization and management was in the accounting system itself. In the account books and ledgers, there was a well-constructed system to come to grips with accounting for factory costs and expenses. There was a factory account which included such items as belt leather, candles, glue, twine, iron, soap, and sig. It also included Sacriste's work and raw materials for dyeing. There were also accounts for machinery, wages, wool, and one for drugs that was used after Sacriste was bought out in 1832. The woolen goods account credited the value of production. Hopefully, it represented sales for the most part, but also must have included goods kept as stock on hand. In some accounting systems this would have been called the stock account. Production of course related to sales, but with such an elastic market, production and sales seldom coincided, so care must be taken not to equate the woolen goods account with the sale of goods. The debits in the woolen goods account were returned items, and amounted to a significant sum only in 1827 when a large amount of goods were inventoried and returned to stock. The wages account received credits in the form of rents from employees.[84]

Perhaps the most interesting aspect of the du Pont accounts in these years was the very small sums spent for machinery. The du Pont company had a well equipped factory at its start in 1809, continued to buy up-to-date machinery through the teens including the Brewster spinner, but after 1822 there were few major machinery purchases, and little evidence that productivity increased notably at Charles I. du Pont and Company before 1832. The du Pont company had built five of their own power satinet looms before 1827; at least that seems the most plausible explanation for

[84]Ledgers 56 and 57, Chas. I. du Pont & Co., Acc. 500, EMHL.

their presence in the inventory of Victor du Pont's will.[85] There was no record of power loom purchases until 1832. Labor costs did decline at the company, but not as much as at the Massachusetts factories. Furthermore, it must be acknowledged that the figures presented for quantities of production are purely estimates, although hopefully they are based on sound assumptions.

As bookkeeping systems are compared, it should be noted that no accountant at Charles I. du Pont and Company prepared a summary account. This summary was derived from ledgers for this paper. The critical amount shown here is from woolen goods. This was not sales, but the amount of goods produced at hoped for market prices. After 1827 drugs were part of the account with Sacriste and included under the factory account. Dyeing was sub-contracted to Sacriste until he was bought out in 1832. Profit and loss here included interest payments, commissions, insurance, and bad debts.[86] In view of the average annual losses of a little over $2,500 per year, it would be well to note that Charles I. du Pont's salary from the company was $1,000 per year.[87]

---

[85]Hartmann, "The du Pont Woolen Venture."

[86]Ledgers 56 and 57, Chas. I. du Pont & Co., Acc. 500, EMHL.

[87]Ibid.

SUMMARY ACCOUNTS:CHARLES I. DU PONT & COMPANY[88]

1827 (April 1-December 31)

	Dr	Cr	
Machinery	-	-	
Factory	6,226.32	1,420.01	
Drug	2,264.41	683.99	
Wages	9,064.30	1,277.78	(rents, board)
Wool	10,393.10	28.56	
Woolen goods	10,215.61	31,588.43	
Profit & loss	3,687.18	3.89	
	$41,850.92	$35,002.69	($6,848.23)

1828

	Dr	Cr	
Machinery	-	-	
Factory	12,497.45	1,496.88	
Drug*	-	-	
Wages	11,587.48	991.69	
Wool	18,963.82	74.83	
Woolen goods	505.96	46,071.97	
Profit & loss	4,529.48	25.90	
	$48,084.19	$48.661.27	$ 577.08

1829

	Dr	Cr	
Machinery	595.00	-	
Factory	13,657.18	682.28	
Drug*	-	-	
Wages	9,363.47	790.08	
Wool	15,858.54	74.83	
Woolen goods	405.96	41,765.58	
Profit & loss	9,033.46	541.38	
	$48,913.61	$43.854.15	($5,059.46)

1830

	Dr	Cr	
Machinery	321.20	100.00	
Factory	10,115.83	552.82	
Drug*	-	-	
Wages	8,823.49	398.45	
Wool	22,256.86	541.68	
Woolen goods	2,835.95	43,966.45	
Profit & loss	4,616.04	226.22	
	$48.969.37	$44,785.62	($4,183.75)

---

[88] Journals 38, 39, Ledger 57, 58, Chas. I. du Pont & Co., Acc. 500, EMHL.

1831

	Dr	Cr	
Machinery	163.00	-	
Factory	11,423.70	719.02	
Drug*	-	-	
Wages	9,932.80	-	
Wool	32,964.35	2,609.42	
Woolen goods	12.25	54,209.63	
Profit & loss	6,039.36	-	
	$60,535.46	$57.538.07	($2,997.39)

1832

	Dr	Cr	
Machinery	710.84	-	
Factory	10,250.18	523.44	
Drug	961.47	-	
Wages	9,356.60	629.54	
Wool	16,733.39	-	
Woolen goods	172.45	45,031.94	
Profit & loss	4,165.30	-	
	$42,450.28	$46,184.92	$3,734.64

---

*Nothing in the drug count, because all dyeing was done by Sacriste. Average payment to him for four years--$3,257.86 per year. In 1832, he was bought out for $1,478.77.

Losses from April 1, 1827 to December 31, 1832 amounted to $14,777.11, an average annual loss of $2,569.93.

The du Pont woolen factory was clearly less dynamic, more paternalistic, and more traditionally oriented than its counterparts in New York and New England. Lack of interest in new machinery and slow productive growth are apparent from the figures and information above. The paternalism showed up in such institutions as the Sunday school run by Victorine du Pont for all the children working in du Pont factories. In 1828, E. I. du Pont testified that, "All the children employed in, and dependent on, our factories, are regularly taught in Sunday schools until they acquire the rudiments of a tolerable education."[89] This was no idle boast; in 1827 there were 200 pupils in the "Brandywine Sunday School."[90] A doctor was retained by the company to treat hands.[91] Injured workmen were given small jobs to do on the property and retained on the payroll.[92] Even a dancing master was hired at one point to provide lessons for workers.[93]

The reasons for the lack of dynamism do not require an intensive search. The main interest of the du Pont family was in gun powder. Gun powder made the family fortune in America, and gun powder claimed most of the energies of the family until and through the Civil War. But more important was the lack of competition. Wilmington boasted another important woolen manufacturing owned by William Young, but by 1832, the son claimed that the company had turned its attention to the manufacture of cotton rather than wool. There were small woolen factories in Pennsylvania, a number of satinet factories in New Jersey, but nothing like the numbers in New York and New England. The Charles I. du Pont

---

[89]U.S. Congress, Evidence on Woollens, 1828, p. 125.

[90]Raymond G.Betts, "Eleuthère Irénée du Pont and the Brandywine Sunday School," Delaware History 8 (September 1959):342-53.

[91]Petit ledger 63, Chas. I. du Pont & Co., Acc. 500, EMHL.

[92]Winterthur Mss., Grp. 3, Victor du Pont, W3-4653, EMHL.

[93]Petit ledger 62, Chas. I. du Pont & Co., Acc. 500, EMHL.

and Company provided comfort for its owner, and to 1832 at least, an adequate living for those who worked for the company. Its products were mostly cheap woolen goods that literally suffered no competitors.

Of the three companies studies in some depth, the most dynamic was certainly Babcock's Dudley Woollen Manufacturing Company. It was the most modern in its bookkeeping and accounting systems, and it continually purchased newer, more up-to-date machinery. Compared to Charles I. du Pont and Company, its profit and loss accounts fluctuated wildly, and those fluctuations were rooted in three basic causes:

1. The price of raw wool ranged from thirty-two cents per pound to eighty-two cents from 1817 to 1837. (See appendix.) Fine wool was expensive, and it was, of course, the essential raw material. All through the teens and 1820s there were continual meetings among wool manufacturers to promote a protective tariff for manufactured goods. Yet, very little evidence was found for efforts to reduce the cost of raw wool; ironically, the tariff on goods more than offset the tariff on raw wool which was 7 1/2 percent in 1815, and raised to 15 percent in 1824. By the tariff of 1828 duties on goods and raw wool were so high that they literally invited fraud.[94]

2. The elasticity of the market for finished

---

[94]Taussig, Tariff History of the United States, 79-86; Heaton, Yorkshire Cloth Traders in the United States, passim.

woolens especially fine broadcloths was also a major factor in the fluctuating profitability among woolen manufacturers. One way to escape this problem was to concentrate more on the cheaper fabrics such as satinet and even cassimeres. By 1832 all three of these companies had begun to place more emphasis on the cheaper cloths; by that time the most expensive cloth the du Ponts manufactured was army kersey. As reported in Mc Lane in 1832 the Dudley Woollen Manufacturing Company made 37,500 yards of cassimere, 30,000 yards of broadcloth. Slater, Howard and Company manufactured 27,750 yards of broadcloth, 14,000 yards of cassimere, and 37,850 yards of satinet.[95] Since 1822 du Pont had been manufacturing primarily satinet, linseys, and other cheap woolens.

3. The efforts of all three manufacturers to keep abreast of new machinery developments was certainly an expense factor for all of them. Babcock can be seen in the forefront in this case, and his efforts to keep up-to-date were certainly part of his wildly fluctuating profit and loss picture. The du Ponts were less concerned with new machines, and the profit and loss picture does not fluctuate as wildly there.

By the late 1820s all three woolen manufacturers had found new accounting techniques to help them come to grips with the analyses of costs. Manufacturing by machinery

---

[95] McLane Report, 1: 376-7, 484-5.

put a premium on cost analysis partly because of the machinery itself. No one had yet had any experience with machinery costs, particularly as machines became worn out or obsolete. Furthermore, manufacturing involved a whole new range of expenses such as commission and insurance payments, advertising and freight, interest payments on debt, a conglomerate of wages calculated over different time periods, and raw materials of different weights and measures. The new accounting systems used by Babcock from the beginning and later by Charles du Pont and Samuel Slater helped to clarify manufacturing costs, and hence profits or the lack of them. Factory agents often were not merely managing manufactories but whole villages--the rent, food needs, and entertainment not only of operatives, but tenant farmers, subcontracting machinists, and traveling salesmen. The new accounting methods brought some order out of the chaos.

CONCLUSION

The American woolen industry was given life by the shortages and consequent high prices brought about by the Napoleonic Wars. The vastly inflated prices of 1813 to 1815 convinced many with excess capital to invest in manufacturing, most particularly woolen manufacturing. By 1820 there were at least 250 small woolen factories in the United States. Almost all were water powered; all had the capacity to full and card, and many had introduced mechanical spinning and finishing to their range of processes. By the mid-1820s, the more progressive factories had harnessed broadloom weaving to their waterpower.

Competition in the quality and price of fine woolens was rampant and came mainly in the United States from the mills of Yorkshire and the western counties of England. The woolen broadcloth industry had roots and traditions dating back to Tudor times. By the Napoleonic wars England too had begun slowly to mechanize a tradition-bound industry. American woolen manufacturing probably never matched the quality of the finest superfine English broadcloths, but mechanization enabled Americans to cut costs and produce much more uniform qualities of goods.

When trade with England was resumed after the wars, Americans could not compete with the quality or the prices of English woolens. Many factories folded or were taken over by other hopeful entrepreneurs. Americans believed the key to cheaper manufacturing lay in machinery, and because New Englanders tended to be a group of literate people, many otherwise ordinary men became extraordinary tinkerers and inventors. Soon after the war, Americans were patenting shearing machines, spinning machines, and power looms. Manufacturing expertise was not only homegrown, but imported as well; even such natives of Yorkshire as Edward Howard began to see the need for machinery.

Americans were convinced, probably not entirely correctly, that wages in England were lower than in America. Machines became a panacea to lower wages. One of the most significant ways to lower wages was to replace skilled male workers with unskilled (and cheaper) women. Skills or even muscle were not required to tend machines; in 1820 the majority of workers in woolen mills were men, in 1832 the majority were women.

Even if wages were higher in the United States than in Great Britain, most English woolen mills relied on steam power requiring coal. Coal costs should have balanced American outlays for higher wages. In New England, commerce was more economically significant than agriculture; in New York state commerce and agriculture competed side by side. In both areas waterpower was plentiful, cheap, and unencumbered by complex upstream and downstream riparian rights. By 1820, manufacturing had become a third and vital economic element in both areas.

Americans had mixed feelings about manufacturing. In some instances, they were unable to come up with a clear meaning for "domestic manufactures." Did one mean manufacturing at home? Or did one perhaps mean home manufacture as opposed to foreign manufacture? During colonial times, one of the premises of the mercantile system was the reliance of the "mother country" on raw materials from the colonies; and the colonies consequent dependence on manufactured goods from "home," or rather, England. For many years, Thomas Jefferson was clearly of the view that Americans were better off allowing their "workshops (to) remain in Europe,"[1] but by 1816 even Jefferson was writing that it was time to "place the manufacturer by the side of the agriculturist."[2] As Jefferson's views changed so too did those of other Americans. Alexander Hamilton, Tench Coxe, and Matthew Carey had been promoters of American manufacturing since the 1790s. Now as such men as Samuel Slater, various du Ponts, Francis Cabot Lowell became manufacturers, both the appeal of profit and ideology turned the tide of sentiment. Americans were aware of

---

[1]Thomas Jefferson, Notes on the State of Virginia (New York: Harper Torchbooks, 1964), p. 158.

[2]Thomas Jefferson to Benjamin Austin, 9 January 1816, in The Government and the Economy, 1783-1861, ed. Carter Goodrich (Indianapolis, Bobbs-Merrill, 1967), pp. 184-87.

conditions in European, and particularly English, factories. What they deplored above all, was the use, abuse and exploitation of children. In the early days before 1832, while child labor was certainly employed, and often employed for long daylight hours, children were encouraged to go to school, and most factories did not employ them for anything like the whole year. Six to eight weeks to six to eight months were common working periods for children.

If the American manufacturer's first love affair was with machinery, his second was with accounting systems. If keeping even with competitors was critical in the matter of machines and their efficiency and productivity, neither of the latter could be measured without a complete knowledge and understanding of costs. Cost accounting was at its very raw beginning in the 1820s. Of the manufacturers studied in this paper, none seemed to have such a genuine grasp of the techniques to completely know his costs. Enough beginnings were in evidence, however, to enable a modern analyst to bring together the important data. That data with the help of instant calculating gadgets enables the present day analyst to affirm what those early manufacturers already knew--machinery did save money. Machinery did allow factories to produce more efficiently.

The final point of this monograph is perhaps even more fundamental. Industrialization and modernization are seen by such economic historians as Walt W. Rostow as virtually identical.[3] Whatever concepts of modernization are considered most salient, those concepts are predicated on something like mass production which in turn is dependent on machinery set in motion by inanimate power. It is a familiar story in cotton textiles in Great Britain and the United States. Productivity in woolens was never so dramatically increased as it was in cottons. Nevertheless, woolen cloth was produced by machinery, inanimately powered, and located in small but integrated factories where the end product of the raw wool was cloth. By 1830 most American woolen machinery was American invention and built in the United States.

The use of machinery brought with it problems in cost analysis never before encountered. It was a relatively simple matter to determine costs for manufacturng if one included only wages and raw materials. But machines not only embraced an initial cost, but running costs, repair costs, and replacement costs. It was these costs that forced manufacturers to revise and update their accounting systems. The new accountng systems enabled manufacturers to place realistic values on machinery.

[3]Walt W. Rostow, The States of Economic Growth, 2nd ed. (Cambridge: Cambridge University Press, 1971), pp. 1-16; Richard D. Brown, Modernization: The Transformation of American Life, 1600-1865 (New York: Hill & Wang, 1976), pp. 3-22; Thomas C. Cochran, "The Business Revolution," American Historical Review 79 (December 1974):1449-66.

Appendix A

PAYROLLS

Payroll, 1822, Victor and Charles I. du Pont and Company

Sorting			
Samuel Lawford	$1.00/day		$ 73.72
Henry Letition	1.00/day		297.50
Scouring			
Joseph Burke (colored)	18/month		205.62
Dye shop			
Louis Sacriste	(see salaries)		
W. Colburn	21/mo.		247.94
Phillip Richards	15/mo.		160.83
Peter Yorbert	8/mo.		32.00
Joseph Yorbert	15/mo.		180.00
Spinning and slubing			
Henry Pierce	$22; 24; 27/mo.		291.00
John Sterling	by the pound (3 to 5¢)		320.70
Samuel Henderson	"		336.04
John Bancroft	(also weaving)		51.60
Henry Clark	"		375.88
Richard Pierce	"		236.53
Robert Hanlan	26/mo.		95.00
Lawrence Savage	by the pound		107.82
John Mitchell	"		143.91
John Lithone	"		142.91
Jeremiah Whitehead	"		113.49
			$3,412.19
Broadcloth waving @ 16 to 31¢/yard			
Andrew Armstrong	(also cassimère)	544 yards	168.64
Henry Finigan	" "	938 yards	201.14
James Nelson		278 yards	47.34
John Quinn	" "	1,237 yards	263.54
Isaac Dickey		1,323 3/4 yards	266.16
Hugh Mulholland	" "	312 3/4 yards	53.66
Thomas Farmer	" "	108 3/4 yards	21.75
John Baltz	" "	205 3/4 yards	35.21
Alexander Mairs	" "	598 1/2 yards	103.35
Henry Courtney	" "	234 yards	42.12
John St. Leger	" "	275 3/4 yards	49.64
William Ferguson	" "	276 1/2 yards	47.09
		6,332 3/4	$1,299.64

Cassimere weaving @ 8 to 14¢yard

Andrew Armstrong		428 yards	$ 43.41
Henry Finigan		738 1/4 yds.	79.18
Bernard McCann		1,498 3/4 yds.	184.67
also	102 1/2 yds. kersey @ 6 1/2¢		6.39
Andrew McGrath		2,145 1/4 yds.	255.68
James Pierce		1,940 1/4 yds.	223.62
James Nelson		1,110 1/2 yds.	143.48
John Quinn		100 1/2 yds.	12.56
Henry Miller		495 1/4 yds.	52.90
Owen McQuade		1,863 3/4 yds.	210.35
Richard Tracy		1,042 3/4 yds.	125.51
Thomas Sherry		1,476 1/2 yds.	173.54
Michael McGrath		1,967 yds.	238.79
Terence McGrand		1,467 1/2 yds.	171.90
Hugh Mulholland		1,263 yds.	159.84
Thomas Farmer		1,415 1/2 yds.	169.18
Michael Wall		1,721 yds.	200.07
also	590 3/4 yds. linsey @ 5¢		29.79
John Connoway		1,573 yds.	183.98
John Baltz		1,364 1/4 yds.	185.20
William McGrath		1,593 3/4 yds.	191.74
John Murdock		798 1/2 yds.	73.02
John Henderson		1,324 yds.	105.92
Alexander Mairs		1,092 yds.	137.20
Abraham Whitehead		220 1/2 yds.	26.80
James Breen		1,243 yds.	128.68
John Stapleton		351 3/4 yds.	43.93
Henry Courtney		1,323 1/2 yds.	161.75
Hugh McGowan		1,031 1/2 yds.	110.54
James McGann		1,454 yds.	156.67
John Bancroft		295 3/4 yds.	33.18
John St. Leger		619 1/2 yds.	76.99
William Frguson		638 1/4 yds.	81.72
James McCrane		98 3/4 yds.	9.77
Francis O'Neale		264 3/4 yds.	30.84
William Holland		1,611 yds.	135.51
also in the country	269 1/2 yds. @ 5 & 5 1/2¢		14.15
Francis Keho		1,550 1/2 yds.	179.08
		39,121	$4,517.86

Fulling and finishing

M. G. Reichenberger	$24/mo.		(fulling)	100.61
Joseph France	13/mo.	(?)	(finishing)	137.66
George W. Powell	24/mo.		(pressing)	281.53
William Lilly		(?)	(finishing) 4 mo.	106.75
John Mitchell	1.25/day		(fulling)	31.25
				$ 651.80

Mechanician

Samuel Saxton	1.25/day	356.88

Apprentices		
Louis Dautremont	3/mo. & board	$ 38.00
William Connoway	2.50/mo. & board & overwork	31.86
		$ 69.86
Adult male labor		
Charles Evans	$24/mo.	249.71
George Bratton	17/mo.	199.45
Francis Petit de Mange	18/mo.	216.00
Joseph Dixon	13 & 20/mo. plus extra work	219.00
Pierre D'Arnauld	19/mo.	228.00
Ezra Evans	16/mo.	179.69
Robert Evans	10/mo. (See Rebecca Evans.)	
Joseph Henderson	19.50/mo.	221.50
Phillip Megren	12.50 & board	190.93
Jack Henderson	10/mo. (Same as John, weaver ?, see Rachel Henderson.)	
		$1,734.28
Adult female labor		
Mary Henderson	8/mo. (warping) & board for Mary and Joseph ($204.00)	89.55
Maria Evans	8/mo. (See Rebecca.)	
Catherine McDermott	6/mo. (See Mary McDermott.)	23.89
Mary McGee	? (burling)	
Mary Baltz	14/mo. (See Daniel Baltz.)	
Mary McCann	7/mo (See John McCann.)	
Mrs. Monk	8/mo. (spooling)	16.36
Ann Reynlds	7/mo.	7.54
Fanny Aikens	7/mo.	44.86
Mariane Petit de Mange	7/mo.	32.50
Eliza Bedford	7/mo.	4.18
Sally Mathews	7/mo.	75.27
Margaret Ann	7/mo.	12.12
Mrs. Powell	(warping, spooling)	130.60
Mrs. Nixon	(spinning, spooling)	46.87
		$ 483.74
Male child labor		
James McDermott	4/mo. (See Mary McDermott.)	
Daniel Baltz	4/mo. (See Mary.)	107.59
Alfred McDonald	3/mo. (See Catherine.)	
Joseph Baldwin	5/mo.)	8.46
Benjamin Baldwin	5/mo.)	
John McCann	4/mo. (See Mary above, Bridget)	145.74
John Breen	3.50/mo.	23.13
William Bratton	5/mo.)	
James Bratton	4/mo.)	133.63
George Bratton	4/mo.)	
Alexander	3/mo.) (Bonus ? to family.)	66.00

Male child labor (cont.)			
James Leonard	3.50/mo.	(See Mary Boyle.)	$ 27.34
George Evans	4/mo.	(See Rebecca Evans.)	
James Smith	4/mo.		22.00
John Aiken	4/mo.		4.53
James Murphy	4/mo.		12.61
James Carrol	3/mo.		5.99
Charles Green	4/mo.		11.39
Denis Calahan	4/mo.		17.22
George Murphy	4/mo.		17.84
Edward Kelly	5/mo.		69.68
			$ 673.15
Female child labor			
Mary McDermott	3/mo.)	Plus Catherine & James	86.36
Bridgit McDermott	3/mo.)		
Catherine McDonald	4/mo.	See Alfred	39.41
Mary Ann Frydy	4/mo.	Ward of John Baltz	
Rachel Henderson	4/mo.)		88.45
Margaret Henderson	4/mo.)		
Bridget McCann	4/mo.	(See Mary, John.)	145.74
Mary Boyle	3.50/mo.	Ward Mrs. Leonard	26.95
Rebecca Evans	4/mo.	(See Robt., Maria, George)	282.65
Bridgit Carrol	3/mo.		10.03
Susan Aiken	4/mo.		32.80
			$ 712.39
Extra work and work on the mill race, 23 men. ($221.86)			
Spooling account			123.84
Salaries			
James White, overseer for 6 mo.			225.00
Charles Evans			249.71
Louis Scriste			1,000.00
Victor duPont			1,000.00
Charles duPont			800.00

Payroll, June 30, 1828, Slater, Howard & Co. (25 days)

Sorting		
William Black	2,219 lb. @ 9/c ($1.50 cwt)	$ 33.21
Jerry Waterhouse	2,545 lb.	38.17
Carding and roping		
William Wait	2,233 3/4 lb. @ 1 1/2¢	33.50
George Clapp	2,653 1/2 lb.	39.80
Picking		
William Hollingshead	549 lb. Spanish wool @ 2¢	10.98
Spinning		
Amos Bartlett	1,300 Runs warp @ 1 3/4¢	22.75
William H. Tourtelott		16.26
Hammon Webster	1,381 R.	24.16
Levi Bartlett	1,931 R.	33.79
Daniel Alridge	1,381 R.	24.17
Martin Walsh	1,870 R.	32.73
Jesse Robinson	116 lb. kersey filling @ 4¢	4.64
	1,103 lb. broad filling @ 3¢	33.10
John Scholfield	470 3/4 fine broad fill @ 4¢	18.83
	35 lb. fine broad fill @ 5¢	1.75
	366 lb. broad fill @ 3¢	10.98
John Brierly	130 1/4 lb. kersey filling @ 4¢	5.21
	694 lb. broad fill @ 3¢	20.82
Setting teasels		
Cornelius Doran	2,148 handles @ 6/ c ($1.00 per 100)	21.48
Kersey weaving		
Hannah Robbins	250 2/4 yards @ 7¢	17.54
Susan Hoyle	224 1/4 yds.	15.70
Lucy White	171 1/4 yds.	11.99
Edward Calvert	27 1/4 yds.	1.91
Joseph Scholfield	96 2/4 yds @ 8¢	7.72
	769 3/4	
Broadcloth weaving--hand loom		
Robert Burns	189 yards @ 14¢	26.46
Henry Anderson	107 3.4 yards	15.09
John Brierly	1 3/4 yds.	.25
John Archer	136 3/4 yds.	19.15
John Buckley	174 2/4 yds.	24.43
William Archer	9 3/4 yds.	1.37
Edward Calvert	86 2/4 yds.	12.11
Robert Tomlinson	156 2/4 yds.	21.91
Samuel Booth	55 3/4 yds.	7.81
	24 yds. fine broadcloth @ 20¢	4.80

Broadcloth weaving--hand loom (cont.)

Samuel Johnson	139 1/4 yds. broad @ 14¢	$	19.50
William Cline	75 yds.		10.50
Robert Wilson	139 3/4 yds.		19.57
George Booth	135 yds.		18.90
John Shaw	56 yds.		7.84
	48 2/4 fine broadcloth @ 20¢		9.70
Owen Quin	72 3/4 yds. broadcloth @ 14¢		10.19
Joseph Wood	89 yds. fine broadcloth @ 25¢		22.25
James Jones	112 1/4 yds. broadcloth @ 14¢		15.72
	1,810	$	748.74

Broadcloth weaving--power loom

Almira Brown	197 1/4 yards @ 9¢	17.75
Elmira Bolton	191 1/4 yds.	17.21
Sally Sweet	170 2/4 yds.	15.35
Thomason Penniman	158 2/4 yds.	11.09
Jonana Perry	193 2/4 yds.	17.42
Charlotte Barclay	132 3/4 yds.	11.95
Almira Powers	168 3/4 yds.	15.19
Eliza Shaw	Labor 4 10/12 days @ 15/6 per week	2.08
	117 3/4 yds. @ 9¢	10.60
Jane Herbison	17 3/4	1.60
	1,347 1/4	

Adult male labor

Henry Platt	6/ per day ($1.00)	25 days	25.00
Edward Huslin	$17.50 per month	22 1/2 days	15.14
Josiah Moulton	16 " "	25	15.39
Day Harris	10.83 " "	25	10.41
Ezra Munyan	13 " "	25	12.50
Thomas S. Chishold	6/ per day	25	25.00
Daniel Skinner	$16 per month	25	15.39
Mathew Ryan	40 " "	25	38.48
Charles Ryan	20 " "	25	19.23
John Ryan	20 " "	25	19.23
Kyan Ryan	20 " "	12	9.23
Elisha Todd	16 " "	22	13.50
William Herbison	16 " "	9	5.54
George Greaves	7/6 per day ($1.25)	25	31.25
Abel Davis	89¢ per day	24	19.20
Dan Munyan	7/6 per day	24	30.00
Zephiniah Bartlett, per bill			2.16
Asa Bartlett	$20 per month	25	19.23
Jonathon Perry	5/6 per day (83¢)	24	22.00
Arba Graves	$15.83 per month	23	14.00
George Hill			
Reuben Loomis	$15 per month	21 1/4	12.26
Horace Vinton	12.50 per month	22	10.58
William Price	9/ per day ($1.50)	25	37.50
James Fenton	$21 per month	24	19.38
Joseph Halliwell	6/ per day	25	25.00

Adult male labor (cont.)			
John Frazier	$17.15 per month	23	$ 15.17
Edward Kennedy, Sr.	3/6 per day (58¢)	25	14.58
Oliver Parsons	$17 per month	25	16.35
James Booth	16 " "	24 1/2	15.08
Joseph Booth	17 " "	5	3.27
Adam Graham	16 " "	10 3/4	6.62
Gideon Brown	7/6 per day	7 3/4	9.69
Arnold Brown	6/ per day	7 3/4	7.75
J. Munyan	6/ per day	2 3/4	2.75
John Case	7/6 per day	11 1/4	14.06
Asa Wood	$1.05 per day	5	5.25
Anson C. Sawfell	$17.50 per month	5	3.37
Laren Pope	10/ per day ($1.66)	3 1/2	5.83
George Smith	$21.50 per month	24	19.84
John Field			
Mason Eldridge	Chimney and underpinning		35.00
William Smith	$25.50 per month	1	.98
William Booth	$6 per week		25.71
John Booth	Cutting wood and pasting		4.47
			$ 792.61

Adult female labor ($2.00 or more per week)			
Harriet Munyan	15/6 per week ($2.58)	25 days	$ 10.76
Almira Joy	14/ per week ($2.33)	11 3/4 days	4.57
Persis Mellen	15/6	25	10.76
Sarah Mellen	15/6	25	10.76
Mary Booth	15/6	23 1/4	10.00
Sally Davis	12/ per week	24 1/2	8.17
Abigail Davis	12/ per week	23 1/2	7.83
Polly Larned	15/6 per week	20 1/2	8.82
Nancy Larned	15/6	23 10/12	10.26
Louisa Taft	15/6	24 5/12	10.51
Dinah Joslni	15/6	24 1/2	10.55
Sarah Plumstead	15/6	25	10.76
Mary Sloan	14/	25	9.71
Matilda Kingsbury	14/	23	8.94
Cynthia Barnes	14/	24 1/2	9.52
Eliza Frazier	14/	22	8.55

Male child labor (Paid by the week.)			
W. Hudson (ward of John Shaw)	12/ per week ($2.00)	24 1/4 days	8.08
Peter Quin	6/ per week	24 days	4.00
James Quin	6/	24	4.00
John Platt	12/	24	8.00
Mark Moulton	21/ ($3.50)	24	14.00
Jack Moulton	12/	24 3/4	8.25
James Moulton	9/	25	6.25
Josiah Moulton, Jr.	6/	24	4.13

Male child labor (cont.)			
Otheniel Moulton	4/6	23 3/4	$ 2.97
Jerimiah Herbison	12/	2 3/4	.92
Able Davis, Jr.	6/	20 1.2	8.82
Rufus Bartlett	18/	25	12.50
Jeremiah Bartlett	6/	25	4.17
Charles Perry	4/	25	2.78
Robert Hill	4/	24 1/2	2.73
Female child labor			
Elizabeth Moulton	6/6 per week	23 3/4	4.28
Lucy Munyan	6/ per week	24 3/4	4.13
Loring Munyan	7/6	25	5.21
Harriet Greaves	7/ per week	24 3/4	4.81
Lament Davis	7/6	25	5.21
Elizabeth Perry	7/6	25	5.21
Persis Perry	10/ per week	25	6.95
Isabella Hill	6/	25	4.17
			$1,823.44

66 male adults plus 12 outside laborers	57%
27 female adults	23%
8 female children)	
15 male)	20%
116	

Payroll, June 30, 1830 Dudley Woollen Manufacturing Company

Sorting			
Henry Work	4,661 lb. @ 6/6 per 100 ($1.083)		$ 50.49
Geo. Albe for H. Work, 3,031 lb. @ 1¢ = $30.31			
Amos Platt	2,055 lb. @ 6/6		22.26
Scouring			
Ezra Work	23 days @ 6/ per day		23.00
John May	26 days @ $100 per year		8.33
Dye house			
Joseph Pratt	27 days @ $7 per month		7.27
Carding and roping			
Rufus Pachen	3,012 lb. @4¢		120.84
2 men) 6 girls) paid $61.90 2 boys)			
George Munyan	2,482 lb. @ 4¢		99.28
2 men) 4 girls) paid $50.23 2 boys)			
Spinning			
James Taunton	24 3/4 days @ 7/ per day		28.88
Elijah Bugbee	3,460 R(uns filling @ 8/10		27.68
Lera Bugbee	2,534 R. " @ 7/10		17.75
John Thornton (by Thomps.)	1,663 R. " @ 8/10		13.30
	1,935 R. warp @ 9/10		17.42
Spinning on Brewster			
Theresa Richardson	25 days @ 15/ per week		10.42
Louisa Whitemore	25 1/2 days @ 10/ per week		6.96
Emily Clemens	25 days @ 7/6 per week		5.21
Weaving			
James Platt	1,984 1/4 yards broadcloth @ 9¢	$178.58	
	4,519 1/4 yards cassimere @ 5¢	225.96	
			404.54
10 females) 1 male)	1,819 1/2 yards broadcloth @ 6¢ =	$109.17	
14 females	4,308 1/2 yards cassimere @ 3 1/2¢ =	$150.79	
Raising knap			
Aaron Billings	958 3/4 yards broadcloth @ 3¢ =	$ 28.76	
	3,235 3/4 yards cassimere @ 1¢ =	32.36	
			61.12
4 men) 1 boy)paid $31.79			

Finishing			
William Knapp	958 3/4 yards broadcloth @ 4¢	$ 38.35	
	3,235 3/4 yards cassimere @ 1 3/4	56.62	
			94.97
2 men) 7 girls) paid $37.91			
Fulling			
Thomas King	22 1/4 days $13 per month		11.12
Dan'l Fairbanks	22 3/4 days $ 6 per month		5.46
Factory account			
Nathanial Lyon	@ $700 per annum		58.33
			$1,094.63
Expense account			
John Brown	@ $500 per annum		41.66
Chester Clemens	@ $600 per annum		50.00

Weavers pay own board, rest paid by the company, about $200 per month.
Twenty houses rented to hands and others from $20 to $33 per year.

Appendix B

SPECIFICATION OF WHITTEMORE'S CUT, PRICK AND SET MACHINE

Vol. 1

p. 43-5
June 5, 1797

AMOS WHITTEMORE

Letters Patent

The schedule referred to in these Letters Patent and making part of the same, containing a description in the words of the said Amos Whittemore himself, of an improvement in manufacturing cards.

A general specification of a machine for manufacturing sheet cards, suitable for wool or cotton cards, hatters cards, clothiers, jacks, & cards of every kind, size or denomination. This machine is put in motion by a cylinder, on which are a number of knobs to give the different motions. This cylinder may be turned by hand or other power. On one end of the cylinder is a balance wheel, with two or more arms; on one of the arms is a handle to turn it, on the other end is a section wheel which plays into a pinion which turns two rollers, which roll the wire into the former the proper length; immediately after a crowner (so called) is let off by a knob on the cylinder, and forced up by a spring against the wire, so rolled into the former and holds it against the head, while the shears forced up by another knob cuts the wire off. A pricker is forced up by another knob, & pricks two holes in the leather, and falls back, while the wings forced up by another knob form the wire into a staple. Around the head a conductor is let off by a space in the cylinder, and is forced up by a spring to its proper place to conduct the wire or staple into the leather, which is held in the carriage and extended by screws so as to be tight.

Immediately the whole apparatus for forming the wire is forced forward and places the wire or staple into the leather, and holds it until the crooker which is on the other side of the leather and moved by another knob, forces the points of the wire or staple down over a stationary piece placed the same side of the leather with the crookers which completes the wire; immediately the head is lifted up by another knob, the crowner advances further forward and sets the wire close up to the leather, then the apparatus which forms the wire and crowner falls back together to their place and receive another wire.

While the wire is rolling into the former, the carriage is moved by a cog taking one tooth in a toothed rack, which cog is moved by another knob on the cylinder and moves the carriage and leather to receive another wire or staple, it continues on until it goes once through the card or sheet lengthwise. The instant this cog is raised and held up by a piece which is governed by a spring and a straight piece which gives the length of the card or sheet, another cog at the opposite end of the machine falls into another toothed rack, & moves the carriage and sheet back in the same manner it was carried forward; this cog is moved by the same knob which moves the first mentioned cog, by being connected with it, at the same time these cogs shift; another cog which is moved by a small wheel on the end of the cylinder, being connected with a piece, which falls into a blank or space in the small wheel, by which means the cog takes one tooth in a cog wheel, which is placed on an arbour above the small wheel; on which arbour are two small wheels, on which wind two chains or straps which are confined to the carriage or piece which the carriage slides on; the piece connected with the cog rises immediately as the small wheel on the fist mentioned arbour revolves around, and forces the cog to move the cog wheel and winds the chains or straps; which raises the carriage and leather sufficiently for another row of wires to be let; it holds the cog wheel in the same place until the row of wires be full; this piece which is connected with the cog which moves the cog wheel is also connected with another piece under it which rests and slides on a straight piece, the same length of the straight piece that gives the length of the card or sheet and governs the other two cogs; this piece so connected with the cogs slides on the straight piece as the carriage is moved and end (the straight piece being confined to the carriage) until it slips off the end of the straight piece and lets the piece above connected with it and the cog fall into the blank or space in the small wheel on the first mentioned cylinder, to let the dog take one tooth in the cog wheel and using again by the small wheel revolving around is catched on the straight piece and held up until the row of wire is full and then slips off the other end. Continues to operate in the same manner until the card or sheet is complete, or has the complement of wire let in; two or more cards or sheets may be set at the same time on the same machine by the addition of a former to each sheet or card.

Witnesses present at signing

Nath[l] Abraham　　　　Amos Whittemore
Thomas Edwards

Elxd M.N.J.

880 wds,　　Ex

(Drawing)

(Rec[d] & Recorded anew 3rd June 1852)

Appendix C

SPECIFICATIONS FOR WILLIAM H. HOWARD'S POWER LOOM

Vol. 10

p. 139
Feb. 12, 1830

WILLIAM H. HOWARD

Letters Patent

The schedule referred to in these Letters Patent and making part of the same containing a description in the words of the said William H. Howard himself of his improvement in the Power Loom called the "improved vibrating cam Loom.

To all persons to whom these presents shall come. William H. Howard of Worcester in the County of Worcester & State of Massachusetts machinist sends greeting. Be it known that I the said Howard have invented made & applied to use a new & useful improvement n the power loom called the "Improved vibrating cam Loom" & specified in the words following. Power looms such as have been and are now in general use are constructed with a frame of sufficient length to receive the desired width of cloth & of width enough to admit the lathe to vibrate and the harness to open the warps for the passage of the shuttle. It has a shaft called the mainshaft extending the length of the loom & is placed nearly in the centre of the frame. On each end of said main shaft are members or sweeps. The lathe is supported on pivots at the bottom and near one corner of the frame. The perpendicular parts of the lathe at the ends on which it rests & vibrates are called "Lathe Standards." The lathe is put in motion by means of an arm extending from the crank on the main shaft to the back side of the lathe. The shuttle and harness are put in motion by means of cams on a shaft lying under the main shaft & connected with the said main shaft at one end by geers. The cams are in the centre of the loom & supported by a cross girt. The looms as above described are called "crank looms" & are found to answer a valuable purpose for weaving narrow cloth, but for weaving broad cloth they are not considered suitable on account of the motion of the lathe as produced by the cranks not giving sufficient time for the shuttle to pass before the lathe advances to beat in the weft. To obviate this difficulty various methods have been introduced. The most effectual one I will endeavour to describe in the words following. A piece of iron about two feet in length is placed perpendicularly at each end of the main shaft, the bottom of which is supported in a pivot made fast to the end of the loom frame directly under the main shaft. In the top of this iron is a mortice of a circular form & the pin in the crank enters this mortice and as it revolves produces a vibrating motion to the upright piece as above described which is called the "vibrating cam." The motion is given to the lathe in the same manner as in the crank loom. The two looms already described resemble each other in every other respect than that of giving a desired motion to the lathe by means of the vibrating cams. I do not however claim any improvements in the looms already specified as my improvement, but I do claim the particular method of applying the vibrating cams more directly, simply, & effectively than ever before done & also that of the cross girt. In pointing out my improvement reference is to be had to the drawing deposited in the Patent Office. My improvement consists 1st in making the circular mortices called "vibrating cams" as above in the Lathe standards instead of having a separate piece for that purpose alone; 2nd that of applying the cross girt & that part called the "swag staff" being hung on a pivot on the cross girt. In testimony that the above is a true specification of my improvements as above described, I have hereto set my hand and seal this twenty-fifth day of November in the year of our Lord one thousand eight hundred and twenty-nine.

Witnesses
Joel Dewing
Emory Washburn

William H. Howard

742 wds

Ex'd
ChSW

Appendix D

ENGLISH TEXTILE MILLS AND MACHINERY

CIRCA 1835

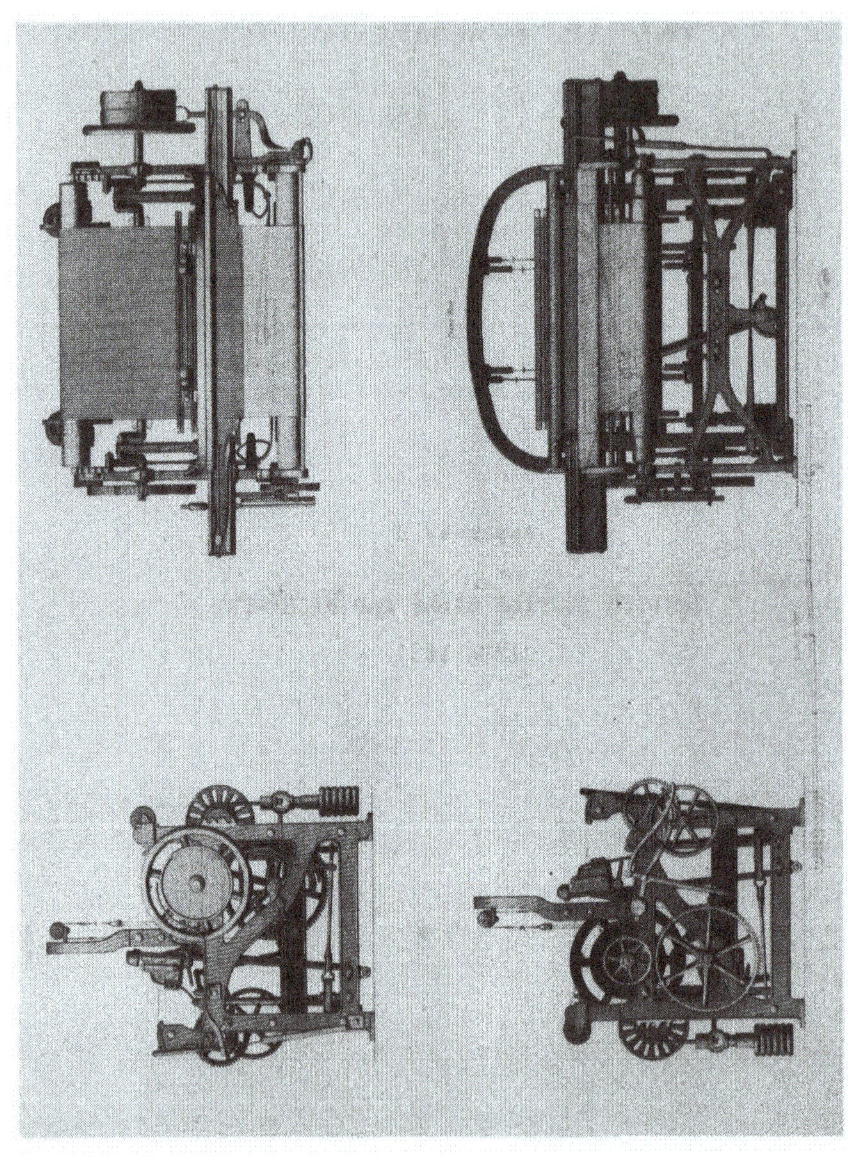

DRAWING AND

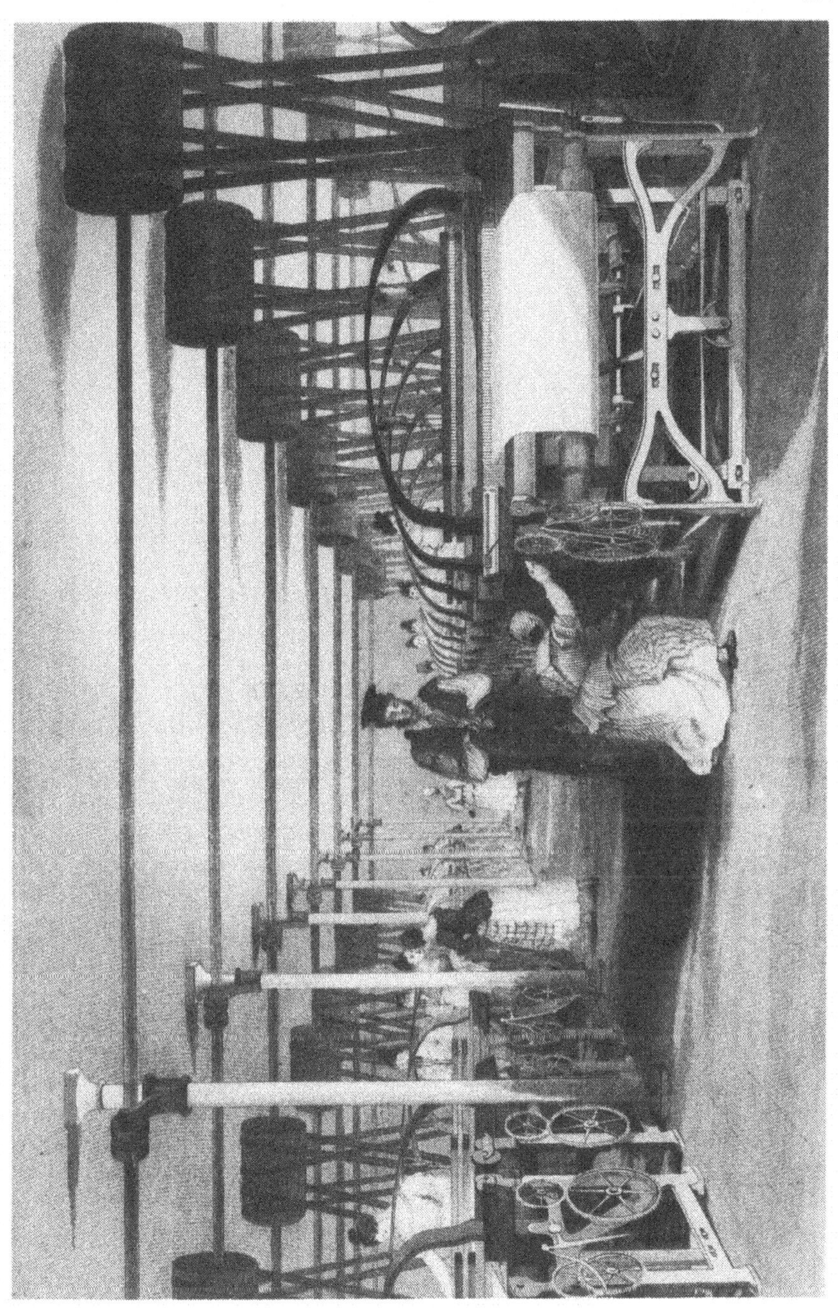

Appendix E

SCHEMATIC OF A POWER TRAIN

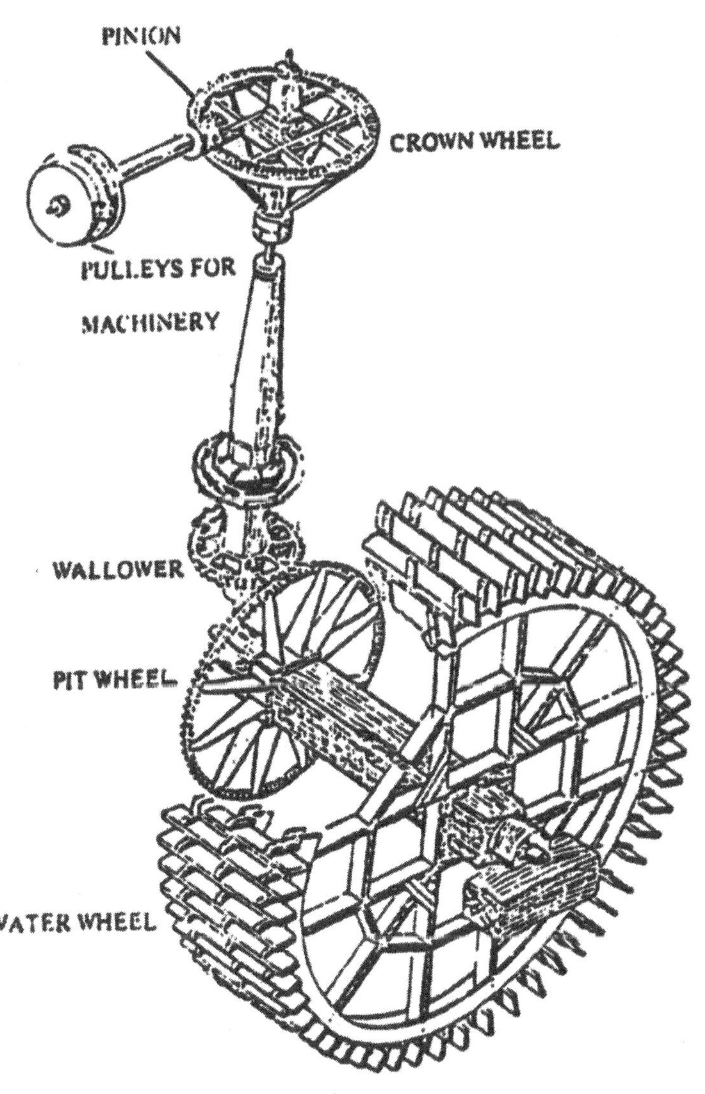
PINION
CROWN WHEEL
PULLEYS FOR
MACHINERY
WALLOWER
PIT WHEEL
WATER WHEEL

Appendix F

WHOLESALE PRICE INDEX COMPARED TO COMMON WOOL AND MERINO WOOL PRICES

Year	Wholesale Price Index 1835 = 100.0	Price Common Wool New York City[2]	Index	Price Merino Philadelphia[3]	Index
1813	162			2.75	470
1814	182			3.31 1/4	566
1815	170			1.33 1/3	228
1816	151	.46 3/4 (Phila.)	134	.975	167
1817	151	.34 1/4 (NYC)	101	.75	128
1818	147	.35	103	.81 2/3	140
1819	125	.38 3/4	114	.82 1/4	141
1820	106	.35	103	.75	128
1821	102	.35	103	.75	128
1822	106	.38 3/4	114	.75	128
1823	103	.35	103	.71 2/3	123
1824	98	.32	94	.55	94
1825	103	.33	97	.53	91
1826	98	.30 2/3	90	.39 1/4	67
1827	98	.25	74	.33	56
1828	97	.25	74	.35	60
1829	96	.22	65	.32	55
1830	91	.22	65	.47	80
1831	94	.275	81	.63	108
1832	95	.275	81	.48	82
1833	95	.32	94	.56	97
1834	90	.30 1/3	89	.56	96
1835	100	.34	100	.585	100
1836	114	.43	126	.59	101
1837	115	.45	132	.502/3	87

[1]Lance E. Davis, "Banks and their Economic Effects," in <u>American Economic Growth: An Economist's History of the United States</u> Lance E. Davis, et al. (New York: Harper & Row, 1972), p. 364.

[2]Cole, <u>Wholesale Commodity Prices</u>, 1: 364

[3]Ibid

BIBLIOGRAPHY

Unpublished Manuscripts

Boston, Mass. Harvard Business School, Baker Library.
Slater Collection.
Pearson Family MSS.

Greenville, Del. Eleutherian Mills Historical Library.
Antietam Woolen Manufacturing Company Papers.
Charles I. du Pont & Co. Papers.
Winterthur Mss., Papers of Victor du Pont.

New York, N.Y. Cooper Union Archives.
Peter Cooper Letter File.

New York, N.Y. New York Historical Society Manuscript Collection.
Isaac Young and Solomon Fancher, Factory Day Book.

North Andover, Mass. Merrimack Valley Textile Museum.
Merino Wool Factory Company MSS and Accounts.

Philadelphia, Pa. Historical Society of Pennsylvania.
William Young Papers.

Providence, R.I. Rhode Island Historical Society.
Zachariah Allen MSS.

Sturbridge, Mass. Old Sturbridge Village Research Library,
Merino/Dudley Woollen Manufacturing Company Records.
Papers of Mr. & Mrs. H. Willis Babcock.

Washington, D.C. National Archives.
Record Group 29, "Records of the 1820 Census of Manufactures."
Record Group 241, "Restored Patents, Specifications."

Unpublished Theses

Conrad, James Lawson, Jr. The Evolution of Industrial Capitalism in Rhode Island, 1790-1830: Almy the Browns, and the Slaters. Ph.D. dissertation, University of Connecticut, 1973, 73-26571.

Hartmann, Thomas B. "The du Pont Woolen Venture," unpublished Research Report for the Eleutherian Mills Historical Library, Greenville, Del., August 1955.

Spalding, Robert Varnum. The Boston Mercantile Community and the Promotion of the Textile Industry in New England, 1813-1860. Ph.D. Yale, 1969. 69-15742.

Published Material

Albion, Robert Greenhalgh. The Rise of New York Port (1815-1860). New York: Scribner's, 1939; repr. 1970.

Allen, Zachariah. "Upon the Relative Advantages Possessed by England, France, and the United States of America, as Manufacturing Nations." In Memoir of Samuel Slater, George S. White. Philadelphia: 1836; repr. New York: A. M. Kelley, 1967, pp. 339-44.

Ammidown, Holmes. Historical Collections. 2 vols. New York: By the Author, 1874.

Bagnall, William R. The Textile Industries of the United States Including Sketches and Notices of Cotton, Woolen, Silk and Linen Manufacture. Cambridge: Riverside, 1893; repr. New York: A. M. Kelley, 1971, Vol. I.

_____. Vol. II of above in typed manuscript at Baker Library. "Contributions to American Economic History." (Unpubl. materials) Sketches of Manufacturing Establishments in New York City, and of Textile Establishments in the Eastern States. (1908) 4 vols.

Bailyn, Bernard. The New England Merchants in the Seventeenth Century. Cambridge: Harvard 1955; repr. New York: Harper & Row, 1964.

Barber, John Warner. Connecticut Historical Collections, 2nd ed. New Haven: Durie, Peck and J. W. Barber, 1836.

_____. Historical Collections . . . of Every Town in Massachusetts. Worcester: Dorr Howland & Co., 1839.

_____. Historical Collections of the State of New York. New York: Tuttle for the Author, 1841.

Bathe, Greville and Dorothy. Oliver Evans: A Chronicle of Early American Engineering. Philadelphia, 1935; repr. New York: Arno Press, 1972.

Baumgarten, Linda R. "The Textile Trade in Boston, 1650-1700." Winterthur Conference Report, 1974, Arts in the Anglo-American Community in the Seventeenth Century. Edited by Ian M. G. Quimby. Charlottesville: University of Virginia Press, 1975, published for the Henry Francis du Pont Winterthur Museum, Winterthur, Delaware.

Benton, C. and Barry, S. F. A Statistical View of the Number of Sheep. Cambridge, Mass.: Folsam, Wells, & Thurston, 1837.

Betts, Raymond G. "Eleuthere Irenee du Pont and the Brandywine Sunday School." Delaware History 8 (September 1959):343-53.

Bidwell, Percy Wells and Falconer, John I. History of Agriculture in the Northern United States, 1620-1860. Washington, D.C.: Carnegie Institution, 1924; repr. New York: Peter Smith, 1941.

Bischoff, J. A Comprehensive History of the Woollen and Worsted Manufacture. 2 vols. London: Smith, Elder, 1842, repr. London: Frank Cass, 1968.

Bishop, J. Leander. A History of American Manufactures, 1608-1860. 3 vols. Philadelphia: Edward Young, 1868; repr, New York: Johnson, 1967.

Bowden, Peter J. The Wool Trade in Tudor and Stuart England. London: Macmillan, 1962.

_____. "The Wool Supply and the Woollen Industry." Economic History Review, 2nd series, 9 (August 1956):44-58.

Bradford, William. Of Plymouth Plantation, 1620-1647. Edited by Samuel Eliot Morison. New York: Modern Library, 1952.

Bremner, Robert H., ed. Children and Youth in America: A Documentary History. 3 vols. Cambridge: Harvard University Press, 1970.

Bridenbaugh, Carl. Fat Mutton and Liberty of Conscience. Providence: Brown University Press, 1975; repr. New York: Atheneum, 1976.

Brown, Ralph H. Mirror for Americans--Likeness of the Eastern Seaboard 1810. New York: American Geographical Society, 1943.

Brown, Richard D. "The Emergence of Urban Society in Rural Massachusetts, 1760-1820." Journal of American History 61 (June 1974):29-51.

_____. "Modernization and the Modern Personality in Early America, 1600-1865: A Sketch of a Synthesis." Journal of Inderdisciplinary History. 2:3 (Winter 1972).

_____. Modernization: The Transformation of American Life, 1600-1865. New York: Hill and Wang, 1976.

Burke, Edmund, Comp. List of Patents for Inventions and Designs, Issued by the United States, from 1790 to 1847. Washington, D.C., 1847.

Cameron, Edward H. Samuel Slater, Father of American Manufactures. Portland, Me.: Bond Wheelwright, 1960.

Carrier, Lyman. The Beginnings of Agriculture in America. N.Y.: McGraw Hill, 1923.

Carus-Wilson, E. M. "An Industrial Revolution in the Thirteenth Century." In Medieval Merchant Venturers. London: Methuen, 1955.

Catling, Harold. The Spinning Mule. Newton Abbot, Devon: David & Charles, 1970.

Clark, Victor S. History of Manufactures in the United States. 3 vols. Washington, D.C.: Carnegie Institution, 1929; repr. New York: Peter Smith, 1949.

Clarkson, L. A. The Pre-Industrial Economy in England. London: Batsford, 1971.

Cochran, Thomas C. "The Business Revolution." American Historical Review 79 (December 1974):1449-66.

_____, and Miller, William. The Age of Enterprise: A Social History of Industrial America. New York: Macmillan, 1942; repr. New York: Harper & Row, 1961.

Cole, Arthur Harrison. "Agricultural Crazes." American Economic Review 16 (1926):622-39.

_____. The American Wool Manufacture. 2 vols. Cambridge: Harvard University Press, 1926; repr. New York: Harper & Row, 1968.

_____. (ed.) Industrial and Commercial Correspondence of Alexander Hamilton. Chicago: A. W. Shaw Co., 1928; repr. New York: A. M. Kelley, 1968.

Cole, Arthur Harrison. "The Tempo of Mercantile Life in Colonial America." Business History Review 33 (1959):277-99.

_____. Wholesale Commodity Prices in the United States, 1700-1861. Cambridge: Harvard University Press, 1938.

Coleman, D. C. "An Innovation and its Diffusion: 'the New Draperies.'" Economic History Review, 2nd series. 22 (1969):417-29.

Coleman, Peter J. The Transformation of Rhode Island, 1790 1860. Providence: Brown University Press, 1963.

Compact Edition of the Oxford English Dictionary. 2 vols. Oxford: Clarendon Press, 1971.

Cooke, Jacob E., ed. The Reports of Alexander Hamilton. New York: Harper & Row, 1964.

_____. "Tench Coxe, Alexander Hamilton and the Encouragement of American Manufactures." William & Mary Quarterly, 3rd ser. 32 (July 1975):369-92.

Coxe, Tench. View of the United States. Philadelphia, 1794; repr. New York: A. M. Kelley, 1965.

_____. A Brief Examination of Lord Sheffield's Considerations on the Commerce of the United States. Philadelphia: 1791.

_____. A Statement of the Arts and Manufactures of the United States for 1810. Philadelphia: Cornman, 1814.

Crump, W. B. (ed.). The Leeds Woollen Industry, 1780-1820. Leeds: Thoresby Society Publ., Vol. 32, 1929; repr. New York: Johnson, 1967.

_____ and Ghorbal, G. History of Huddersfield Woollen Industry. Huddersfield: Tolson Memorial Museum Handbook no. 9, 1935.

Cunnington, C. Willet and Cunnington, Phyllis. Handbook of English Costume in the 17th Century. 3rd ed. Boston: Plays, Inc., 1970.

_____. Handbook of English Costume in the 18th Century. Boston: Plays, Inc., 1972.

_____. Handbook of English Costume in the 19th Century. Boston: Plays, Inc., 1972.

David, Paul A. "The Growth of Real Product in the United States before 1840: New Evidence, Controlled Conjectures." Journal Economic History 27:2 (June 1967), pp. 151-97.

David, Paul A. Technical Choice Innovation and Economic Growth: Essays on American and British Experience in the Nineteenth Century. Cambridge: Cambridge University Press, 1975.

Davidson, Philip. Propaganda and the American Revolution, 1763-1783. Chapel Hill: University of North Carolina Press, 1941.

Davis, Joseph Stancliffe. Essays in the Earlier History of American Corporations. Cambridge: Harvard University Press, 1917; repr. New York: Russell and Russell, 1965.

Davis, Lance E.; Easterlin, Richard A.: Parker, William N.; Brady, Dorothy S.; Fishlow, Albert; Gallman, Robert E.; Lebergott, Stanley; Libsey, Robert E.; North, Douglass, C.; Rosenberg, Nathan; Spolensky, Eugene; & Temin, Peter. American Economic Growth: An Economist's History of the United States. New York: Harper & Row, 1972.

Deane, Phyllis. "The Output of the British Woolen Industry in the Eighteenth Century." Journal of Economic History 17 (1957) 207-223.

_____. The First Industrial Revolution. Cambridge: Cambridge University Press, 1965.

_____ and W. A. Cole. British Economic Growth, 1688-1959. 2nd. ed. Cambridge: Cambridge University Press, 1969.

Derry, T. K. and Willians, Trevor I. A Short History of Technology. Oxford: Oxford University Press, 1969.

Descriptions des Arts et Metiers, (1765), s.v. "Art de la Draperie." By Henry Louis Duhamel du Monceau.

Dickman, Howard. "Technological Innovation in the Woolen Industry: The Middletown Manufacturing Company." The Connecticut Historical Society Bulletin. 37 (April 1972):52-58.

Dunn, Richard S. Puritans and Yankees: The Winthrop Dynasty of New England, 1630-1717. Princeton: Princeton University Press, 1962; repr. New York: Norton, 1971.

Dwight, Timothy. Travels in New England and New York. 4 vols. New Haven: T. Dwight, pp. 1821-22.

East, Robert E. Business Enterprise in the American Revolutionary Era. New York: Columbia University Press, 1938; repr. Gloucester, Mass.: Peter Smith, 1964.

Fannin, Allen. Handspinning: Art and Technique, New York: van Nostrant Reinholdt, 1970.

Ferguson, E. James, ed. Selected Writings of Albert Gallatin. Indianapolis: Bobbs-Merrill, 1967.

Fisher, F. J. "London's Export Trade in the Seventeenth Century." In The Growth of English Overseas Trade in the Seventeenth and Eighteenth Centuries. London: Methuen, 1969.

Fogel, Robert W. and Engerman, Stanley L. The Reinterpretation of American Economic History. New York: Harper & Row, 1971.

Foner, Philip S. The Factory Girls. Urbana: University of Illinois Press, 1977.

Franklin Journal and American Mechanics' Magazine (Philadelphia), 1825-1850.

Freudenberger, Herman. The Waldstein Woolen Mill. Cambridge: Harvard University Press, 1963.

Friedmann, Karen J. "Victualling Colonial Boston." Agricultural History 47 (July 1973):189-205.

Gallatin, Albert. "Report on Manufactures, 1810." American State Papers: Finance Vol. II, Washington, 1832.

George, M. Dorothy. London Life in the Eighteenth Century. New York: Capricorn Books, 1965.

Gibson, George H. "The Delaware Woolen Industry" Delaware History 12 (October 1966).

_____. "Fullers, Carders, and Manufacturers of Woolen Goods in Delaware." Delaware History 12 (April 1966).

_____. "The Growth of the Woolen Industry in Nineteenth Century Delaware." Textile History Review 5 (October 1964):125-57.

Gordon, Thomas F. Gazeteer of the State of New York. Albany: By the Author, 1836.

Grant, Ellsworth S. Yankee Dreamers and Doers. Chester, Conn.: Pequot Press, [1975].

Habakkuk, H. J. American and British Technology in the Nineteenth Century: The Search for Labour-Saving Inventions. Cambridge: Cambridge University Press, 1967.

Harte, N. B. & K. G. Ponting, eds. Textile History and Economic History: Essays in Honour of Miss Julia deLacy Mann. Manchester: Manchester University Press, 1973.

Handlin, Oscar, ed. This Was America . . . as Recorded by European Travelers to the Western Shore in the Eighteenth, Nineteenth, and Twentieth Centuries. Cambridge: Harvard University Press, 1949.

Hayes, John Lord. American Textile Machinery. Cambridge, Mass.: University Press, 1879.

Hazard, Thomas Robinson. Facts for the Labouring Man, by a Labouring Man. Newport, R.I.: By the Author, 1840.

_____. The Jonny-Cake Papers of "Shepherd Tom." Boston, 1915.

Heaton, Herbert. "Benjamin Gott and the Anglo-American Cloth Trade." Journal Economic & Business History 2 (1929).

_____. "Benjamin Gott and the Industrial Revolution in Yorkshire." Economic History Review 3 (1931):45-66.

_____. "The Industrial Immigrant in the United States, 1783-1812." Proceedings of the American Philosophical Society 95 (October 1951): 519-27.

_____. Yorkshire Cloth Traders in the United States, 1770-1840. Leeds; Thoresby Society Publication, 37 (1941).

_____. The Yorkshire Woollen and Worsted Industries from Earliest Times up to the Industrial Revolution 2nd ed. Oxford: Oxford University Press, 1965.

Hills, Richard L. Power in the Industrial Revolution. Manchester: University of Manchester Press, 1970.

History of Worcester County. 2 vols. Boston: C. F. Jewett & Co., 1879.

Hummel, Charles F. *With Hammer in Hand: The Dominy Craftsmen of East Hampton, New York*. Charlottesville: University of Virginia Press, 1968; published for the Henry Francis du Pont Winterthur Museum.

Hurd, D. Hamilton, comp. *History of Worcester County, Massachusetts*. 2 vols. Philadelphia: J. W. Lewis & Co., 1889.

Jefferson, Thomas. *Notes on the State of Virginia*. New York: Harper & Row, 1964.

Jenkins, D. T. *The West Riding Wool Textile Industry, 1770-1835: A Study of Fixed Capital Formation*. Edington, Wilshire: Pasold Research Fund, 1975.

Jenkins, J. Geraint, ed. *The Wool Textile Industry in Great Britain*. London: Routledge & Kegan Paul, 1972.

Jensen, Merrill. *English Historical Documents: American Colonial Documents to 1776*. Vol. 10 of *English Historical Documents*. Edited by David C. Douglas. 12 vols. New York: Oxford University Press, 1955.

Jeremy, David John, ed. "British and American Yarn Count Systems: An Historical Analysis." *Business History Review* 45 (Autumn 1971):3.

_____. "British Textile Technology Transmission to the United States: The Philadelphia Region Experience, 1770-1820." *Business History Review* 47 (Spring 1973):1.

_____. *Henry Wansey and His American Journal, 1794*. A.P.S. vol. 82. Philadelphia: American Philosophical Society, 1970.

_____. "Innovation in American Textile Technology during the Early 19th Century." *Technology & Culture* 14 (January 1973):1.

Johnson, Emory R. *History of the Domestic and Foreign Commerce of the United States*. 2 vols. Washington, D.C.: Carnegie Institution, 1915.

Kalm, Peter. *Travels in North America* (1750) English version of 1770. Edited by Adolph B. Benson. 2 vols. New York: Peter Smith.

Kranzberg, Melvin, and Pursell, Jr., Carroll W., eds., Technology in Western Civilization, 2 vols., New York: Oxford University Press, 1967.

Leavitt, Thomas W., ed. The Hollingsworth Letters: Technical Change in the Textile Industry, 1826-1837. Cambridge: Massachusetts Institute of Technology and the Society for the History of Technology, 1969.

Leblanc, Robert G. Location of Manufactures in New England in the Nineteenth Century. Hanover, N.H.: Geography Publications at Dartmouth, no. 7, 1969.

Lemon, James T. The Best Poor Man's Country: A Geographical Study of Early Southeastern Pennsylvania. Baltimore: Johns Hopkins University Press, 1972.

_____. "Household Consumption in Eighteenth-Century America and Its Relationship to Production and Trade: The Situation Among Farmers in Southeastern Pennsylvania." Agricultural History 41 (1967):59-70.

Lipson, E. The History of the Woollen & Worsted Industries. London: A. C. Black, 1921.

Lunt, Dudley C. "The Farmer's Bank--An Assurance Co." Delaware History (March 1958):54-74.

McLane Report on Manufactures, Documents Relative to Manufactures in the United States, House Document, no. 308, 22nd Cong. 1st Sess. 2 vols. Washington, D.C., 1833; repr. New York: A. M. Kelley, 1969.

Mann, Julia deLacy. The Cloth Industry in the West of England, 1640-1880. Oxford: Clarendon Press, 1971.

Manufacturers' and Farmer's Journal: Providence and Pawtucket Advertiser, Jan. 3, 1820-Nov. 26, 1831.

Mathias, Peter. The First Industrial Nation. London: Methuen, 1969.

Navin, Thomas R. The Whitin Machine Works since 1831: A Textile Machinery Company in an Industrial Village. Cambridge: Harvard, 1950.

Nevins, Allan, ed. America through British Eyes. New York: Oxford University Press, 1948.

_____. The Diary of Philip Hone. 2 vols. New York: Dodd, Mead, 1927.

New York Assembly Journal. 49th Sess., 1826, Part 2, Appendix C.

New York State Census, 1845. 3 vols. Albany: 1846.

North, Simon N. D. A Century of American Wool Manufacture. Bulletin of National Association of Wool Manufacturers (n.p.), 1894.

______. "The New England Wool Manufacture." In The New England States. Edited by W. T. Davis. Boston: D. H. Hurd, 1897.

Partridge, William. A Practical Treatise on Dying of Woollen, Cotton, and Skein Silk with the Manufacture of Broadcloth and Cassimere Including the Most Improved Methods in the West of England. New York: H. Walker and Co. for the Author, 1823; repr. Edington, Wiltshire: Pasold Research Fund Ltd., 1973.

Pemberton, Thomas. "A Topographical and Historical Description of Boston in 1794 by the Author of the Historical Journal of the American War." Collections of the Massachusetts Historical Society, Vol. 3. Boston: Massachusetts Historical Society, 1795.

Pierson, George Wilson. "The M-Factor in American History." American Quarterly 14 (Summer 1962):275-89.

Pitkin, Timothy. A Statistical View of the Commerce of the United States of America. New Haven: Durrie and Peck, 1835.

Pollard, Sidney. The Genesis of Modern Management: A Study of the Industrial Revolution in Great Britain. Cambridge: Harvard University Press, 1965.

Ponting, K. G., ed. (Sir Edward) Baines's Account of the Woollen Manufacture of England from Yorkshire, Past and Present, (1875). New York: A. M. Kelley, 1970.

______. The Woollen Industry of South-West England. New York: A. M. Kelley, 1971.

Porter, Glenn and Livesay Harold C. Merchants and Manufacturers: Studies in the Changing Structure of Nineteenth-Century Marketing. Baltimore: Johns Hopkins University Press, 1970.

Postan, M. M. The Medieval Economy and Society. Middlesex, England: Penguin Books, 1972.

Potter, J. "The Growth of Population in America, 1700-1860." In Population in History: Essays in Historical Demography. Edited by D. V. Glass and D. E. C. Eversley. London: Edward Arnold, 1965.

Pressnell, L. S., ed. Studies in the Industrial Revolution Presented to T. S. Ashton. London: Athlone, 1960.

Pursell, Carroll W., Jr. "E. I. Du Pont, Don Pedro and the Introduction of Merino Sheep into the United States, 1801: A Document." Agricultural History 33 (April 1959):86-88.

_____. "E. I. Du Pont and the Merino Mania in Delaware, 1805-1815." Agricultural History 36 (April 1962): 91-100.

Randall, Henry S. Sheep Husbandry. New York: Orange Judd & Co., 1860.

Rees, Abraham. The Cyclopaedia or Universal Dictionary of Arts, Sciences, and Literature. 1st American edition revised. 39 vols & 6 vol. plates. Philadelphia: S.F. Bradford, 1805-24.

Rezneck, Samuel. "The Rise and Early Development of Industrial Consciousness in the United States, 1760-1830." Journal Economic and Business History 4 (1932):784-811.

Riggs, John Beverley. A Guide to the Manuscripts in the Eleutherian Mills Historical Library. Greenville, Delaware: Eleutherian Mills Historical Library, 1970.

Rosenberg, Nathan. Technology and American Economic Growth. New York: Harper & Row, 1972.

_____. Perspectives in Technology. New York: Cambridge, 1976.

Rostow, W. W. The Stages of Economic Growth, 2nd ed., Cambridge: Cambridge University Press, 1971.

Schlebecker, John T., ed. Eighteenth-Century Agriculture, A Symposium. Agricultural History 43 (January 1969):1.

_____. "Agricultural Markets and Marketing in the North, 1774-1777." Agricultural History 50 (January 1776): 21-31.

Schumpeter, Elizabeth Boody. English Overseas Trade Statistics, 1697-1808. Oxford: Clarendon Press, 1960.

Scott, Franklin D. Trans. Baron Klinkowstrom's America, 1818-1820. Evanston: Northwestern University Press, 1952.

Sheffield, Lord John B. Observations on the Commerce of the American States. 6th ed. London, 1784.

Shepherd, James F. and Walton, Gary M. Shipping, Maritime Trade and the Economic Development of Colonial North America. Cambridge: Cambridge University Press, 1972.

Smith, Adam. The Wealth of Nations. New York: Random House, 1937.

Spofford, Horatio Gates. Gazeteer of the State of New York. Albany: B. D. Packard, 1824.

Springer, Semon H. "Peter Cooper in Hempstead, 1812-1818." Nassau County Historical Journal (Autumn, 1951).

Strassmann, W. Paul. Risk and Technological Innovation: American Manufacturing Methods during the Nineteenth Century. Ithaca: Cornell University Press, 1959.

Supple, Barry E. Commercial Crisis and Change in England, 1600-1642: A Study in the Instability of a Mercantile Economy. Cambridge: Cambridge University Press, 1959.

Taft, Royal C. Some Notes on the Introduction of the Woolen Manufacture into the United States. Providence, 1882.

Tann, Jennifer. Gloucestershire Woollen Mills. Newton Abbot: David and Charles, 1967.

_____. The Development of the Factory. London: Cornmarket Press, 1970.

Taussig, F. W. The Tariff History of the United States. New York: Putnam, 1888; repr. New York: Capricorn Books, 1964.

Taylor, George Rogers. The Transportation Revolution, 1815-1860. Vol. 4. Economic History of United States. Edited by Henry David, et al. New York: Holt, Reinhart & Winston, 1951; repr. New York, Harper & Row, 1968.

_____. "American Economic Growth before 1840: An Exploratory Essay." Journal Economic History 24 (1964):427-44.

_____. "American Urban Growth Preceeding the Railway Age." Journal Economic History 27 (September 1967):309-39.

Thirsk, Joan. "Farming Techniques" in Agrarian History of England and Wales, 1500-1640. Vol. 5. Finberg, H.P.R., genl. ed. Cambridge: Cambridge University Press, 1967.

Tredwell, Daniel M. Personal Reminiscences of Men and Things on Long Island. Brooklyn: Charles Andrew Ditmas, 1912.

Tryon, Rolla Milton. Household Manufacture in the United States, 1640-1860: A Study in Industrial History. Chicago: University of Chicago Press, 1917.

U. S. Congress. House. Committee on Manufactures. Minutes of Evidence on Woollens, 20th Cong., 1st sess., 1828, H. Rept. 115.

Volume Relating to the Early History of Boston Containing the Aspinwall Notarial Records from 1644-1651. Thirty-second Report of the Record Commissioners of the City of Boston. Boston: 1903.

Wallace, Anthony F. C. and Jeremy, David J. "William Pollard and the Arkwright Patents." William & Mary Quarterly 3rd ser. 34 (July 1977):404-25.

Ware, Caroline F. The Early New England Cotton Manufacture: A Study in Industrial Beginnings. Boston: Houghton Mifflin, 1931; repr. New York: Johnson Repr., 1966.

_____. The Early Woolen Industry of New Jersey. Trenton, New Jersey: Agricultural Society, 1958.

Warner, Sam Bass, Jr. The Private City: Philadelphia in Three Periods of Its Growth. Philadelphia: University of Pennsylvania Press, 1968.

Weiss, Harry B. and Ziegler, Grace M. The Early Fulling Mills of New Jersey. Trenton, New Jersey: Agricultural Society, 1957.

_____. The Early Woolen Industry of New Jersey. Trenton, New Jersey: Agricultural Society, 1958.

White, George S. Memoir of Samual Slater. Philadelphia, 1836: repr. New York: A. M. Kelley, 1967.

Wilson, Charles. England's Apprenticeship, 1603-1763. London: Longman's, 1965.

Worden, D. A Statistical, Political, and Historical Account of the United States of North America. 2 vols. Edinburgh: Archibald Constable and Co., 1819.

Worst, Edward F. Foot-Power Loom Weaving. 6th ed. Milwaukee: Bruce Publishing Co., 1924; repr. New York: Dover, 1974.